The Mythic Fantasy of
Robert Holdstock

CRITICAL EXPLORATIONS IN SCIENCE FICTION AND FANTASY
(a series edited by Donald E. Palumbo and C.W. Sullivan III)

The Mythic Fantasy of Robert Holdstock

Critical Essays on the Fiction

Edited by
DONALD E. MORSE *and*
KÁLMÁN MATOLCSY
Foreword by Brian W. Aldiss

CRITICAL EXPLORATIONS IN SCIENCE FICTION AND FANTASY, 26
Donald E. Palumbo *and* C.W. Sullivan III, *series editors*

McFarland & Company, Inc., Publishers
Jefferson, North Carolina, and London

Frontispiece: Robert Holdstock (used by kind permission of the photographer Sarah Biggs).

Library of Congress Cataloguing-in-Publication Data

The mythic fantasy of Robert Holdstock : critical essays on the
   fiction / edited by Donald E. Morse and Kálmán Matolcsy ;
   foreword by Brian Aldiss.
         p.   cm. — (Critical explorations in science fiction
         and fantasy ; 26).
         [Donald Palumbo and C.W. Sullivan III, series editors]
         Includes bibliographical references and index.

      ISBN 978-0-7864-4942-2
      softcover : 50# alkaline paper ∞

      1. Holdstock, Robert — Criticism and interpretation.
      2. Fantasy fiction, English — History and criticism.   I. Morse,
      Donald E., 1936–   II. Matolcsy, Kálmán.
      PR6058.O442Z76   2011
      823'.914 — dc22   2010044519

British Library cataloguing data are available

Cover photograph © 2011 Shutterstock

Manufactured in the United States of America

*McFarland & Company, Inc., Publishers
   Box 611, Jefferson, North Carolina 28640
   www.mcfarlandpub.com*

In Memoriam
Robert Holdstock
Mapmaker of Regions Unknown

Table of Contents

Contents

Acknowledgments

Grateful acknowledgment is given to Gollancz, an imprint of the Orion Publishing Group, London, for permission to quote from previously published material in Robert Holdstock, *Mythago Wood*, copyright © 1984 by Robert Holdstock.

Portions of Chapter 1 appeared in an earlier form in W. A. Senior, "The Embodiment of Abstraction in the Mythago Novels," *Hungarian Journal of English and American Studies* (*HJEAS*), 14.2 (2008): 302–16. Donald E. Morse, editor. Used by permission of Donald E. Morse, editor. Copyright © 2009 by *HJEAS* (*Hungarian Journal of English and American Studies*).

Portions of Chapter 2 appeared in an earlier form in Kálmán Matolcsy, "Masks in the Forest: The Dynamics of Surface and Depth in Robert Holdstock's Mythago Cycle," *Journal of the Fantastic in the Arts* (*JFA*) 17.4 (2007): 350–70. Brian Attebery, editor. Used by permission of Brian Attebery, editor. Copyright © 2007 by the *International Association for the Fantastic in the Arts*.

Portions of Chapter 5 appeared in an earlier form in Marek Oziewicz, "Profusion Sublime and Fantastic: Robert Holdstock's *Mythago Wood*," *Journal of the Fantastic in the Arts* (*JFA*) 19.1 (2008): 94–111. W. A. Senior, editor. Used by permission of W. A. Senior and Brian Attebery, editors. Copyright © 2008 by the *International Association for the Fantastic in the Arts*.

The bibliography is courtesy of the Robert Holdstock website, *Robert Holdstock's Mythago Wood*, at http://robertholdstock.com. Modifications to the bibliography were made from the kind suggestions of Sarah Biggs and Malcolm Edwards. Used by permission of the late Robert Holdstock.

The photograph of Robert Holdstock by Sarah Biggs is used by kind permission of the photographer.

Acknowledgments

We also wish to thank Paul Stark of the Orion Group; Jo Fletcher, Robert Holdstock's editor at Gollancz; Malcolm Edwards, Holdstock's collaborator; and Sarah Biggs, Holdstock's long-time partner, for their support of and contributions to this book.

We dearly thank our wives, Csilla Bertha and Éva Kopócs, for helping turn this dream into reality through their tangible and intangible support without which this project would have languished.

Finally, this book was begun as a tribute to the imagination and genius of Robert Holdstock but, unfortunately, was brought to conclusion as a memorial to his work. His death at 62 has robbed readers of one of the most engaging and engaged minds in contemporary fiction and friends and family of one of the truly generous, loving spirits of our time. He is and will be much missed.

Foreword: Under the Spell
of a Magician

Brian W. Aldiss, O.B.E.

Yes, I knew, or thought I knew, Rob Holdstock. He was a friend. I persuaded him to attend the International Conference on the Fantastic in the Arts, where he found himself in his element among other writers. I have a photo of six of us sitting around in shades, looking like a real bunch of crooks. But Rob was shy, a modest man. He had already written *Mythago Wood*.

You can check the place up on a map of England. Or almost. There's Herefordshire, a peaceful little county, "Middle England," as we say; it looks westwards towards the Welsh border. The Ryhope estate might be approximately *there*, and Oak Lodge, and also that ancient aforestation, the primary woodland of oak, ash, beech, and the like, with its untrodden dark interior, which gives Rob's novel its magical name: "Mythago Wood."

It is hard to believe that the Wood does not exist in reality. Happily, it exits in Unreality. And there in Unreality, it seems, Steve Huxley's brother Christian has married Guiwenneth, who has emerged from the Wood — the beautiful, pungent-smelling, elemental Guiwenneth.

Guiwenneth opens the tale as a stinking corpse, buried near the house, Oak Lodge. Later, she is all about the house, sumptuous, lively, and cooking a rabbit. "She served the carcass whole, head and all, but had split the skull so that the brains would cook.... Guiwenneth ate with her fingers, using her short knife..." (*Mythago Wood* [1984] 87).

As for Christian, it seems he is lost in the vastness of that ancient eponymous forest.

The story is enriched by the sons' father's, Huxley Senior's, tale and

1

Foreword by Brian W. Aldiss

by his notebooks. It is the father who first glimpsed those "various forms from the latter part of the first millennium AD" (24). Such frightening forms begin to invade the house. We, like Steven, are not clear what they may be or what shapes they may take. And not the human-like forms only: in the middle of the night, a great tree breaks into Oak Lodge.

However, I should not be telling the story, or fragments of the story. Inevitably we enter the wildwood with its stench of ash, blood, and animal. And there is the Urscumug. There are the creatures; there, too, are "the strange men from cultures unrecognizable" (127). Why do we welcome all this, even to the extent of finding it, or believing we find it, all mistily memorable?

Why? Because we are under the spell of a magician. It holds us like a poem. "A thing of terror is a spell forever; its dreadfulness increases...."

Mythago Wood exists as a whole. It is no ordinary horror story, with its extraordinary beauty. Rather it is about time, time solidified, death pickled, and the way we might have lived, might have had to live, once upon a time. That's awful enough.

More than that, Rob Holdstock has shown us here an arrangement of inherited memories, feelings, thoughts, and childlike fears which lie like a fertilizer just below consciousness. These elements are uniquely designed in a pattern that pleases and disturbs us.

Which is the function of all valid art.

Brian W. Aldiss, O.B.E., has three Hugo awards, three BSFA awards, a Nebula award, a John W. Campbell Memorial award, and a SFFWA Grand Master award among others. He wrote with David Wingrove what may well be the most influential history of science fiction, The Trillion Year Spree (1986). One of his short stories was the basis for Steven Spielberg's A.I. (2001).

Introduction: Mythago Wood — "A Source of Visions and Adventure"

Donald E. Morse

"I hadn't realized until I found them — the books, that is — how compact they were, how..." He tried to find the word. "How useful. They're tiny! They would hardly make a fire. You can hold them in the palm of your hand! And yet they are a source of visions and adventure." (Robert Holdstock, *Avilion* 316)

The Story-Teller

Robert Holdstock's agent once wryly remarked of a new novel the author had just completed that it was not exactly "beach reading" — a description that greatly amused Holdstock. And it is true, there is nothing frivolous or trivial about his fiction, for he raises some profound and often difficult questions while exploring people driven to the very edge of sanity: a husband gloating over his wife's suicide, a young girl sacrificing her life to pursue her brother's dream, brother battling brother to the death, a young son assuming responsibility for his mother's demise. Children leave home never to return. Lovers part and reunite only to part again. Such topics do not, it is true, make very suitable "beach reading," but beyond this and similar caveats these novels do illustrate what happens when humans meet their limits as humans, as well as the consequences of transgressing those limits. In this sense, among others, the novels add to our knowledge of the human heart and mind.

A story-teller *par excellence*, Holdstock wrote with considerable insight about the power of dreams, the unconscious, and human desire. W. B. Yeats believed that "in dreams begin responsibilities," and Holdstock's novels continually probe the limits and extent of this responsibility. To dwell only in the dream is to neglect, if not to avoid, living, as happens to Tallis in *Lavondyss: Journey to an Unknown Region* (1988), who expends her spirit in continual pursuit of a dream — a dream that is not even her own but her brother's. To pursue a powerful dream to the exclusion of all else can be disastrous, as illustrated by Christian, who commits fratricide and rapes his brother's wife. Both are extreme examples of those that follow the lead of George Huxley, original discoverer of the strange nature of the Mythago Wood (*Mythago Wood* [1984]). Following a medieval warrior princess he, then both of his sons, disappears into the wood for substantially long periods to be significantly transformed by his experience there.

Holdstock began by writing science fiction, but although his early books were well received, they remain under-realized. "[T]he three early science-fiction novels prefigur[e], and to some extent wrestl[e] with, the kind of fusion of science fiction and fantasy that Holdstock was to crystallize in *Mythago Wood*," Andy Sawyer has concluded. Clearly, Holdstock had yet to find his true subject and mode that would allow him to write with passion and depth — which would occur in the Mythago Wood novels.

A prolific author, Holdstock created a considerable body of work often under various pseudonyms and pen names. He wrote not only science fiction but also mysteries and horror, did novelizations of films, and edited collections, but whatever he did, as Jon Grimwood remarked, he did quickly, publishing a book "every three or four months, under numerous names." But not the mythago novels. Those took time: time to percolate through his sensibility, time to accumulate the images, time to select the many myths to be used, time to write. Like many, perhaps most, writers, he only gradually realized that he had come upon his treasure lode of story, that all his stories were waiting for him in that sentient wood. So he kept returning to Mythago Wood over some twenty-five years and each time explored and deepened the possibilities inherent in his subject, but then the subject itself began to expand, for the Wood, though compact, is deep and within it time and space do not conform to the rules of this world. "Time is strange in Mythago Wood" (*Avilion* [2009] 1), with seasons sometimes succeeding one another over a few days and space often malleable with one mythic world intersecting others. Like Euripides, Holdstock "dramatized the intersection of myth and reality, one turning upon and challenging the other" (Said 142). And as Brian Aldiss writes in his foreword to this volume: "It is hard to believe that the wood does not exist in reality. Happily, it exits in Unreality."

The Mythago Wood Cycle

Robert Holdstock's Mythago Wood novels are among those rare books that add to our experience rather than simply reflecting that experience back to us. Looking over his career it is possible to see now an almost inevitable trajectory of work that led again and again back to Mythago Wood. His last, culminating novel, *Avilion*, presents a fully realized portrait of the "sentient" wood, exploring what had been implied in earlier works: that the beings in the wood produced through human desires, thoughts, and dreams were far more than reflections of those desires, thoughts, and dreams — they were themselves actual beings.

> Ryhope Wood is as ancient as the Ice Age, primal, undisturbed for twelve thousand years; and it is semi-sentient. As small as Ryhope Wood seems, it contains a vast world. Within its apparently impenetrable boundaries, legendary figures and landscape come alive, born from the collective memory of those who live in its proximity [*Avilion* 1].

In this last novel, Holdstock explores a conundrum posited by science fiction in the nineteenth and early twentieth centuries: What if a being created by humans became aware of itself as a created being? What would happen? Would that creature bless or curse his creator? Might she contemplate — or even commit — suicide out of despair at never being fully human? Alternatively, might being less than human lead to frustration or would being more than human lead to exaltation? Frankenstein's creature lived to curse his creator for making him so monstrous. Guiwenneth, the continuing presence in the Wood, appears in most of the Mythago novels as the would-be or actual lover of two generations of Huxley men. Knowing that only a human desire and dream will lead to her rebirth in Lavondyss, she asks of Christian as she once more "dies" or withers away to the twigs and leaves of the forest from which she was created: "Dream me well" (*Gate of Ivory, Gate of Horn* [1998] 336). The process by which life is created in the Wood contrasts sharply with other more familiar stories, such as Dr. Frankenstein's creation of life out of inanimate material or the sculptor's bringing to life the statue Pygmalion, an already idealized woman carved in stone. In the Mythago Wood human dreams filtered through any of the world's many mythologies come to life as mythagos. As George Huxley explains, mythagos "are formed ... from the unheard, unseen communication between our common human *unconscious* and the vibrant, almost tangible sylvan mind of the wood itself. The wood watches, it listens, and it draws out our dreams..." (Holdstock, "The Bone Forest" 9).

This image of the human appearing out of nature occurs in one of Holdstock's favorite poems by W. B Yeats, "The Song of Wandering Ængus," where Ængus, the Celtic god of love, himself falls in love with a magical woman who metamorphoses from a trout only to "disappear ... into the brightening air." The conclusion of the poem pictures the god wandering the earth in search of the "glimmering girl." The god of love, in pursuit of love, strangely ages during his quest but never gives up, "though old with wandering." Similarly, the Huxley men pursue their dream of the ideal woman and, like the god, they, too, grow old with wandering. Yet, unlike the god, each does realize his dream at least partially and — in one sense or another, in one way or another — does capture his "glimmering girl." And here is where Holdstock seizes the opportunity to introduce pathos, violence, tragedy, and loss, for in each instance the meeting or union, if there is union, is but fleeting. The girl abandons the man, disappears or dies, leaving behind he who dreamed her into life. This compelling metaphor for love found, love enjoyed, and love lost reflects the central experience in human life of loss that is mirrored again and again in these powerful fictions.

But Holdstock goes further, especially in *Avilion*, where he ponders an ancient conundrum: what if a human were to mate with that dream creation? What if anything would, could, might result? Such questions have long teased philosophers, dreamers, and psychologists, and in *Avilion* they are explored in profound depth. This intriguing "thought experiment" becomes fully fleshed in the children of the human male, Steven, and the mythago woman, Guiwenneth, with results that appear in hindsight as inevitable as they are tragic for both human and mythago: the children leave to go not just their separate ways but leave in such a way as to sunder primary relationships and dissolve the family because of their contrasting, and perhaps ultimately incompatible, natures. Together the boy and girl illustrate the need for both intuition gained from a mythago mother and reason inherited from a human father. Jack, the child dominated by his human inheritance, attempts to integrate into the human world, while Yssobel, dominated by her mythago inheritance, goes questing deep into Mythago Wood.

Besides profoundly exploring the central human experience of loss, *Avilion* becomes a striking parable of the life cycle of birth, growth, maturation, old age, and death. Children grow and go their own ways searching and maturing; love is found, lost, found again, only to be once more lost. The constants in the novel included within the life cycle are predominately growth and change occasioned by the struggle to survive against encroaching darkness, threatening violence, and the stink of decay and decomposition. The life cycle inevitably revolves away from youth and idealized love, as birth leads to death by way of adventure, growth, pain, and love. Yet, life in all its facets is again and again affirmed within Holdstock's dark vision, perhaps best summed up in the title of one of the three poems appended to the conclusion of *Avilion*: "He regrets that his dreams are not fulfilled, yet dreams" (340).

A Tribute to Robert Holdstock

This book was begun as a tribute to Robert Holdstock's creative genius and now with his death becomes a memorial to his considerable accomplishment as a seminal writer. The essays are by many of the leading scholars of the fantastic from countries as diverse as the United States, England, Sweden, Poland, and Hungary, for Holdstock is a powerful and growing presence both through his own work and that of his translators.

In the first part, three general essays suggest various approaches, such as tracing the lineage of the novels back to folk and fairy tales, examining them as psychic fantasies of our unconscious life, and dissecting their spatiotemporal order. W. A. Senior in "The Embodiment of Abstraction in the Mythago Novels" traces the genealogy of the "magic wood or enchanted forest ... from medieval folktale and romance to Spenser, Shakespeare, Radcliffe, William Morris, Tolkien, and others.... As a metaphor of human emotions, experiences, and obsessions," he concludes, "the wood enables protean incarnations of the very abstractions that metaphors embody. From primitive myth to mythic figures and lost memory to story, the capacious nature of Ryhope permits all expressions of the incarnation of imagination, memory, or desire." Kálmán Matolcsy in "Masks in the Forest: The Dynamics of Surface and Depth in the Mythago Cycle" questions the simple identification of the Mythago Wood cycle of novels as only or as primarily fantasy, for he claims, "Holdstock's choice of thematics delegates the novels to a category of the literature of psychic life [fusing] ... [l]iterary fantasy and psychoanalytical fantasies ... in the image of the forest as the mysterious world of the unconscious." In his reading the books suggest a "double tragedy of the mythago process [that] resides in the failure of the self to expel the Other once and for all, while this internal Other also experiences its failure to become externalized." The novels also stress the narrative nature of a wholesome human life. In the last general essay, "Exploring the Habitats of Myths: The Spatiotemporal Structure of Ryhope Wood," Stefan Ekman examines "the unique spatiotemporal structure of Mythago Wood under its more prosaic name of Ryhope Wood, charting its evolution over the four novels." In order to fully analyze the forest's spatiotemporal structure, Ekman coins the term *mythotopes*, which he defines as "the habitats of myths" and divides into three categories: *constant* mythotopes, *shared* mythotopes, and *specific* mythotopes — the last are connected to a particular myth.

The discussion of specific novels in Part Two begins with Andy Sawyer's "Time Winds," in which he examines the early science-fiction trilogy that includes Holdstock's first published novel, *Eye Among the Blind* (1976). He concludes that these "three science-fiction novels seem to be set in the same universe, sharing, as many SF sequences do, an imagined locale which serves as a metaphysical mindscape" — a mindscape that will come to dominate the Mythago Wood novels. The first of these books, *Mythago Wood*, may be fruitfully contemplated as an example of the Romantic, natural sublime, as Marek Oziewicz argues in "Profusion Sublime and the Fantastic," where the primary agent for the sublime is Ryhope Wood itself. What Oziewicz concludes about *Mythago Wood* applies equally well to all of the novels under discussion here: that "grasping at the transcendent is fundamental to Holdstock's novel[s]."

Two essays focus on what may well be Holdstock's finest and most tragic novel, *Lavondyss: Journey to an Unknown Region*. In "Tallis, the Feminine Presence in Mythago Wood," Elizabeth A. Whittingham examines what she terms "the challenging presence" of Tallis by considering it under the figures of maiden, mother, and crone — the ever-present threefold goddess of several myths. Her essay throws new light on this character that must be central to any discussion of Holdstock's values. Vera Benczik, looking at the same novel in "Embedded Narratives in *Lavondyss* and Ursula K. Le Guin's *The Left Hand of Darkness*," analyzes "embedded mythological excerpts [that] serve as metaphorical maps" in the two novels. She concludes that both books "draw heavily upon mythology, but *The Left Hand of Darkness* uses an anthropological approach whereas *Lavondyss* relies heavily on the Jungian system of archetypes and ancestral memory.... While bridging the gaps in the narratives by supplying relevant information," she insists, "the embeddings themselves are the source of uncertainty and miscommunication."

Uncertainty and miscommunication lie at the heart of *Gate of Ivory, Gate of Horn*, which Donald E. Morse in "Stories to Illuminate Truth and Lies to Hide Pain" claims is "one of the most psychologically complex novels within the mode of contemporary fantasy." The focus here is a boy's daring confrontations with the traumatic experience of his mother's suicide in which he and his father are implicated. Holdstock's mythago proves an almost ideal invention for metaphorically dealing with what often cannot be confronted directly in experience. The novel presents both false and true dreams, but identifying and separating out which is which proves as difficult for the characters involved as it may for the reader.

In "'A Heap of Broken Images'—The Mythological Wasteland of the Mind," Ildikó Limpár argues that both *The Hollowing* (1993) and *Ancient Echoes* (1996) lead the reader into the self, or, "more precisely, within the self's psyche, which functions as a classic otherworld known from the literature of fantasy, yet also operates according to the rules of reality." In our contemporary world, she contends, "the perfect site for the unknown is not to be found in another galaxy but within the unconscious." She continues that "the novels use the psychic landscapes for the same purpose: the 'hero' must enter it in order to fulfill his personal quest, that is, to reclaim his child."

Holdstock's last series of novels, the Merlin Codex books—*Celtika* (2001), *The Iron Grail* (2002), and *The Broken Kings* (2007)—in many ways, runs parallel to the Mythago Wood novels. Before his death Holdstock had completed three and may have contemplated a fourth book in the series where he experiments with a different form of narration having Merlin tell all the various stories down through the centuries. C. W. Sullivan III in "'So many names in so many tongues...': Allusive Mythology in *Celtika*" focuses on exactly how Holdstock is able to explore and uniquely amalgamate Celtic and Greek myth. He concludes that "Holdstock can interweave a Greek tale with a Celtic/Arthurian tale secure in the knowledge that the two will fit together because they have similar structures and themes." Finally, Tom Shippey in "Thresholds, Polders, and Crosshatches" argues that these three novels are neither history nor geography as we know it but Holdstock's recreation of both from within myth, which goes to the heart of Holdstock's literary method as a mythic fantasy writer of considerable power and range.

"A great voyager of the mind"

Like many writers, Robert Holdstock, inadvertently, or perhaps intentionally, left behind an appropriate epitaph. He often quoted from one of his favorite poets, Alfred Lord Tennyson, and chose for the epigraph to *Avilion* lines from "The Passing of Arthur," the mythic king from Tennyson's *Idylls of the King*. The lines capture the focus of Holdstock's fiction — his life's work that centered on the journey to be undertaken always in hope but also always in doubt and, above all, with the certain knowledge that life does cause "grievous wound[s]" and some of those beyond all healing.

> But now farewell, I am going a long way
> With these thou seest — if indeed I go
> (For my mind is clouded with a doubt)—
> To the island-valley of Avilion;
> ... Where I will heal me of my grievous wound.

As a person, unlike the characters in Mythago Wood who were "such stuff as dreams ... made," Holdstock knew both the value and limit of dreams — even those of healing: "He regrets that his dreams are not fulfilled, yet dreams" (*Avilion* 340). Perhaps it lies in our human nature that no dream remains utterly fulfilled or unfulfilled. Still, as a writer, Robert Holdstock — this magician of words — dared to dream Mythago Wood and the Merlin Codex into several extraordinary novels that will be read, reread, treasured, and shared down through the years. His words have the power to come alive in us, his readers, as we absorb the mythic fantasy of a sentient wood and its mythagos. As Brian W. Aldiss wrote in a foreword to the collected mythago novels: "We have here a powerful and profound work of creation which I believe will be read, not merely in the present, but in a hundred years' time, and in the eternal entanglements and winters yet to come" ("Foreword"). Tom Shippey's conclusion to his essay is also that of this volume as a whole: Robert Holdstock "is undoubtedly a great creator of otherworlds, a great transcender of resemblances, a great voyager of the mind."

WORKS CITED

Aldiss, Brian. "Foreword." *The Mythago Cycle*. Vol. 1. London: Gollancz, 2007.

Grimwood, Jon Courtenay. "Robert Holdstock Obituary." *The Guardian* 2 December 2009.

Holdstock, Robert. "The Bone Forest." *The Bone Forest*. London: Grafton, 1991. 1–82.

Said, Edward W. *On Late Style: Music and Literature Against the Grain*. New York: Vintage, 2006.

Yeats, W. B. "The Song of Wandering Ængus." *Collected Poems of W. B. Yeats*. 2nd ed. London: Macmillan, 1973. 66–67.

1

The Embodiment of Abstraction in the Mythago Novels

W. A. Senior

Stories of the magic wood or enchanted forest proffer a lengthy genealogy for the fantasy scholar, from medieval folktale and romance to Spenser, Shakespeare, Radcliffe, William Morris, Tolkien, and others. Although the wood itself changes little physically from era to era, from author to author, its enabling malleability bequeathes writers immense possibility, both in plot and in metaphor. Medieval ballads, folktales, and romances such as *Sir Orfeo* tell of mortals who wander into the wood, meet the Queen of Elfland and her train, and never return; or if they do, they find that decades have flown by in what seemed only days or weeks, that friends and family are dead or vanished. In the comic image of the Forest of Arden in *As You Like It*, enchantment becomes possible as the characters move out of the constraints of the city and into what C. L. Barber, in his masterwork *Shakespeare's Festive Comedy*, terms the "green world," where the trammels of society evaporate and the laws of the heart rule, the cynicism of Jacques aside. In the complex interlace of the *Faerie Queene*, Spenser's heroes, heroines, and villains begin by "pricking across the plain" but end up bewildered and wandering in deep woods of moral and mortal danger. Lothlórien, perhaps the ultimate haven in Tolkien's Middle-earth, incorporates power with stability; an isled wood out of time, it recognizes its own realities and casts an enchantment over all who enter it. Finally, in the line "Two roads diverged in a yellow wood," I would argue that Robert Frost takes a tentative step not only toward fantasy, toward the unknown, the mystery, and the heart of darkness, but also toward the limitlessness of creative potential offered by the enchanted forest.

The perilous wood is not always easy to find, though; and often characters must enter through a doorway of sorts.[1] Most portal fantasies feature a hidden or unrecognized entrance to the enchanted land: over the rainbow or through a wardrobe, down a water passage, in an eidolon of power such as Stonehenge, or simply through a rift between worlds, as in works by C. S. Lewis, Stephen R. Donaldson, Philip Pullman, Jane Yolen, and various others. The protagonists meet with a secondary or parallel world replete in itself, governed by its own internal rules or laws and populated by races and creatures with a depth of intertwined legend, story, and history. After the conclusion of their adventure or quest, the characters return, often after almost no passage of time.

The locus of Robert Holdstock's contemporary myth narrative, Ryhope Wood, although its external physical dimension is only three square miles, appears to have no boundary to those within it and represents the unlimited potential of the mind and creative impulse. While the time dilation in many fantasies makes weeks seem days, in Ryhope, mere minutes can encompass lifetimes. Here the past impinges on the present as figures from earlier ages and tales are generated by the power of the imagination and need of those in the present. As Colin Manlove comments,

> The wood, which is a small remnant in Herefordshire of the old British wildwood, is the recurrent home of living archetypes ... spawned down the ages by neighboring humanity's unconscious minds. To seek to enter the wood is to journey into the mind, and bring about one's psychic unravelling as deeper layers are exposed. Everything met in the wood (which once entered becomes vast), whether its trees or its inhabitants, is the mythic creation of some mind [61].

George Huxley's journal entry in "The Bone Forest" accounts for the power of Ryhope Wood:

> I have coined the word "mythago" to describe these creatures of forgotten legend. This is from "myth imago," or the *image of the myth*. They are formed, these various heroes of old, from the unheard, unseen communication between our common human *unconscious* and the vibrant, almost tangible sylvan mind of the wood itself. The wood watches, it listens, and it draws out our dreams... [9].

As Ursula K. Le Guin explains it,

> The great fantasies, myths, and tales are indeed like dreams: they speak *from* the unconscious *to* the unconscious, in the *language* of the unconscious — symbol and archetype. Though they use words, they work the way music does: they short-circuit verbal reasoning, and go straight to

the thoughts that lie too deep to utter. They cannot be translated fully into the language of reason, but only a Logical Positivist, who also finds Beethoven's Ninth Symphony meaningless, would claim that they are therefore meaningless. They are profoundly meaningful, and usable — practical — in terms of ethics; of insight; of growth [62]

Thus, in Holdstock's creation, the denizens of the Wood spring from the unconscious of the characters who enter it: that is, the Wood itself draws upon cultural memories to provide the embodiment of figures embedded within those memories. The magic, if it can be called that, is not due to spells, enchantments, or the conventions of genre fantasy. There are no witches, wizards, centaurs, dragons, elves, dwarves, trolls, or any of the usual forms of characters drawn from the library of myth, folktale, or fantasy. This is not the wild of faery, the Gothic, Scott's romances, Tolkien, Lewis, or any other fantasy writer. The primary power resides in the nature of the Wood itself, which functions as a passage to another, more primal, time; and the inhabitants of the ghost wood are variations on earlier figures elicited from the minds of those who can penetrate the Wood and pass through the portals, or "hollowings," that guard it. As Brian Aldiss comments in *Trillion Year Spree*, "The heartland of the wood is not a refuge but a confrontation with the most primitive images of self" (442).[2] Stephen R. Donaldson, in *Epic Fantasy in the Modern World*, argues that "in fantasy the entire out there, with all its levels and complexities and dimensions, is an externalization ... of what is in here" (5–6). Certainly, Donaldson's work differs greatly from Holdstock's, but the creative and mythic impulses intersect. Donaldson's hero, Thomas Covenant, finds himself in a world which reflects and animates his own internal world: Lord Foul, for instance, is the reification of his own self-disgust and hatred because of his leprosy and of its corruptive effects. However, in Holdstock's wood, the externalizations are drawn from a well of cultural stories and memories as each person has internalized them.

The essential difference between Holdstock's vision and the more traditional rendition of the enchanted forest entails the notion of abstraction. The word "abstraction" itself invokes a tension of opposites or contraries: the Latin prefix "abs" means "away" or "from"; yet "tract" (L "*trahere*") means "to pull" and denotes motion in one direction, as in "tractor." So, my stipulation lies not in the usual dictionary denotation of the term that indicates the separation of an idea from a form, but in fact a metaphorical capacity for a reversal of mythopoesis that involves the essence of creation in that *the physical is drawn from the concept*, matter attracted by *nous*—the Greek notion of mind and intelligence. In Holdstock's Mythago sequence, characters pull from the Wood and concomitantly from their own unconscious to give form to airy nothingness. The inhabitants of the Wood, such as the Hood, Twigling, Jacks, Shamiga, and so on, are ideas, inchoate desires, or needs clothed in bodies, an employment of abstraction that transcends dream vision, allegory, or even Jungian archetype from which Holdstock borrows heavily.[3]

Among modern fantasists, Holdstock is perhaps the writer whose work most attempts to unpack the heart of such abstraction in *Mythago Wood* (1984), *Lavondyss: Journey to an Unknown Region* (1988), *The Hollowing* (1993), and *Gate of Ivory, Gate of Horn* (1997). In the enchanted forest, Ryhope Wood, his characters — the Huxleys, Harry and Tallis Keeton, Richard Bradley and his lost son, among others — seek discovery and come at last to the recognition of what they already knew in some form or other. They, and we, can arrive at that consummation only through story, the element that John Clute asserts in the *Encyclopedia of Fantasy* structures the genre:

> Fantasy texts, in this understanding, can be characterized as always moving towards the unveiling of an irreducible substratum of Story, an essence sometimes obscure but ultimately omnipresent; the key events of a fantasy text are bound to each other, to the narrative world, and ideally to the tale's theme that permits endless retellings..., endless permutations of the narrative's unbound motifs, and a sense of ending [900].

Myth and story function to explain what cannot be explained, to articulate the numinous and make comprehensible the mysteries of nature, life, death, birth, past times, and lives.

> Helen reminded Richard that all things in Ryhope Wood were connected with legend, be they Palaeolithic hunters or chivalrous knights, but also the structures and landscapes associated with the lost tales. At some time in the past, this crude shrine had not been real but mythic, a place of aspiration in the dreams of people, a place unreachable, unattainable, except in story [*The Hollowing* 156].

Thus, the abstraction draws us in two directions: the chthonic or physical and the inchoate or spiritual. As Richard Bradley in *The Hollowing* experiences, there are "paths down into the odd world, not of dreams, or the real, but a place between the two" (279).

1. *The Embodiment of Abstraction* (Senior)

Mythagos inhabit the Wood but do not exist until summoned. Clute defines a mythago as

> one of the metamorphic figures that tend to attack those who attempt to invade the polder and that take their essence from the collective unconscious of the British people. The mythagoes wear MASKS of various HEROES and other darker persons whose lives, real or imagined, have been central to the MATTER OF BRITAIN [Clute and Grant 475].

Accurate as Clute's assessment is, it does not do justice to the panorama of characters that confront Steven Huxley in *Mythago Wood* alone, never mind the mythic *dramatis personae* who populate *The Hollowing*. First, not all mythagos are hostile; some are friendly while others simply pass through the story, as their tales intersect with the point of view character's experiences, whether Steven's, Christian's, Tallis's, or those of the others. Second, Ryhope Wood swarms with incarnations of lost memories and ages: a mounted French knight from the twelfth century, a family of wandering Saxons, a tribe of Neolithic hunter-gatherers, a survivor of the trenches in World War I, Bronze Age warriors, and, of course, the mysterious Urscumug, a proto-human figure with the characteristics of a boar.

To add to the distinction, we should note that the term "mythago" is a portmanteau word, another indication of the tension to which I have alluded. "Myth" and "imago"—a mythago is the living embodiment, the image, of the myth itself; and what is a myth if not an attempt to explain through story the inexplicable, to abstract or create significance from the seemingly inchoate? Commenting on the nature of story and his own creative process in an interview with *Locus* magazine, Holdstock suggests that "myth and legend work through the familiar being expressed in a new and innovative voice. We retell stories and that is what makes them so powerful" ("Lost Landscapes" 7). In Holdstock's work, however, myth or image metamorphoses in relation to the projecting impulse of the person within the Wood; each person thereby creates a different imago-version based on his or her conception of the myth or story itself. Another, connected closely to the first, is that historical and cultural influences also play a role in the creation of the mythagos, which are, in fact, not so much created as rediscovered, or perhaps reinspired, brought back to life by living need.

Christian explains:

> The old man believed that all life is surrounded by an energetic aura....
> In these ancient woodlands, *primary woodlands*, the combined aura

17

> forms something far more powerful, a sort of creative field that can
> interact with our unconscious. And it's in the unconscious that we carry
> what he calls the pre-mythago — that's *myth imago*, the image of the
> idealized form of a myth creature.... The form of the idealized myth,
> the hero figure alters with cultural changes, assuming the identity and
> technology of the time. When one culture invades another ... the heroes
> are made manifest ... [*Mythago Wood* 37].

Thus, depending upon which version of Arthur inhabits the cultural landscape of an age, a different form would emerge in the Wood. Invention,
that most elusive of constructs, taken literally from the Latin (*invenire*),
means to come upon, meet with, or discover; the term implies, therefore,
that what has been "invented" or created has been in existence already but
in other guise or apprehension. The oft-cited valediction to Arthur at the
end of Malory's *Mort d'Arthur*—"*rex quondam, rexque futurus*"—encap-
sulates the promised reiteration of mythago figures as they are called forth
in different semblances by the version of the story being revivified. One
example is the hostile Hood figure who threatens Steven at various ages
in *Mythago Wood*.

   As I have pointed out, Holdstock's mythagos are not allegorical figures
of any sort, although they inhere to the same principle, the creative act of
attempting to give idea and act a physical presence or mask. The mythagos
and their generation bring us to the essence of poetics, the art of sub-
creation as Tolkien terms it (see 60 and 68–75); and in part, Holdstock
is writing about the nature of art, of being a writer, and his work falls
cleanly into what we may call mythopoetic fantasy. In his researches on
"mythogenetic process," the elder Huxley wonders over the "mythopoetic
energy flows in my cortex — the *form* from the right brain, the *reality* from
the left" (*Mythago Wood* 34). Characters as creators within their own worlds
hold up a mirror to the author.

   An anguished George Huxley attempts to explain the figure to his
son Christian: "They reflect our needs.... They *take* from us. I should have
known that. They reflect us, and *take* from us. We are them. They are us.
Mythagos! Two shadows from the same mind" (*Gate* 29). Thus, the same
character drawn from myth may find various manifestations, depending
upon whose interaction with the Wood generates her. For instance, each
of the Huxley men co-creates or invents a different Guiwenneth, the Celtic
princess who later in the Arthurian sequence becomes Guenevere, and
enters one redaction of the protean myths or legends attached to her. To

help explain the phenomena to him, Christian tells Steven in *Mythago Wood* that "[s]he was my father's mythago, a girl from Roman times, a manifestation of the earth goddess, the young warrior princess" (39). This imago clearly differs at various points with its later cousins and reveals possibilities of what the generated figure could be. George Huxley even ponders at one point about how a Hercules mythago, shorn of battle fever, because of his "creator's" conception, would fare. The same malleability is true of the protean settings within Ryhope's limited physical compass. In "The Bone Forest," Huxley muses to himself "that mythagoscapes changed subtly, and that they could be brought into existence by different minds and therefore with slightly different features" (67).[4]

Mythagos are not exactly the same as their distant relations, Jungian archetypes, because of their embodiment of a different form of abstraction. Graham Dunstan Martin observes of the entire series, but of *Mythago Wood* in particular, that "[m]any of the novel's characters have an archetypal quality, and one may easily be tempted to apply Jungian psychology to its study.... I am not sure that such an analysis, however, would not be too facile" (167). Rather than individual or monolithic, like the figure of the shaman or wise man, they are often cumulative; there is no real one-to-one correspondence, but rather an intuition or resonant association. Holdstock implies the distinction in one of George Huxley's early journal entries:

> ... no society of primitives inhabits this wonderful WILDNESS of unshorn hill and rough-banked river I penetrate day by day, adventure by adventure. But ... a mixture of forms and figures, ... strangely familiar images from my studies, that seems to suggest ALL of myth, something timeless yet ever-changing, fragmented, and at any time, in whatever place I occupy, somehow ever-present [Gate 96–97].

This notion of "a mixture of forms" creates the distance from a strict identification with the archetype. For instance, the bogeyman figure of *The Hollowing*, whom Alex calls the Giggler, is indistinct and composite, a horrifying amalgam of the toys, paintings, pictures, and experiences with the always perplexing world of adults that have all deeply affected him with fear and anxiety. In *Lavondyss*, Tallis Keeton plunges toward an Ice Age winter where iterations of the earliest wanderers are generated, those who moved from the continent after the retreating glaciers. Spud Frampton, the World War I character Steven and Harry meet, is, for instance, generated out of the despair of soldiers in the Great War lost in tunnels or in No Man's Land, looking for someone to guide them back. "Mythago forms as recently as that," exclaims Steven (*Mythago Wood* 228). Yet while he does fit the profile of the guide figure, there is a subtle distinction: Frampton, culled from Steven's unconscious by Sorthalan, destroys himself as he becomes unmoored from his own mythic history and time.

The ultimate example of the tendency toward abstraction finds its quintessence in the concept or place of Lavondyss, a mythical or metaphorical quest objective within Ryhope Wood that few can comprehend or even articulate. Lavondyss, "*the place where the spirits of men are not tied to the seasons*" (*Mythago Wood* 214; see also *Lavondyss* 213), is implicated in both the definition of abstraction I have stipulated as well as the more general denotation as something abstruse, something separated from a concrete, physical reality, or the formulation of an idea unweighted by material objects. It is the reification of hope, desire, recovery, restitution. Tallis, before she hears its name, mourns her vision of the dying Scathach and thinks she has sent him to "where the hunting would never end, where every man could sing well, and where the loving was as fierce in the winter as it was in the spring. To that many coloured land.... To that bright side of the forbidden place..." (*Lavondyss* 109; see also 177). A place that exists but does not, it ironically corresponds to More's Utopia, a pun on the no-place which conveys the good-place. Christian, Harry Keeton, various scientists in *The Hollowing*—all pursue a partially felt, partially sensed, partially apprehended vision they struggle to describe or evoke. Harry Keeton confesses that he is unable to make clear his meaning: "Utopia? Peace? A sort of future vision of every people. A place like heaven" (*Mythago Wood* 252). During his final confrontation with Steven, Christian struggles to explain his understanding, mingling various mythologies with a sense of wonder and transcendence: "*Tir-na-nOc*.... Avalon. Heaven. Call it what you like. It's the unknown land, the beginning of the labyrinth.... The realm guarded ... against Man's curiosity." He continues that place is "inaccessible," a thing from the past "unknowable, forgotten" (*Mythago Wood* 265).

The protean physical representation of Lavondyss implicates the articulation of desire of those who seek it. For Keeton, it is a place of healing and recovery; for Tallis, a hope of reunification with her half-brother; for Christian, an opportunity for redemption and safety from the Urscumug; for McCarthy in *The Hollowing,* a redemption as he searches for both his dead partner, killed while exploring a medieval castle in the Wood, and "the key of mytho-genesis," the *bête noir* of Huxley père (100). Even the mythagos themselves are tied to it; each of the Jaguth must pass back through the valley to Lavondyss, for it is a "potent symbol, a place of spiritual strength" (*Mythago Wood* 253). And of course, the Urscumug/George Huxley will take Guiwenneth back there so that she may return.

Yet each has a different voyage and a different vision. For Harry, shot down over France during World War II, the glimpse into Lavondyss recalls the iconographical city in the medieval dream vision *The Pearl*; a place out of time and history, it is a city of light in a dark place, guarded by powerful creatures, which "glowed in the night ... alien to them, unlike any city of history, a glowing, gorgeous place, which beckoned them emotionally and had them stumbling blindly towards it" (*Mythago Wood* 253).[5]

Not a conventional afterlife, a heaven or a hell, it is in fact the stuff that dreams are made on, but it is abstracted from those dreams as well. It is referred to by different people as the ghost place or ghost world, Ryhope as the "ghost wood." The current usage of "ghost" leads us in a false direction, for here again, Holdstock delves back into an earlier use of the term, from the enabling Old English "*gast*," which returns us to the etymological root of inspiration: breath, soul, spirit, life, or man or human being (see Hall). For Lavondyss is not only the Ice Age, source of our first unconscious memories

> of Europe, source therefore of the savage myths which people Mythago Wood, but it is also the Other World, the world of rebirth and immortality, and is derived from the words "Avon, Lyonesse, Avalon (the Celtic after-death Paradise), lave, abyss, and Dyss" (= Dis, an Ancient Greek name for Hades) [Martin 168].

Paradoxically, Lavondyss is both the place of life and death, drawing qualities of both in a complex metaphor that lies on the horizon of understanding.

The concept of Lavondyss, the lost place that all search for, suggests another central characteristic of fantasy implicated in the notion of abstraction, that of loss, the recovery of the past. Detractors of fantasy often sniff that it melts, thaws, and resolves into a dew of coddling nostalgia; that fantasy is a childish form of wish fulfillment presenting a comfortable quasi-medieval world in which everything turns out well. The evidence is, of course, against such a view, represented prominently in the elegiac ending of *The Lord of the Rings*, the utter destruction and horror of Stephen R. Donaldson's Thomas Covenant series, Ged's disempowerment and sacrifice in Ursula K. Le Guin's Earthsea works, or even the attrition Harry Potter feels as parents, godparent, mentors, friends, and allies are stripped from him year by year. Nor can we find much comfort or reassurance in any of Holdstock's work, least of all the Mythago novels. As I commented in the *Dictionary of Literary Biography*, Holdstock does not shy away from the savage in any of his work: *Ancient Echoes* (1995) "is perhaps Holdstock's most brutal book ... filled with cruelty that exceeds even the ferocious early sword-and-sorcery books" (247).[6]

I would argue that in fantasy particularly the essence of loss is a form of abstraction, of something or someone being pulled away leaving an emptiness, a perceptible void. In Holdstock's novels, such absence becomes transubstantiated into presence insofar as the emotion of loss recognizes something, but something that has departed. Loss of the past thus exists in a sense as abstraction, as characters pull from a past wealth of myth, story, legend, folktale, oral narrative, and dim memory, linking the urge to rediscovery to recreation. Entry to Ryhope Wood deracinates one from the present and forces him or her to rediscover a vanished reality.

The narrative engine that propels the Mythago novels is the reiterated loss of Guiwenneth by the three Huxley men, the loss of Harry and Tallis Keeton, and then the disappearance of Alex Bradley in *The Hollowing*, or even Wynne-Jones' rift with his daughter, both before and after his immurement in the Wood (see *Mythago Wood* 100ff). The doomed romance of Steven and Guiwenneth has undertones of the Arthur/Guenevere story, or perhaps more aptly the Tristan/Iseut tale of separation. What accelerates the tension is that both realize that their story cannot end happily, in part because they understand they are caught up in a lost story itself, although Steven will not at first admit it. After they attempt to leave the Wood and Oak Lodge and discover they cannot, Steven tries to comfort her:

> "I don't mind," I said.
> "I do," she said softy. "I'll lose you."
> "You won't. I love you too much."
> "I love you very much too. And I'll lose you. It's coming, Steven, I can feel it. Terrible loss" [*Mythago Wood* 146].

This same poignant and terrible loss sends Christian on a desperate journey in *Gate of Ivory, Gate of Horn*, a quest which eventually warps him until he has, in fact, lost himself, one of the overhanging dangers of Ryhope and its shifting realities as one plunges more deeply into his own unconscious. Of the increasingly withdrawn and bosky McCarthy, Lacan tells Richard, "'You see? He's sitting there dreaming, listening to the wood.

There's nothing to hear. Not in *here*, at least,' he tapped his right ear. 'But there is so much to hear more deeply'" (*The Hollowing* 99).

One poignant loss occurs, or perhaps does not, at the end of *Lavondyss*, when Tallis seems to be separated from her distraught father. "As Frye implies — although he does not develop the idea in detail — the hero monomyth encompasses not just romance, but tragedy as well. The sorrows of the hero who refuses the call to adventure, or who gets trapped in the special world and never finds his way out, constitute one form of tragedy," Kathryn Hume argues (180). It is never clear to the reader, given the ambiguous narrative in *Lavondyss*, whether in one possible outcome Tallis emerges to be reunited with her father, or if she becomes trapped, like Harry, within the wood, within the story, and does not find her way out. John Clute asserts in a review of *The Hollowing* that "[t]he story is the story Holdstock tells most often: The tale of the Lost Child searching for its Parent or whose parent is searching for it" ("Canon" 59). Richard Bradley's immersion in the Wood to find his son, Alex, appears to be motivated by a version of the tale in which Tallis has not come back and Richard fears the same for Alex, whose own mythagos reflect the home and place he has lost.

Perhaps we can most cogently summarize Ryhope Wood as the place of lost hopes, dreams, loves, and possibilities, but paradoxically and equivalently as a place where each or any can be reclaimed. As Carroll Brown points out, "[w]e know ... that Ryhope Wood is more a psychic landscape than a physical one, that a journey inward is a journey into the inner space of a human being and humanity in general and that the external terrain does not, in a sense exist in its own right" (160). In his odd journal-based conversation with his own split mythago-ego, Huxley learns that "[t]*hrough Ash there is a strange continuity. No matter what has been destroyed, it lives in* her, *and one day can be summoned back*" ("Bone Forest" 53). The Coda at the end of *Mythago Wood* accentuates the possibility of what Tolkien labels recovery (see 77–78). And there are no guarantees, given the interlay of story. Will Christian return? Steven, now in another variation of the tale, waits for Guiwenneth to reappear, and the story turns once more. As a metaphor of human emotions, experiences, and obsessions, the Wood enables protean incarnations of the very abstractions that metaphors embody. From primitive myth to mythic figures and lost memory to story, the capacious nature of Ryhope permits all expressions of the incarnation of imagination, memory, or desire.

23

As Hume observes in *Mimesis and Fantasy*, "[t]he power of fantasy increases if it offers us something genuinely new and compelling" (165). Robert Holdstock's Mythago novels and stories represent some of the standard elements of fantasy in an entirely different way than what we are accustomed to. While Holdstock observes many of the standard stages of the monomyth or quest structure of genre fantasy, he alters them, often radically. In particular, he omits the final stage, which Joseph Campbell calls the "return and reintegration with society" (136). At the end there is no reunion of Huxleys, Wynne-Joneses, or Keetons, no reassertion of domestic normalcy, because they have all become lost and found in the Wood and its tales; in a sense they have become abstractions themselves, stories for another time and another people.

NOTES

1. The passage through the gateway often corresponds to an elemental test of earth, air, fire, and/or water. Bilbo Baggins in *The Hobbit*, for instance, has to escape from the goblin caves under the Misty Mountains (earth), the elves' dwelling in the Mirkwood (water), and Smaug's lair under the Lonely Mountain (fire). Such passages also inhere to the threshold stage in the monomyth as set forth by Joseph Campbell in *The Hero with a Thousand Faces* (77ff). For a good early discussion and outline of the portal fantasy itself, see Hilary Thompson, "Doorways to Fantasy."

2. *Trillion Year Spree* deals with the history of science fiction, and Aldiss, similarly to others such as Carrol Brown, posits that the Mythago novels draw much of their resonance and power from their "science fictional mode" (Aldiss 442). That said, the setting remains a potent evocation of both primal British forests and the mythic wood itself.

3. I would like to reiterate the generally held position that both allegory and dream vision effectually undercut the intent and import of fantasy since both posit a world that does not exist in its own right, and thus that fantasy, and all it contains, is simply an artificial construct with a didactic purpose or the result of a "bit of undigested beef," as Scrooge tells himself in "A Christmas Carol."

4. If fantasy is in fact a literature of desire, as Rosemary Jackson would have it, then the desires born of Ryhope Wood are those abstracted from desires that the characters in the novels may not even realize they have.

5. Keeton's description is redolent of a number of medieval representations of the celestial city, most notably here in fourteenth-century *Pearl*. See E. V. Gorden, ed., *Pearl*, especially lines 61–144 and 985–1080.

6. On the other hand, in an interview with Catie Cary in *Vector*, Holdstock says of the reunion at the end of *The Hollowing*, "If you are saying, 'My God, Holdstock's written a happy ending story,' and this *has* been said to me, I'm sorry but occasionally I want my stories to end happily" (3).

WORKS CITED

Aldiss, Brian, and David Wingrove. *Trillion Year Spree.* 1986. New York: Avon, 1988.

Brown, Carroll. "The Flame in the Heart of the Wood: The Integration of Myth and Science in Robert Holdstock's *Mythago Wood.*" *Extrapolation* 34.2 (Summer 1993): 158–72.

Campbell, Joseph. *The Hero with a Thousand Faces.* 2nd ed. Princeton: Princeton University Press, 1968.

Clute, John. "Canon at the End of Time." Reviews. *Interzone* November 1993: 59+.

_____, and John Grant, eds. *The Encyclopedia of Fantasy.* New York: St. Martin's, 1997.

Donaldson, Stephen R. *Epic Fantasy in the Modern World.* Kent, OH: Kent State University Libraries, 1986.

_____. *The Illearth War.* New York: Holt, 1977.

_____. *Lord Foul's Bane.* New York: Holt, 1977.

_____. *The Power That Preserves.* New York: Holt, 1977.

Gorden, E. V., ed. *Pearl.* New York: Clarendon, 1974.

Hall, J. R. Clark. *A Concise Anglo-Saxon Dictionary.* 4th ed. Cambridge: Cambridge University Press, 1975.

Holdstock, Robert. "The Bone Forest." *The Bone Forest.* London: Grafton, 1991. 1–82.

_____. *Gate of Ivory, Gate of Horn.* New York: ROC, 1997.

_____. *The Hollowing.* 1993. New York: ROC, 1994.

_____. *Lavondyss: Journey to an Unknown Region.* New York: Morrow, 1988.

_____. *Mythago Wood.* 1984. New York: Berkeley, 1986.

Hume, Kathryn. *Fantasy and Mimesis: Responses to Reality in Western Literature.* New York: Methuen, 1984.

Le Guin, Ursula K. "The Child and the Shadow." *The Language of the Night: Essays on Fantasy and Science Fiction.* Ed. Susan Wood. New York: Perigee, 1979. 59–72.

Manlove, Colin. *The Fantasy Literature of England.* New York: St. Martin's, 1999.

Martin, Graham Dunstan. *An Inquiry into the Purposes of Speculative Fiction: Fantasy and Truth.* Studies in Comparative Literature 58. Lewiston, NY: Edwin Mellen, 2003.

"Robert Holdstock." Interview. By Catie Cary. *Vector* October/November 1993: 3–6.

"Robert Holdstock: Lost Landscapes, Grand Obsessions." Interview. *Locus* April 1996: 6+.

Senior, W. A. "Robert Holdstock." *Dictionary of Literary Biography.* Vol. 261. British Fantasy and Science-Fiction Writers Since 1960. Ed. Darren Harris-Fain. Detroit: Gale, 2002. 239–47.

Thompson, Hilary. "Doorways to Fantasy." *Canadian Children's Literature* 21 (1981): 8–16.

Tolkien, J. R. R. "On Fairy-Stories." *The Tolkien Reader.* New York: Ballantine, 1966. 33–99.

2

Masks in the Forest: The Dynamics of Surface and Depth in the Mythago Cycle

Kálmán Matolcsy

In interpretation it is tempting to declare that a novel is "about" something. Robert Holdstock's Mythago Cycle, the single most notable effort in British fantasy since the works of J. R. R. Tolkien and C. S. Lewis, is thus, among others, "about" the human mind. Nevertheless, the "about" of the Mythago novels that investigate deeply into the recesses of the mind could also appear, by an inversion of some final analysis, to have resulted from the reader's probing into his or her own mind. These books may deal with some of the traditional mythic figures of fantasy, but they also sport a certain amount of self-reflexivity. They present a mirror to the searching intellect through their self-reflexive quality, and thus, in a recoil of the epistemological quest, interpretation could finally appear to have ferreted out a representation of the hermeneutic project itself. The "about" may, at the end of the day, remain just as circular as the protagonists' first tentative movements when feeling their ways around the magical paths of Ryhope Wood. In these cyclical returns to the outset of "pathfinding," the primary light of the "about" flickers around the reader and takes on the characteristics of the pre-mythagos — the primeval forms of mythic archetypes which are, according to the novels' logic, perceived in the form of "movement at the edge of ... vision" (*Mythago Wood* 48).

The novels constantly turn us back to the outset of interpretation, just as Ryhope Wood prepares circular paths for those uninitiated into the secret gateways, "hollowings," into the heartwood. As one of the protagonists, Steven Huxley, explains, "The wood turns you around. It defends itself.... You walk for hours and come in a circle" (*Mythago Wood* 111). The major dynamics and rules of the Wood are best investigated through the diary of Steven's father, who was the initiator of various scientific investigations into the nature of Ryhope; yet, Steven admits that his journal "locked me out of its understanding" (8). The cyclical pathways of interpretation, the "locking out of understanding" and the opening of such locks runs along the magical pathways of Ryhope Wood. It could well be that the "about" of the Mythago novels proves to be cunning interpretations of our interpretations of them, their interpretations through myth of our interpretations of myth in them.

First Steps in the Forest

The monomyth of cyclicality keeps reappearing in the books, manifested in the circularity of "ley matrices" (*Mythago Wood* 35–37), the circular forest pathways, and the eternal return of mythagos themselves. The first novel, *Mythago Wood*, sets the rules of mythago-formation. One of the various mythic characters, Guiwenneth (a bronze-age British princess) qualifies as "a manifestation of the Earth Goddess," a form of the legendary character of Boedicea or Boudicca (39), and perhaps of Arthur's Guinevere. The fascinating twist is that Guiwenneth, a mythic image lost to us modern-age people, is a fleshy being, regenerated from the collective mythic memories of the Huxleys inhabiting the outskirts of the Wood; thus she is a "mythago." Due mainly to the novel's rationalizing moves and naturalist techniques, Guiwenneth gradually loses her magical quality as a lost storybook figure and becomes a living, human young lady. Her human quality is, paradoxically, further emphasized by her awareness of her non-human origin: "I am wood and rock, Steven, not flesh and bone" (147). Part of Steven's quest is directed at her transformation from mythago to something more human, a possible partner for life: "I want to know about you.... Not the image figure that you represent," he tells her (150). In the meantime, through a process contrary to mythago-formation, the Wood takes on a magical quality, since it is a place that "sucks at the mind," the contents of the unconscious: "it sucks out the dreams" (*Lavondyss* 280). This magic, however, yields itself to scientific observation, since George Huxley, the father-scientist figure in *Mythago Wood* seems to have detected energy vortices which "suck at the mind"; they enhance mythogenesis and create the legendary figures of the Jungian collective

Part One: Approaches

unconscious from wood and leaf litter — Holdstock's uncanny imagination ignited by a simple but nonetheless revolutionary idea.

In the motif of mirroring, Ryhope Wood becomes a mythical well of ancient power, reflecting our unconscious being and animating the archetypes we carry in our head.[1] The return of Guiwenneth in several different forms — in *Mythago Wood* she is George Huxley's mythago, then his two sons similarly induce her unawares — is thus the return of a mythic image from the irrational mind. Mircea Eliade analyzes the image of the return in his seminal *The Myth of Eternal Return: Cosmos and History.* Eliade asserts that every religious action and place reiterates an action of or revelation by the gods or ancestors at the place and time of the beginning. Archaic "life is the ceaseless repetition of gestures initiated by others," he argues (5), and the archaic individual thus reenacts these myths to escape historical time and enter a cyclical, mythical time, the sacred place and time of hierophany: "[F]or archaic man, reality is a function of the imitation of a celestial archetype" (5). Eliade is also adamant on his use of "archetype." In the preface to *Eternal Return* he contrasts his usage — archetype as "exemplary model" or "paradigm" (xv) — to Jung's idea of the archetypical image residing in the collective unconscious. Nonetheless, I think that the two lend themselves easily to fusion when analyzing Holdstock's work, since the Jungian archetypes in the Mythago series all reiterate an original mythic image or example. The archetypes of Guiwenneth and Robin Hood, among many others, reside in the collective unconscious as they each are different receptacles for and reservoirs of some original action.[2] In *Lavondyss: Journey to an Unknown Region*, the major archetypes of the shaman, myths of bone, and bird magic all derive from an original Ice Age act of infanticide and cannibalism, of the gruesome murder of young Arak in the midst of a soul-gripping, hopeless winter (434). In an interview Holdstock admits, "I'm not interested in legend and myth as we *know* it, but in what went before! What events, what terrifying and wonderful tales, now forgotten, were remembered sufficiently in darker ages to create what we think of as legend now" (Lightbody par. 4).

The image of the return in the Mythago Cycle's magical world necessitates the return of the archetype. The traumas and desires of the Huxleys reinforce the repeated appearance of Guiwenneth, the warrior-princess, a representation of the object of love and partnership for reclusive men. Guiwenneth is the key to the fates of the scientist George Huxley, who regards her as the objectification of his scientific research into the mysteries of the forest[3]; of Christian Huxley, first a lover, later a brutal warrior chieftain searching after his bounty; and of the youngest son, Steven, a real soul mate to the girl, who lingers at the edge of the heartwood waiting for her to return.

The circularity of the mythago world — the circular forest, the vortices and ley matrices, the mythagos themselves, and the return of mythago thematics in the different mythago novels and other stories of Holdstock's — is in contrast to the quests which basically, and by definition, have a clear purpose, rendering them teleological and linear. Holdstock's quest structure is somewhat different from Northrop Frye's definition as represented by the mythos of romance. In Frye, the romantic hero in the romance journeys in a circular route: rejected by society, he crosses over into an unknown realm and finally returns glorified to reestablish him or herself (187–88). By contrast, the questing heroes and antiheroes of the Mythago Cycle can never ultimately return to their homelands: Steven chooses to stay in the winter land, a valley "where the hunter waits" (*Mythago Wood* 274), and Tallis Keeton is destined to grow old, trapped in an Ice Age community without other humans, except for the human-mythago hybrid Scathach (*Lavondyss* 467–73). The hero's and heroine's linear quests thus appear to cut through the circular lines of myth, perhaps implying that, although the unconscious is able to produce the same images over and over again, any person taking the route in and choosing to trespass on the tangled hinterland of their own psyche must remain, in one way or another, trapped in the world of the fantasy.

A Fantasy of Fantasies

The Mythago books have unquestionably been identified as works of fantasy. Holdstock's choice of thematics, however, also delegates the novels to a category of the literature of psychic life. Literary fantasy and psychoanalytical fantasies[4] are fused in the image of the forest, which gives life to "[t]hings from the unconscious.... Ghosts that we all carry" (*Lavondyss* 74–75).[5] The mythagos are ghosts, which is emphasized by the old name of the forest, "Shadox Wood," and Gaunt the villager's description of mythagos as "moonshadows," "[s]hadows that creep out of the dreams of sleeping folk" (72). Collating literary fantasy and the psychoanalytical theory of fantasies bears fruitful results, as Kathryn Hume asserts: "The very condensation of fantasy images, their ability to resonate with the different emotional needs in the members of the audience, gives fantasy a power and effectiveness that are different from anything achievable by mimesis alone" (191). Rosemary Jackson identifies the fulfillment of these emotional needs, fantasy's psychoanalytic content, as inherently transgressive, ready "to subvert and undermine cultural stability" (69). In its exploitation of the uncanny, fantasy performs a "transgressive function" (70). This transgressive character is doubly enforced through the revolutionary ghastly figure of the mythago, a borderline character, always lurking in the shadow of the undergrowth; neither human nor unphysical — neither figure nor shadow — but both.

Mythagos are parts of ourselves, yet different from us; to simplify Jungian theory, they qualify as our "shadows," our "dark characteristics," a kind of dark matter from our unconscious (Jung, "The Shadow" 91). Or, they can qualify as our "anima and animus," "a feminine side, an unconscious feminine figure [in a man] ... and its counterpart in a woman" (Jung, "Conscious, Unconscious, and Individuation" 221). One of the major "myths of the modern fantastic" arises here, as outlined by Jackson, namely, that "the source of otherness, of threat, is in the *self*" (58). Otherness within the self is a necessary conclusion of both Jungian and Freudian psychoanalytic theories. Jean Laplanche, who has done pioneering work in interpreting Freud's writing, emphasizes the "alien-ness of the unconscious": "the unconscious [is] an alien inside me, and even one put inside me by an alien" ("Unfinished Copernican Revolution" 66, 65). The alien at work here bears two faces; on the one hand, it is the other person — the "putting inside" works by way of seduction — and on the other, it is the alien body of the memory of the event, the trauma itself, which is internalized and repressed. The Other of the self is the mythago, simultaneously seducing the self— the Huxleys' quests are directed at possessing, or uniting with, the Guiwenneth-Other, their anima — and residing within it.

In the interplay of self and Other, the distinct mythago becomes part of our own selves. Thus identity observably vibrates with the tension of the fantastic paradox, as in T. E. Apter's approach to fantasy from the viewpoint of Freudian dream analysis: "The impact of fantasy rests upon the fact that the world presented seems to be unquestionably ours, yet, at the same time as in a dream, ordinary meanings are suspended. Everything proliferates with potential meanings and becomes a potential danger" (2–3). The uncertainty of fantasy in the Mythago novels represents the uncertainty of the self, continually merging into the Other. Further, the mythago as the Other is an alien body at once outside and within the self, but, as a product of the unconscious it can stay alive only within the realm of Ryhope Wood and never in the village of Shadoxhurst. Guiwenneth, for instance, in an attempt to escape the forest with Steven, experiences "a physical pain ... as if she were being punished for straying so far from the mother wood" (*Mythago Wood* 145). Like a nymph, she needs quickly to reconnect with the forest (see 145–46). The Jungian mythic image aspires to a life of its own, but tragically fails. This is coupled by the fate of the tragic hero or heroine of the Mythago books. Wynne-Jones, for one, is prepared to die in Ryhope Wood; he has been sucked dry and has no strength to leave the forest. The mythago process reminds us that we, ultimately, are creatures of our own minds, shadow-beings that, whatever the strife, cannot escape the tangled undergrowth of our mental life.

The double tragedy of the mythago process resides in the failure of the self to expel the Other once and for all, while this internal Other also experiences its failure to become externalized. The tension is maintained by the tug-of-war of unconscious forces portrayed by Holdstock as emergent and chaotic; the play of negativity threatens to throw the self into abjection.[6] In addition to the chaotic nature of space and time in Ryhope Wood, the gravitation towards grime, sweat, smells, and animal filth (for example, in the representation of the primal boar-spirit, the Urscumug [see 166], or the process of becoming "bosky" in the woods and indulging in a "miasma" of fetors and odors [*The Hollowing* 243–51]); violent death, necromancy, cannibalism, and necrophagy (or the essentially abject practice of bringing up the devoured human carcass in *Lavondyss* [434]); as well as inexplicable phenomena are as evident and frequent in the woods as the faint but menacing occurrence of mythagos; providing a double sense of wonder and abject horror. The tragedy of the hero or heroine and their mythagos lies in the fact that sublimation of the unconscious content may not finally arrive, but, instead, the loosening of taboos in the unconscious can swallow up the self, as in the case of Tallis, Wynne-Jones, and the Huxleys, who get trapped in and are never released by the forest — the chaos of their own unconscious.[7] The transgressive function of Holdstockian fantasy borders on horror in that it repeatedly affirms our innately chaotic nature. The whole of the Mythago Cycle records the borderline moment where the heroic might collapse into the cosmological.[8]

Nonetheless, the hidden content of the unconscious does not primarily threaten the integrity of the self but rather holds the key to a unique way of self-constitution. Jung repeatedly emphasizes the necessity of integrating the unconscious contents in the conscious self on the path of individuation and self-knowledge. Jung interprets alchemical texts with the purpose of tracing this integration, the *coniunctio* of the alchemists, the amalgamation of opposites: "The factors which come together in the coniunctio are conceived as opposites, either confronting one another in enmity or attracting one another in love" (*Mysterium Coniunctionis* 3). In *The Hollowing*, Helen Silverlock, an American woman of Lakota Sioux descent, embarks on a quest to confront and defeat Coyote, the ultimate trickster, to "make him come out of the shadows" (161), to erase him from her mind. As Helen explains, "'I carry the curse in my head ... Trickster is in here.' She tapped her skull" (161). Jung contends:

> The shadow is a moral problem that challenges the whole ego-personality, for no one can become conscious of the shadow without considerable moral effort. To become conscious of it involves recognizing the dark aspects of the personality as present and real. This act is the essential condition for any kind of self-knowledge ... ["The Shadow" 91].

As Helen Silverlock believes, "If I can get Trickster to come out into the wood, to be made solid, then I can kill him" (*The Hollowing* 166). At first Helen's quest appears as personal as Steven's in *Mythago Wood*. Nonetheless, Helen's shadow has more in common with a collective image than a private unconscious[9]: "[Trickster] shares his spirit between all the minds of my family" (161). Helen wishes to sweep the collective unconscious of her family clean from the moral and historical blemishes, which can be ultimately seen as an attempt to liberate the minds of her ill-fated native people. The scientific explanation and extension of mythago process paraphernalia — a minor flaw of *The Hollowing* as a novel — is counterbalanced by Holdstock's brilliant collation of North-American and European myth and shamanism, perhaps wielded as a testament to his underlying belief in Jung's conclusion to the collectiveness and universality of archetypes. Coyote thus threatens other characters throughout the book as well, although appearing through personal images: for Alex he appears as a braying monster, the "giggler," mixed with features of the Green Knight; while for Richard, the questing father, he appears as a Jack, a pre–Celtic, mythical shape-shifting trickster later to became the fairy tale character to climb the beanstalk, most famously recorded by the Brothers Grimm.

Part of Steven's quest, defeating his brother the warlord Christian, tells about a similar confrontation with the shadow, the brother here being Steven's dark side projected; while his other quest of finding Guiwenneth lays bare the desire for synthesis of conscious self and anima in the "chymical marriage" (Jung, *Mysterium Coniunctionis* 89).[10] Although Jung identifies the anima with the collective and the shadow with the personal unconscious (106), for my purposes it will suffice to merely grasp the central aspect of the conjunction — the unification of conscious and unconscious, of "coming to terms with the Other" (496), essentially the most important phase of the *Bildung* of the Mythago Cycle's hero or heroine (496). Steven's "development or ... advance towards some goal or end," is thus "the dialectical discussion between the conscious mind and the unconscious" (Jung, "Problems of Alchemy" 254). His urge to re-unite with the girl in a "royal marriage" derives from a sensation of seceding parts within the same mind (*Mysterium Coniunctionis* 380). When Guiwenneth is gone, he feels a vast rift opening in him, rendering him incomplete: "Legendary role or no, Guiwenneth from the greenwood was the woman I loved, and my life could not continue until she was safe again" (*Mythago Wood* 173). This confession points to the fact that, beyond the well-known psychopathology of the unconscious which both the Jungian and Freudian theories stress, the unconscious is also a part of the mind that is necessary for wholesome life. As R. D. Laing emphasizes, "Adaptation to reality and reality-thinking require the support of concurrent unconscious phantasies" (19). However wholesome, the representation of such unconscious content remains unnerving in Holdstock's fantasy, since one of the major transgressive tendencies of the mode is, as Jackson argues, "to erase ... distinction itself, to resist separation and difference, to re-discover a unity of self and other" (52).

Mythago Hermeneutics and Shamanistic Topography

For the hero or heroine of the Mythago novels to navigate between different aspects of the mind, a special hermeneutic method is needed in interpreting the hidden contents of the unconscious. It would be too easy to dismiss such hermeneutics as a perfect copy either of the Freudian method, where the hero would prove a self-analyst excavating the "true" effects of traumas from his own unconscious contents, or of the Jungian one, where the presence of mythagos as archetypes would alone justify the direct link between cause and effect. I regard these tendencies in the light of what Paul Ricoeur identifies as either Romantic hermeneutics in the fashion of Schleiermacher (seeking out "a living relation with the process of creation") or epistemological quest (through the scientific distancing of object and subject) by way of Dilthey ("The Task of Hermeneutics" 46). George Huxley is closer to the Diltheyan approach, applying a scientific analysis to the problematics of Guiwenneth while collecting stories, fables, and legends, seeking the cause, the originating impetus of her myth. His friend Wynne-Jones interprets Jungian archetypes, primarily through the totem-poles or rajathuks which represent different archetypical images: he submerges in an organic connection, giving in to a Romantic identification with the unconscious, to the point where the forest drains all his energy from him, and yet the mere existence of mythagos as projections of unconscious images explains but a tiny portion of their actions.

Since neither the Freudian nor the Jungian method of interpretation yields much utilizable knowledge of Ryhope Wood, mythago hermeneutics are caught up in a particularly dynamic moment of a shift between interpretational strategies. Ricoeur identifies Heidegger's hermeneutics as a movement away from epistemology and towards ontology, from the problem of method towards the problem of being ("The Task of Hermeneutics" 53–54). "It is ... not astonishing," Ricoeur asserts, "that it is by a reflection on *being-in*, rather than *being-with*, that the ontology of understanding may begin; not *being-with* another who would duplicate our subjectivity, but *being-in-the-world*" (55–56). Steven's, Tallis's, and Richard's quests represent such a move, giving in to the tug of their *Dasein*, freely experiencing the call of the psychic land, of the forest. The Other is always already an aspect of this territory, a shift in perspective that requires meditative attention on the part of the hero. While Steven starts his failing attempts at translation by language (see *Mythago Wood* 120), Richard, father of the thirteen-year-old Alex who later disappears into the Wood, similarly cannot make sense of his son's irregular case of autism (or recognize the nature of the land where they live) through personal communication (*The Hollowing* 30).[11] Yet, images and explanations come to Steven from the experience of union through pure — albeit narcissistic — love, and Richard finds true love and his son only after engaging in a situation that primarily requires his immersion. Partial understanding is gained through Romantic or epistemological analysis, but richness of interpretation is achieved by trudging into the dense undergrowth of experience, as signified by the epigraph to *Lavondyss*, taken from Walt Whitman's "Darest Thou Now, O Soul":

> *Darest thou now, O soul,*
> *Walk out with me toward the unknown region,*
> *Where neither ground is for the feet nor any path to follow? (9)*

While Steven and Richard finally dissolve in their experience of love and loss as conveyed by the land of Ryhope, Tallis, from the first moment on, intuitively fuses with her environment in a permanent shamanistic trance. Roger C. Schlobin analyzes the shaman figure in fantasy literature in connection with the society he or she is assisting (40); yet, the obscure ways of the shaman also indicate his or her personal journey: Shamans are "crisis creatures.... They are saturated with too much individualism" (41). Tallis — whose identification with the shaman figure is facilitated by the association with magical practices, trance, bones, birds, mirrors, the constant urge to enter the otherworld, and her ability of "oolerinnen," "hollowing" (*Lavondyss* 214) — apart from helping to maintain the social and familial order through the quest for her brother, also embarks on a spiritual journey toward her own self-integration. From an early age, she sees mythagos skirting the forest near their family house and becomes repeatedly possessed by them. Tallis is a neophyte, and her youth is a single constant initiation into the rites of Ryhope Wood by three hooded old women who tell her stories and legends, the myths of the origins, all of which later turn out to hold the clues for her journey in the forest and for finding her brother Harry.

In a deeply mythopoetic manner, Tallis's initiation into the ways of a shaman starts out by the process of naming. Three days after her christening, she is unofficially named Broken Boy's Fancy after the legendary hart which at the end of the novel turns out to be Harry's mythago; the broken antler a projection of Harry's facial burn mark which, according to *Mythago Wood*, connects him to his secret reason for entering into Ryhope Wood.[12] Furthermore, on the day of his death, her grandfather Owen composes a letter for Tallis to be given to her on her fifth birthday, setting off her shamanistic learning. He writes: "*You will learn names.... And as you do so, you are treading an old and important pathway*" (15). Tallis soon appropriates the naming game as an exhilarating but necessary way of entering and fusing with the land, of learning names in order not to be trapped "on the other side" (47).

Tallis's search for "secret names" (18) — apparently based on a theory of the Adamic language, in that every object is rightly named after its innate characteristics — correlates with an investigation into her unconscious. As she confesses to her peculiar friend, the composer Ralph Vaughan Williams, secret names are "in a part of the mind that is very closed off from the 'thinking' part" (18). The names that Tallis the shaman has to find during her initiation process are names from her own mind, names that will help her enter the land of Ryhope, to cross a brook, a meadow — names of the land. As Owen's letter claims, "*The naming of the land ... conceals and contains great truths*" (45).

J. Hillis Miller in *Topographies* contends that "topographical considerations, the contours of places, cannot be separated from toponymical considerations, the naming of places" (1). He observes that "place names *seem* to be intrinsic to the places they name.... The place is carried into the name and becomes available to us there" (4; emphasis added). The Mythago novels play with this notion of the name as "intrinsic" to the place and vice versa, but also highlight a similar ambiguity that is contained by Miller's "seem," since Tallis ultimately draws the place names from her own unconscious. The labels and legends, therefore, instead of simply showing Tallis the way, *create* the path of her journey; a unique path carved into the land, a new plot unfolding, signified by Tallis's own archetypal projections altering the rajathuks and various parts of the Wood: "There was new memory coming to the land; there was change" (*Lavondyss* 253). The word "topography," Miller stresses, "contains the alternation between 'create' and 'reveal'" (6). Tallis, by naming, both creates and reveals a terrain, both shapes and discovers the "*unknown region*," where there previously had been "*neither ground ... for the feet nor any path to follow*" (Walt Whitman qtd. in the epigraph to *Lavondyss*). The archetypal vision of the novel is, nonetheless, far from being incompatible with such a view. As Ursula K. Le Guin observes, "The only way to the truly collective, to the image that is alive and meaningful in all of us, seems to be through the truly personal" ("Myth and Archetype" 74).

Dani Cavallaro in *The Gothic Vision* labels fictions of the Gothic, horror, and the fantastic collectively as "narratives of darkness" or "dark fiction" (16). The darkness of the narrative becomes its epistemological strength: certain types of darkness can be ultimately revealing, since in their undefined, homogeneous state they point to the contents they conceal or which are concealed in them. These contents appear, through being hidden, in Tallis's "unknown region." Furthermore, through mythogenetic conceptualization, where she creates part of the Wood and mythagos herself, Tallis is the primary agent setting fantasy rules. Eric S. Rabkin in *The Fantastic in Literature* emphasizes the function of certain ground rules that instruct the reader into the mode of reality in the work and which "the fantastic contradicts" (4–5). Tallis's mythopoetics contradict these ground rules, since the fantasy world does not simply engulf Tallis, but she brings it alive in the first place, she fills the "*blank before us*" by dreaming what "*waits undream'd of in that region, that inaccessible land*" (Whitman, "Darest Thou Now, O Soul" qtd. in *Lavondyss* 251). This basic observation can be supported by the simple fact that Tallis is not easy to astonish. The fantastic contradiction of the ground rules is always indicated in the text, Rabkin asserts, most often by character bewilderment (10), such as Alice's astonishment at talking plants in Lewis Carroll's seminal story (3–4). Yet, Tallis is no Alice. The thirteen-year-old derives no astonishment from her games with masks and hollowings. She does not observe the world as strange, it comes naturally to her, for her unconscious originates the fantasy.

The delineation of rules, the double process of both revealing and creating the memory of the land, proves crucial in the entry to the otherworld, an otherworld of the mythic undermind which parallels the land of myth. The questing heroes in Ryhope are heroes of love — Steven is after Guiwenneth, Richard after his son, and Tallis after her brother and her would-be lover — entering the world of death, in a reenactment of the Orphic or Osiric myths. The *descensus ad infernum* is emphasized throughout the novels through a plethora of images of the wood as the underworld, the otherworld, and a ghost wood. A rather common feature of initiation processes, as Eliade stresses, is "initiatory death, ... the symbolic descent to Hell" (*Rites and Symbols of Initiation* 110). Tallis's games similarly prepare her for the shamanistic journey to the otherworld, to the chaotic inferno of the unconscious.

The shaman's journey usually incorporates the themes of suffering, ordeal, and dismemberment, as does his initiation. The shaman, like his mythic archetypes, that is, the dismembered god or hero, descends into the inferno, or is killed in gruesome ways. Such grisly symbolism is a major feature of *Lavondyss* and usually centers on flesh and bone: from the bones of dead birds Tallis makes Bird Spirit Land; via the Ice Age boy's flesh devoured by birds Harry's spirit becomes liberated; Tig sucks at bones to gain the wisdom of the ancients; and Tallis's final transformation at the end of the novel — where she painfully dies and lends her body to the generation of a tree — is similarly inscribed in the code of shamanistic disintegration. The ordeals of Ryhope justify Eliade's observation that forgotten "historical or primordial" past "is homologized with death" (*Myth and Reality* 121).

The images of the underworld, dismemberment, and bones are paired up with the business of masks. Tallis's masks, Gaberlungi, Sinisalo, Falkenna, Skogen, and the others, are implements that enhance her ability to hollow, to enter other dimensions. The shaman, by taking up a mask, assumes a mythical role and intends to mirror an ancient function, perhaps that of the gods or the ancestors. Tallis, by wearing her masks, evokes certain archetypal forces or functions that aid her on her journey; she regains primordial memory of stories, figures, and places. She wears Gaberlungi, for instance, for "*memory of the land*," at which time "the stories crowded and jostled her mind," while Skogen is "*shadow of the forest ... a landscape mask*," through which she can see patterns on the earth that show ancient woodlands and formations (*Lavondyss* 66–67). The masks and the journey into the underworld focus on the topographical and metaphysical relations between surface and depth. Holdstockian fantasy not only establishes the interplay of different levels of surface and depth but also disorders the network of relations. The surface of the mask, in its function of evoking archetypal memory, is in reality far from representing a mere surface — it represents a mytho-psychic depth. Wynne-Jones tells Tallis about the "concealed places in your mind, many *forbidden* and *forgotten* places," which, he assures her, are connected to the masks (341).

The interplay of surface and depth feeds an entire forest of transformations, creating countless meandering paths. From *The Hollowing* we learn that the mythago world is a "fragile, tentative land. It's in a state of flux" (130). This tendency to transform affects every aspect of the novels, most of all, the characters. Tallis turns into a holly-jack, a mythical ancient shrub-woman — "Leaf Mother" (*Lavondyss* 122), and through an utterly confusing feedback loop, meets her human self on the way. The reader encounters the exact same scene some fifty pages prior to that, observed from the opposite angle, from Tallis's human point of view. Also, Tallis herself at the end of the novel, quite naturally and inescapably, is transformed into an old and dying woman. In *Gate of Ivory, Gate of Horn*,

Christian's mother is "transformed" through her death. The focus on the inevitability of change in the Mythago books pivots on this tension between love and loss.

Out of the Forest: Into the Forest

While during the endlessly circular transformational games the mythagos come unnervingly close in resembling human beings, humans themselves transform into legendary figures. Steven and Harry realize that in the Wood they become part of an all-compassing myth: "I had become a part of legend myself. Christian and his brother, the Outlander and his Kin, working through roles laid down by myth, perhaps from the beginnings of time" (*Mythago Wood* 230). Richard in *The Hollowing* gets involved with the mythical Jason and his Argonauts, while Christian in *Gate of Ivory, Gate of Horn* joins the band of the legendary Night Hunt. Tallis also becomes a myth character, "voice of the oak" (*Lavondyss* 235), through helping Scathach from the cover of the foliage, just as Scathach has to fill his role as the dying hero at the battle of Bavduin (*Lavondyss* 125). Holdstock's heroes and heroines cannot escape the ultimate mythogenetic force exerted by the novels and become inscribed into the mythic world. Eliade interprets the same possibility of reinscribing the modern into the mythical as "the metamorphosis of a historical figure into a mythical hero" (*Eternal Return* 42). Harry speculates: "If we *do* become legends to the various historical peoples scattered throughout this realm ... what would that *mean?* ... Will the *real* world have distorted tales of Steven and myself...?" (*Mythago Wood* 244). Through a journey into the narrative landscapes of the mind, these heroes and heroines transform into myth characters, they become full-fledged components of the tales, and in acquiring such a narrative nature their crises and desires reveal the crises and desires of the text.

Similarly, the quests of the characters added up may be viewed as constituting the quest of the text. The major desire of most narratives is manifested in closure, as Catherine Belsey argues: "the story moves inevitably towards *closure* which is also disclosure, the dissolution of enigma through the re-establishment of order..." (70). The mode of such stories, "realism," in Belsey's interpretation becomes a wide category, only partially meeting the historical classification of realist fiction, a "literature which creates an effect or illusion of reality," with "the inclusion of all those fictional forms which create the illusion while we read that what is narrated is 'really' and intelligibly happening" (51). Major works of fantasy and science fiction, therefore, are not to be excluded either, since "[e]ven in fantasy events, however improbable in themselves, are *related* to each other in familiar ways" (52). As Brian Attebery similarly observes, fantasy "needs consistency. Reader and writer are committed to maintaining the illusion for the entire course of the fiction" (*Fantasy Tradition* 2). The internal rules of the fantasy world itself, hardly realistic in comparison to extra-textual reality, become plausible concerning internal correspondences.

Moreover, fantasy is exceedingly prone to develop a desire for closure due to the interim state of disorder and chaos the fantastic content generates. In *Alice's Adventures in Wonderland*, "a true Fantasy," according to Rabkin (37), the text strives to complete Alice's nonsense journey, to come full circle, and, although the strange qualities of Wonderland are not explained, the validation of why the journey took place arrives in the end in the form of a dream.[13] Such a narrative utopia is also delineated in the Holdstock novels, paralleling the utopia of Lavondyss, a city of shining light that Harry has presumably seen in the French forest, and the linear quest for this placid island; the text urges a narrative settlement at the textual location of its imaginary settlement. Not all of the Mythago novels touch this final point, but they all establish the desire for approximating it, comparably to the adventurers in the texts who have long cherished their imaginary achievements. These textualized adventurers — all turned storybook characters of some kind in the whirlpool of the mythogenetic wood — represent the utopian quest of the text.

Quite unusually for the utopian, closure-seeking narratives that they are, the Mythago novels finally unveil their own desire to reach the final settlement precisely when they turn the characters into mythic heroes, when they delineate the map to this utopia and draw the heroes as textual markers in the narrative, that is, when they disclose the textuality of their narrative world. Tallis sings: "*A fire is burning in Bird Spirit Land. / My bones smoulder. / I must journey there*" (*Lavondyss* 140). These are not her words, actually, but the words from an echo in her mind, the words of myth — the myth of the text. All of the Mythago novels express this shamanistic desire to "journey there," to touch that other side, the textual utopia. Moreover, in line with their overarching cyclical-linear matrices, they also delineate their desire to draw a full circle, to return to the original starting point, such as the breathtakingly beautiful imagery of return upon

Tallis's death (*Lavondyss* 472–73). The self-reflexivity of the Mythago novels is manifested in a doubly linear and circular movement: in seeking some metaphysical center, they travel from surface to depth, but then, by laying bare the narrativity of the characters, they again rise above the textual surface. The shaman Tallis has to take a similar path: apart from assuming identities through masks, she descends into the underworld and dies in a mythic death, which grants her a new life. The fantastic transformations of characters, scenes, and times parallel those of the text itself.

The interplay of surface and depth — oscillating through every aspect of the novels — yields a vision where the desire of the stories is to unveil themselves as narrative, as myth, with the further consequence that characters exist only as components of the narrative, as mythic images in a fantasy. This is, however, far from being a nihilistic experiment. When the text writes its own myth and points to the process of writing, it makes haste to assert the ultimately benevolent effects. Attebery maintains: "Fantasy is not myth, which is generally held to be ancient, anonymous, and traditional, but it is one of the many endeavors we have undertaken to continue the process of mythmaking into a literate, individualistic age ... and the closest to the original in its narrative form" (*Fantasy Tradition* 166). Tallis, Steven, and Richard exist in their narrative reality indeed to point out the mythic nature of the world to us readers. As Attebery observes in *Strategies of Fantasy*,

> the postmodern fantastic, by adopting a playful stance toward narrative conventions, forces the reader to take an active part in establishing any coherence and closure within the text.... Unlike more sophisticated genres, fantasy can be self-referential without being self-destructive; artificial without being arch [53].

Through participating in de-transforming the transformations, the reader, while untying magical knots — "encouraged to exercise [his or her] own storytelling powers to draw a connection from beginning to end" (Attebery, *Strategies* 67) — is writing his or her own story. The text points out our questing instinct; it asserts that we can become myth characters, heroes or heroines. Through the text's endless mirroring and eradicating the difference between surface and depth, self and Other, as well as owing to the possibility to repeat, to reread, to follow the circular plots in newer and newer stories, we become the fascinated Wynne-Joneses, the obsessed and love-stricken Huxleys, the lost-and-found Alexes, and the journeying

Tallises. By seeing ourselves as what we are by way of observing ourselves as something other, we can finally start to make connections, construct narratives, and heal our disjointed place and time. Attebery remarks (in a statement strikingly similar to Eliade's main argument about myth and history in *Eternal Return*):

> It is unlikely that any of the indigenous fantasists intend readers to begin ... expecting the fairies to bring about a transformation in their lives. When you convert history into story, you end up with precisely and only that — a story. Yet, stories, by being different from nature or history, make nature accessible and history meaningful [141].

The subject of the quest, the good place, "eu-topia," is not to be approached "out there" in the world; it resides in the mind. The narrativity of the world mirrors the narrativity of the mind, and mythopoetics can reach just that spot of utter creation. As psychoanalysis similarly suggests, the narrativity of mental life is the key to complete healing.

NOTES

1. Carroll Brown similarly asserts, "Ryhope Wood is more a psychic landscape than a physical one" (160), which identification is further enhanced by the boundlessness of Ryhope Wood — unfathomably vast and yet contained within Ryhope estate — just as the human mind defines an internal, subjective space and time and is nonetheless bound physically by the physiognomy of the human brain and skull.

2. It is faulty to think that mythical archetypes register only mythical events, such as the genesis or the primal fratricide. In Holdstock's wonderful touch — his "playful Euhemeristic speculation," as Brown calls it (170) — in the war veteran's mythago Billy Frampton, we encounter the archetype of the World War I British officer, a popular trench-born legend (see *Mythago Wood* 228). The trauma of the war suffices to generate a myth of quasi-religious nature, which from then on continues to be imprinted in the minds of those inventing and listening to the tales.

3. However theoretical and problematic the ontology of the unconscious — let alone, of the collective unconscious — may prove to be, Huxley and his partner Wynne-Jones are not simple psychoanalysts, but natural scientists of the mind, early twentieth-century representatives of cognitive science. In the move where science, the rational mind, strives to "capture" its irrational counterpart, Guiwenneth becomes the image of nature, female in gender, which the male scientist has to possess in order to perfectly understand. George's love for science culminates in the love of a woman who is the object of his study. In this, Huxley is a late successor to the first sixteenth-century scientists or "philosophers." His desired union with Guiwenneth is reminiscent of Francis Bacon's gender-laden imagery of interpreting nature: Bacon wrote "in terms of a 'chaste, holy and legal wedlock' between the philosopher and Nature, and in terms of binding 'her' to the philosopher's service" (qtd. in Henry 139).

4. As a tongue-in-cheek aside directed at his own writing, Holdstock even names two of his characters in *The Hollowing* after occult fantasist Edward Bulwer-Lytton and poststructuralist thinker Jacques Lacan.

5. The ghastly imagery of dark shapes emerging from the Wood is mirrored by the creation process of *Lavondyss*. Holdstock confesses that *Lavondyss*

was a novel built from dreams. I dreamed of "Old Forbidden Place" and "The Mortuary House," which feature very powerfully in the novel. The book took three years to write and there is no question that I became depressed in the middle of the writing. I wrote about this at the time: that I reached too deeply into my unconscious. I spent days meditating and trying to "touch" the world I was creating, and some very sinister and frightening waking horrors emerged as a consequence ["The Mythago Process" par. 4].

6. According to Julia Kristeva, the abject is detected in the moment when the subject "finds the impossible within; when it finds that the impossible constitutes its very *being*, that it *is* none other than abject" (5).

7. Taboo here is also intended in a Freudian sense, denoting the "uncanny, dangerous, forbidden, and unclean" (Freud 41). According to Freud, the impulses toward transgressing compulsion prohibitions can easily become repressed into the unconscious, and these repressed and proliferating contents continue to remain in tension with the prohibition (57–58).

8. For the contrast between the heroic and cosmological modes in literature, see Hume 177–83.

9. Jung delegates the shadow to the personal unconscious. See *Mysterium Coniunctionis* 106.

10. Incidentally, in the endless permutation of Holdstock's psychoanalytic imagination, Helen — through her behavior as the seducing *femme fatale* (she is in part portrayed as sexually enhanced) and playing regular tricks on Richard — also becomes Richard's (projected) Other, his anima.

11 Since it is mythagos that establish contact with the minds from which they have sprung, they are constantly inquiring into this place of creation. Guiwenneth quickly acquires English, even before Steven could learn bronze-age Celtic (*Mythago Wood* 120). Holdstock's interest in part lies in the tension between the linguistic and non-linguistic aspects of hermeneutics, and the Mythago novels are obsessed with language, its barriers, and the elimination of those.

12. Tallis's naming is doubly shamanistic, since the source for her christening lies in Taliesin, name of the inspired and adept Celtic bard. I will not here take into account the sixteenth-century composer Thomas Tallis and the fact that the girl makes friends with Ralph Vaughan Williams.

13 Alice's older sister is dreaming about Alice's travels, and finally comprehends that her little sister has grown more mature through her own oneiric adventures: "Lastly, she pictured to herself how this same little sister of hers would ... be herself a grown woman ... and how she would gather about her other little children, and make *their* eyes bright and eager with many a strange tale, perhaps even with the dream of Wonderland of long ago..." (148–49).

WORKS CITED

Apter, T. E. *Fantasy Literature: An Approach to Reality.* Bloomington: Indiana University Press, 1982.

Part One: Approaches

Attebery, Brian. *The Fantasy Tradition in American Literature: From Irving to Le Guin*. Bloomington: Indiana University Press, 1980.

_____. *Strategies of Fantasy*. Bloomington: Indiana University Press, 1992.

Belsey, Catherine. *Critical Practice*. New York: Methuen, 1980.

Brown, Carroll. "The Flame in the Heart of the Wood: The Integration of Myth and Science in Robert Holdstock's *Mythago Wood*." *Extrapolation* 34 (1993): 158–72.

Carroll, Lewis. *Alice's Adventures in Wonderland*. 1865. London: Penguin, 1994.

Cavallaro, Dani. *The Gothic Vision: Three Centuries of Horror, Terror and Fear*. London: Continuum, 2002.

Eliade, Mircea. *Myth and Reality*. Trans. Willard R. Trask. Harper Colophon. New York: Harper and Row, 1975.

_____. *The Myth of the Eternal Return: or, Cosmos and History*. 1949. Trans. Willard R. Trask. Bollingen Ser. 46. Princeton: Princeton University Press, 1974.

_____. *Rites and Symbols of Initiation: The Mysteries of Birth and Rebirth*. Trans. Willard R. Trask. New York: Harper Torchbooks. Harper & Row, 1965.

Freud, Sigmund. *Totem and Taboo: Resemblances between the Psychic Lives of Savages and Neurotics*. 1919. London: Penguin, 1938.

Frye, Northrop. *Anatomy of Criticism: Four Essays*. Princeton, NJ: Princeton University Press, 1957.

Henry, John. *Knowledge Is Power: Francis Bacon and the Method of Science*. Duxford, Cambridge: Icon, 2002.

Holdstock, Robert. *Gate of Ivory, Gate of Horn*. 1997. London: Voyager, 1998.

_____. *The Hollowing*. 1993. New York: ROC, 1995.

_____. *Lavondyss: Journey to an Unknown Region*. 1988. London: Grafton, 1990.

_____. "The Mythago Process." April 2003. *Mythago Wood: The Official Robert Holdstock Website*. 20 May 2006 <http://robertholdstock.com/mythback.html>.

_____. *Mythago Wood*. 1984. New York: Berkeley, 1986.

Hume, Kathryn. *Fantasy and Mimesis: Responses to Reality in Western Literature*. New York: Methuen, 1984.

Jackson, Rosemary. *Fantasy: The Literature of Subversion*. New York: Routledge, 1991.

Jung, Carl Gustav. "Conscious, Unconscious, and Individuation." 1939. *The Essential Jung* 212–26.

_____. *The Essential Jung*. Sel. Anthony Storr. Princeton: Princeton University Press, 1983.

_____. "Introduction to the Religious and Psychological Problems of Alchemy." 1944. *The Essential Jung* 253–87.

_____. *Mysterium Coniunctionis: An Inquiry into the Separation and Synthesis of Psychic Opposites in Alchemy*. Trans. R.F.C. Hull. Bollingen Ser. 20. Princeton: Princeton University Press, 1977.

_____. "The Shadow." 1951. *The Essential Jung* 91–93.

Kristeva, Julia. *Powers of Horror: An Essay on Abjection*. Trans. Leon S. Roudiez. New York: Columbia University Press, 1982.

Laing, R. D. *Self and Others*. New York: Penguin, 1980.

Laplanche, Jean. "The Unfinished Copernican Revolution." *Essays on Otherness*. New York: Routledge, 1999. 52–83.

Le Guin, Ursula K. "Myth and Archetype in Science Fiction." 1976. *The Language of the Night: Essays on Fantasy and Science Fiction*. Rev. ed. New York: Harper, 1992. 68–77.

Lightbody, Robert. Interview with Robert Holdstock. *Mythago Wood: The Official Robert Holdstock Website*. 20 May 2006 <http://robertholdstock.com/intervw2.html>.

Miller, J. Hillis. *Topographies*. Crossing Aesthetics. Stanford: Stanford University Press, 1995.

Rabkin, Eric S. *The Fantastic in Literature*. Princeton: Princeton University Press, 1977.

Ricoeur, Paul. "The Task of Hermeneutics." *Hermeneutics and the Human Sciences: Essays on Language, Action and Interpretation*. Ed. and trans. John B. Thompson. Cambridge: Cambridge University Press, 1984. 43–62.

Schlobin, Roger C. "Pagan Survival: Why the Shaman in Modern Fantasy?" Donald E. Morse, Marshal B. Tymn, and Csilla Bertha, eds. *The Celebration of the Fantastic: Selected Papers from the Tenth Anniversary International Conference on the Fantastic in the Arts*. Contributions to the Study of Science Fiction and Fantasy 49. Westport: Greenwood, 1992. 39–48.

3

Exploring the Habitats of Myths: The Spatiotemporal Structure of Ryhope Wood

Stefan Ekman

Ryhope Wood, the central setting of the Mythago Cycle, is not simply a naturalist's fondest dream. Within the impenetrable boundaries of this ancient stand of wildwood, inherited memories of the mythic heroes in our collective unconscious come to life, along with the forests of long-forgotten pasts. These seemingly limitless woodlands, contained within Ryhope Wood's six-mile border, provide a haunting and alluring environment which becomes more than just a setting for the adventures that take place there. The novels of the Mythago Cycle — *Mythago Wood, Lavondyss: Journey into an Unknown Region, The Hollowing*, and *Gate of Ivory, Gate of Horn* — all tell the stories of their protagonists' journeys into the woods, allowing the forest to act on the characters as well as allowing them to act in the forest. Through a closer study of the structures of the forest landscape, it is possible to arrive at a greater understanding of how these journeys are affected by their settings.

Mythago Wood

The spatiotemporal structure that is established in *Mythago Wood* provides the foundation for all four novels. The forest is divided into an unchangeable perimeter and the internal woodlands that change depending on the nature of myths that take place there, providing habitats, or *mythotopes*, for the mythago characters. Mythotopes are either *constant* (set in the perimeter), *shared* by several myths, or *specific* to a particular myth. Among the most interesting shared mythotopes is the river, which figures largely in the myths that outsiders find themselves part of; more than an entrance into the forest, it also becomes a challenge and route to the heart of the forest for them. The path that these structural components form for Steven and Harry may be compared to that of a unicursal, or non-branching, labyrinth.

To an observer outside the forest, the edge wood is dense and forbidding, a tangle of thorn and hazel among enormous tree trunks. Although there are paths and clearings, any intruder that may attempt to penetrate into the depths of the wood gets turned around and so finds him- or herself returning to the edge. Yet, there is a sense of permanence to the edges of this ancient wood, and, as George Huxley demonstrates, it can be mapped, at least up to a point. This unchanging quality, which makes it possible to return to a place, is what separates the *permanent forest* from what the novels refer to as the wildwood or the heartwood. Mythagos begin to form in the edges of the intruders' fields of vision, and eventually the woodland is formed not as a result of natural forces over centuries and millennia but from the visitors' inherited unconscious. The forest is no longer merely "primary oak woodland" but has become something different, with "a quality that defies experience," according to Harry, who continues to reflect that there are "[m]any horse-chestnuts, so the wood is not 'primal,' but a great abundance of oak and hazel, with whole stands of ash and beech. *A hundred forests in one*" (*Mythago Wood* 206; emphasis added). The forest is not a certain type of woodland from a given climate zone and time period. Instead it is a blend, its ancient trees reflecting not a specific time period but many, protean yet changeless. These "hundred forests in one" make up what I have chosen to refer to as the *multifarious forest*, the forest that is itself created to suit the myths brought to life there.

The multifarious forest is not of the same make-up everywhere. The blend of trees reflects the mythagos that haunt a given area, or zone, and the age that their legends come from. Some ten days into the Wood, Steven and Harry suddenly find themselves on the border between two zones in the multifarious forest. The blend of trees changes, suggesting to Harry that they have moved from a medieval wood to "a more primitive forest," and Steven observes that there is "a new quality to this forest, a darker, heavier feel" (249). It is a place of older myths and legends, something which can be inferred from the changes in the forest. The multifarious forest goes through a similar change in make-up further on, when the two companions enter the settings of even older stories in the winter-forest. That "wide, winter landscape of the inner realm" (282) is populated by an early Scandinavian tribe and, further towards the center of the realm, by a Neolithic people.

Each myth or legend is set in a particular type of landscape, and as the myth is passed from era to era, from culture to culture, its setting changes. The settings are more than simply backdrops: they are complex combinations of hero figures (and occasionally their societies), meaningful artifacts, and the natural environment. They are what geographer Yi-Fu Tuan would call places: they have a history and meaning, incarnating the experiences and aspirations of a people (213). A place, Tuan explains, can have a spirit: "space is formless and profane except for ... the sacred places"; but a place also has "personality [which is] a composite of natural endowment ... and the modifications wrought by successive generations of human beings" (234). Places are the central components of Ryhope Wood's spatiotemporal structure, but in the Mythago Wood the requirements of myths define the spirit and personality of places. The history and meaning are mythical, the experiences and aspirations those of legendary heroes. The personality of a mythic place is a combination of a "natural endowment" required by, and meaningful in terms of, the myth, and the modifications are wrought not by successive generations of human beings but by successive versions of the myth. These places are where myths live; they are habitats of myths, that is, environments eminently suited for the myths they harbor. I will refer to such habitats of myths as *mythotopes*, the places where a given version of a myth or legend is set.[1] The word (literally, *myth place*) is created by analogy to *biotope*, an area "characterized by a high degree of uniformity in its environmental conditions and in its plant and animal life" ("Biotope"). Just as the biotic and abiotic components of a biotope are suited to the particular needs of given plants and animals, a mythotope contains components that meet the requirements of given myths and legends. The creation of mythotopes is not explicitly mentioned in *Mythago Wood*, only hinted at; but in *Lavondyss*, George Huxley explains in his journal how, in his friend's, Wynne-Jones's, belief, the mythogenesis "also creates the forbidden *places* of the mythic past" (160). A mythotope comprises the setting for the myth, including buildings and other artifacts, societies and their heroes, animals and landscape features; it even includes seasons. The latter aspect is illustrated by Steven and Harry's journey into

48

the frozen forests of prehistoric myths. In Mythago Wood, miles rather than months separate summer from winter.

A final structural component of the mythotope is the relative passage of time. In *Mythago Wood*, time inside the forest passes more quickly than on the outside. Weeks in the forest correspond to days in Oak Lodge, and the nine months Christian spends there transform him from a young man in his twenties to a man of late middle age (185). This time differential emphasizes the disparity between circumference and area in the first novel. Just as the area of the forest is vastly greater than can be encompassed by its circumference, weeks, months, and years pass at an incredible rate. Time and space inside Ryhope Wood are expanded, ultimately suggesting that even the time that passes in the woodlands is part of the mythotopes. This idea has evolved further in the next two novels, where the passage of time in one mythotope relative to another becomes of central importance. In *Lavondyss*, for instance, Morthen rides off to find a place where she can age faster, and the few hours Tallis spends away from Scathach and Wynne-Jones correspond to two days for them (338, 330). In *The Hollowing*, the time differentials are shown to work both ways, keeping Alex and James Keeton basically unchanged in the forest while years pass outside. On a smaller scale, the relative passage of time is shown to cause problems when Richard hesitates for a few seconds before following Helen through a hollowing, only to find that she has had to wait for him for a day and a half (*The Hollowing* 129–30). In all cases, the passage of time becomes something specific to a mythotope, one of its abiotic factors, as it were, and something which cannot be predicted to be anything but unpredictable. The differentials repeatedly baffle the main characters and, ultimately, the time flow becomes as changeable as the spatial aspects of the forest setting.

Despite the general changeability of the mythotopes, they tend to fall into only a few main categories. Although humans find it difficult to enter Ryhope Wood, and are generally turned around already by the permanent forest, mythago creatures can move in this outer zone; some can even go some distance away from the forest edge. Even so, the edges of the woodland and its surrounding areas, and in particular places such as Oak Lodge and the Horse Shrine, are mythotopes in their own right, holding meaning as parts of specific myths. To the mythagos, the edge of the forest is the end of the world beyond which they cannot move, and Oak Lodge and the Horse Shrine are sacred sites for more than one type of mythago. Nor is the permanent forest the only mythotope through which mythagos from various myths move. The river is a habitat housing several myths, as is Lavondyss, at the heart of the forest. Other mythotopes seem highly specific to certain mythagos. It is thus possible to identify three categories of mythotopes:

1. *constant* mythotopes, places in the permanent forest which are associated with several myths or part of different mythago characters' worlds;
2. *shared* mythotopes, which can be part of various different myths and are shared by several mythagos, and which are created or transformed as part of the multifarious forest;
3. *specific* mythotopes, which are connected to particular myths.

While these categories are useful in understanding the structure of the Mythago woodlands, it is important to realize that they, like the forest they describe, do not form discrete groups as much as a spectrum where the categories run into one another.

Constant Mythotopes

The permanent forest is a haunting place for a great many mythago creatures. Most of them are animals (Steven and Guiwenneth supplement their diet with game from the edgewood [*Mythago Wood* 169]), but there are also mythago people, such as the mysterious Twigling (24–25, 43–44), as well as other forest beings and possibly even mythago communities in the deeper regions (212–13). George Huxley has mapped some constant mythotopes in the permanent forest, such as, for instance, the Horse Shrine, which is mentioned only briefly in George Huxley's journal (45, 75) but described in detail when Richard stays there in *The Hollowing* and which Christian comes across and instantly takes a strong dislike to in *Gate of Ivory, Gate of Horn*. The Shrine, which the mythago Gwyr refers to as "a strange and evil place [at] the edge of the world" (*Gate of Ivory, Gate of Horn* 89), becomes indicative of the most prominent constant mythotope of the edgewood, that of the edge itself.

The edge has a doubleness to it, however. As was previously pointed out, it is the boundary of the mythago creatures' world, beyond which lies a strange and dangerous Otherworld, but it is also the border between the farmland of the Ryhope Estate and the forest wilderness. Lewis Holloway and Phil Hubbard reason that the concept of wilderness "relies on a distinction between farmland and wilderness" (131). They explain that

> [i]n this opposition, the farmland is associated with being settled, with being cultivated, with domestic animals, with relative security and stability. In sum, settled farmland is imagined as "central" to people's lives. On the margins, away from the settled centre, the wilderness, as an "other," is associated with wild animals, wild "uncivilized" people (outlaws or savages), and with danger and insecurity [131].

The doubleness of the powerful, constant mythotope of the edge effects an inversion of the opposition wilderness/civilization. In the primary world, with its focus on civilization, the (seemingly) 2,000-acre Ryhope Wood is marginalized to the point of exclusion from the survey maps (*Mythago Wood* 95). Inside the forest, however, the fields and meadows surrounding it constitute the margin, and not only in a literal sense. The farmland is marginal in that it lies outside the forest world, a perilous, ghostly Otherworld. When mythagos such as Guiwenneth and half-mythagos such as Scathach move too far away from the edgewood, they experience pain and would ultimately die and decay if they were to go further away (compare *Mythago Wood* 166–67; *Lavondyss* 269–70; *Gate of Ivory, Gate of Horn* 20–21, 102). This marginal Otherworld has its antithesis at the heart of the forest, in Lavondyss, and while they are each other's opposites, they also share some common traits. The Otherworld is a place of dying as well as a place of birth through mythogenesis; Lavondyss is a land of death (gloomy or idyllic) but also an origin of myth (compare *Lavondyss* 370–73).

Shared Mythotopes

Just as they travel to the constant mythotopes at the edge of the forest, mythago characters also travel through the multifarious forest on their various quests, particularly those mythagos that journey with or pursue humans entering the forest. Indeed, in *The Hollowing*, a mythago's quest may be to find the human from whose unconscious minds that mythago has formed. Lacan explains to Richard how "[i]t is the function of these creatures. They are compelled to find and touch their maker, their creator" (84). The mythotopes these mythagos travel through become part of their stories as "foreign" land, regions to pass through — inhabited or not.

That other mythagos pass through a mythotope does not make it shared — that requires the mythotope to have distinctive functions in two or more stories. A clear example occurs towards the end of *Mythago Wood*. In the cold valley with the wall of fire, Steven finds the towering megalith which marks Peredur's grave. On one side of the stone, there is a crudely etched shape of a bird, the earliest symbol representing Guiwenneth's father (301). This valley, as far into the multifarious forest as it is possible to go, is a mythotope shared by all versions of the legend of Peredur and Guiwenneth. Nevertheless, it is only shared by versions of a specific legend and has a very special meaning in that legend. More general shared mythotopes occur at the end of *Lavondyss* and *Gate of Ivory, Gate of Horn*. On the timeless battlefield Bavduin, warriors of all legends and times meet, and the Underworld (an aspect of Lavondyss) is the land of death for mythagos of several myths.

The river that flows into the center of the land, to Lavondyss, and out again is a mythotope common to numerous myths in the four books. This universality is evident from the wide variety of dwellings, shrines, and constructions along the shores (compare *Mythago Wood* 280–81; *Gate of Ivory, Gate of Horn* 265): in *Mythago Wood*, both the *shamiga* and Sortha-lan have stories that connect them to a river, stories that refer to different rivers of different times, but in the forest their myths share the same river. The river is particularly interesting as a structural component in the stories of Steven and Harry, Tallis, and Christian. To them, the river mythotope is an entrance into the forest as well as a combined challenge and passage towards the goal of their respective quests. It is along this waterway that Harry and Steven enter the woodlands; Tallis enters via another brook and follows the river ever deeper into the forest; and Christian drifts away in a canoe passing Hogback Ridge. The river leads into but also out of the forest; into but also out of Lavondyss.

Going by the river is not necessarily an easy route, however. The nature of the challenges varies in the three novels, but the way they are overcome reflects how the outsiders must rely on the magic of the mythago world to penetrate the heart of the forest. In a deep gorge, Steven and Harry are set upon and nearly killed by Christian's guards, but for the intervention of Sorthalan, who subsequently offers them passage in his boat and takes them on a short-cut to the winter-forest. In *Lavondyss*, the river is the route to Lavondyss (or the Underworld) for any number of mythagos. It widens into a lake at one point, requiring them to find a way across. When Tallis, Scathach, and Wynne-Jones reach the lake, Tallis's new-found control over her hollowing magic takes the three of them to the far side of the lake. In Kylhuk's quest in *Gate of Ivory, Gate of Horn*, challenge and passage are reversed, the challenge being the whirlpool by the gigantic tree at the end of their voyage. Christian and his friends are saved only by the strange power of Elidyr (who guides the dead to — and from — the Underworld along the river). The magic of Elidyr, Sorthalan, and Tallis's masks are what enable the outsiders to overcome the river's challenge in each case and to reach their goal along this shared mythotope.

Specific Mythotopes

In the chapter "Abandoned Places," Steven and Harry travel through an area of the multifarious forest where they discover numerous hidden buildings of various ages, the first being a ruined broch. Harry identifies it as a mythago in itself, while Steven suggests that it is the core of some legend: "The lost broch. The ruined place of stone, fascinating to the minds of men who lived below steep thatch, inside structures of wicker and mud" (*Mythago Wood* 233–34). In fact, each of the buildings that the two travelers pass while progressing through the trees and thickets is the core of some such legend. Generally, the reader is led to assume that the buildings are situated in the multifarious forest; but one house is set in a forest of a decidedly different type, "a sparsely foliaged pine-forest" (234). This "old Germanic location" is special in that its forest is so obviously not part of the deciduous surroundings. Rather than being a hundred forests in one, this mythotope copies a particular forest type, whose living conditions are drastically different from those of the deciduous forest around it. Mythological rather than ecological factors determine the flora and fauna of the pine-forest mythotope. The difference indicates that the trees in the Germanic setting are relevant to the legend to which that mythotope belongs, ultimately suggesting that special characteristics of a mythotope are determined by relevance to its myth. Few specific mytho-topes turn up in the books. Usually they appear as buildings, such as castles, temples, and fortresses. Albeit themselves quite specific, these build-ings are, like the fairy-tale castle among the abandoned places, set in clear-ings in the multifarious forest — and the multifarious forest is by far the most common component of all mythotopes.

The path Steven follows through the forest to Lavondyss twists and turns but never really leaves him with any choices. In the beginning, he and Harry follow the river (which keeps them mostly on Christian's trail), and then they take the trail towards the mountains. This path conforms to what Umberto Eco calls a linear labyrinth (80) or what is, in Penelope Reed Doob's description, a unicursal labyrinth, where "a single unbranched ... circuitous route leads inevitably, if at great length, to the center" (19). The river along which they travel suggests this circuitous path, curving and curling as it does (*Mythago Wood* 244, 280); and the only fork that is implied occurs where they leave Christian's trail with Sorthalan. The inevitability of the unicursal path is echoed in the inevitability of Steven's quest; the further he pursues his brother and the deeper into the forest he travels the more he becomes the Kinsman of myth, doomed to act out his conflict with the Outsider.

Lavondyss

In the second novel, the main contribution to the structure of Ryhope Wood is the hollowings, but here, too, the mythotopes are more protean and the forest thus becomes more difficult to navigate. Together with Tallis's inability to control where her hollowings lead, this causes the forest to take on the qualities of a multicursal maze, and its branching paths keep Tallis and Scathach lost for years.

Hollowings are connections between two places not necessarily adjacent in space and time. They are generally described as being the creation of characters with a particular ability and provide a focus for much of the story. Their significance to the story and the fact that they evolve into major structural components in *The Hollowing* make them *Lavondyss*'s most important addition to movement in the forest landscape. In his journal, George Huxley describes how Wynne-Jones discovered a mythago he calls "oolering man" on account of the "chanting cry" that he makes preparatory to leaving the woods through the gate to the "*geistzone* which it has created, or made to appear" (*Lavondyss* 160). Bringing the main characters to, or at least connecting them to, *geistzones* is certainly an important, but not the only, function of the hollowings in the stories.

A *geistzone*, Huxley explains, "can be both the desired realm, or the most feared realm; the beginning place or the final place; the place of life before birth, or life after death; the place of no hardship, or the place where life is tested and transition from one state of being to another is accomplished"

(*Lavondyss* 160). This certainly describes the innermost realm of Lavondyss but also includes the cold land bordering it — in *Lavondyss* as well as in *Mythago Wood*. To Steven, the cold valley on the border of Lavondyss becomes the most feared *and* desired place in the forest — the place of confrontation with Christian and of possible reunion with Guiwenneth. Similarly, it is on Bavduin, the wintry battlefield adjacent to Lavondyss, that Scathach passes from one life to another. The similarity of function demonstrates how, in the first novel, Sorthalan anticipates hollowings and oolering men. He is the magical power that brings Steven and Harry to the entrance of the winter forest, a short-cut that takes them to what is the fringe of Lavondyss in *Mythago Wood*. The challenge of the river is overcome with Sorthalan's help, just as Tallis and her companions cross the lake through a hollowing which takes them to the land on the edge of Lavondyss (*Lavondyss* 314–17). Huxley's description of *geistzones* does not fit only Lavondyss, however. I earlier observed how Lavondyss at the center of the forest shares some traits with its opposite, the Otherworld on the margin of Ryhope Wood. Those similarities suggest that the Otherworld is also a *geistzone*: it is a place where mythagos are "before birth" (that is, at a stage antedating mythogenesis), and for outsiders it is definitely a beginning place. To mythagos who see it as the perilous edge of the world, it is the realm most feared, whereas to others (outsiders lost in the wood, for instance) it is the realm most desired. The third book offers a clear example when an oolering man offers a hollowing that takes Richard to a *geistzone*. For Richard, the most desired realm, the place of no hardship, is not to be found in the forest at this stage. When offered a chance to escape he takes it, and is brought out of the forest and back home (*The Hollowing* 175).

Hollowings are not only portals which bring characters closer to (rather than into, as is surmised by Huxley) *geistzones*. It is through a hollowing that Tallis, uncomprehending at first, watches Scathach's death at Bavduin, and it is a hollowing that brings her, Scathach, and their Jaguthin companions deep into the forest. During their eight years of roaming the woodlands, Tallis uses her Hollower mask to open hollowings without reaching her goal, although each attempt brings them closer, at least according to Wynne-Jones (*Lavondyss* 286). Like Wynne-Jones, who becomes forever lost in the forest once he passes through a hollowing (269), Tallis is stuck; and even after she has fashioned herself a new Moondream mask to replace the one she has lost, she is unable to control fully where a hollowing takes her (compare *Lavondyss* 317). Rather than making the journey through the woodlands more efficient and predictable, hollowings have the opposite effect: outsiders are led astray and become trapped in the Mythago Wood.

Not only Tallis's erratic hollowings lead her and Scathach astray. The mythotopes in *Lavondyss* are more protean than in the previous novel. Tallis and her companions try to discover a design to the wilderness; so they leave signs and sites, anticipating finding them again, to impose a structure on their random travel inwards (265). Despite their attempts and Tallis's masks, through which she can see the mystical aspects of the forest, they fail: Tallis lacks Moondream, the mask that allows her to see "the woman in the land," and thus loses herself in the forest; and Scathach is unable to take her back out because his mythago heritage allows him only one journey to the Otherworld. Instead, the forest draws him into the heart of the realm (247, 274).

Mythotopes change as humans pass through and seed them with their dreams. In *Mythago Wood*, seeding is connected to the mythogenesis of mythago characters, who are affected by the unconscious mind of their creator. Christian hypothesizes about the personality of Huxley's Guiwenneth that "[s]he was not violent, perhaps because the old man himself could not think of a woman being violent. He imposed a structure on her, disarming her, leaving her quite helpless in the forest" (*Mythago Wood* 53). In *Lavondyss*, this impact of the original mind is brought to bear on any sort of mythago, and consequently on all aspects of mythotopes. Tallis's arrival at the Tuthanach village is thus portended by, and results in, changes to the mythotope: thorns and undergrowth appear overnight, the totem trees begin to change, and enormous elms are created out of thin air (*Lavondyss* 203–04, 288). Only outsiders notice this, however; the mythagos live in a constant present. The Tuthanach mythotope, as Wynne-Jones explains to Tallis, carries the mark of the mind that seeded it, but there are changes springing from new minds. "Around you are your brother's dreams, later modified by myself, recently modified by you," he tells her and shows how his totems reflect the scarred face of the man from whose mind they sprang (276). The changes wrought by Tallis's mind do not make her journey simpler, however. They hold her back and threaten her, as, for example, the underbrush and thorns in the Tuthanach mythotope (203–04, 246) and the enormous elms which seem to crush only her and which are mythic representations of her fear of the forest (290, 288).

A factor that contributes to the chaotic nature of Tallis's and Scathach's journey is the similarly chaotic and unordered seasons in the Mythago Wood. They make no sense to Tallis, sometimes even coming in an unnatural order (264). In this novel, seasons are not only a result of the characters' progress, but also the seasons themselves are able to perform some movement. During the final stretch towards Bavduin, there is even a "hurricane" of seasons. Its "gusts" vary almost instantaneously, each season lasting only a few seconds (318–20). Just as the multifarious forest implies that certain legends can take place in any kind of forest, the "hurricane" suggests that seasons are irrelevant for the journey to Bavduin — heroes have traveled to the battlefield in all seasons. The mythotope of Bavduin, however, is situated in the eye of the storm, in the grip of constant winter (387). The timeless battle of legend is always fought in the gloom under a sullen winter sky. This is the land on the border of Lavondyss, as cold and unforgiving a place as the icy valley where Steven finds the fiery border to Lavondyss in *Mythago Wood*. Tallis's journey there, however, is much the harder one.

Tallis's path is not the inevitable, unicursal labyrinth of Steven. Her years of wandering lost among the protean mythotopes and through unpredictable hollowings suggest that the forest is one of innumerable forks and dead ends. It is, in Doob's terminology, a multicursal rather than a unicursal labyrinth (18), which Eco refers to as a maze (81). "In a maze," he asserts, "one can make mistakes.... Some alternatives end at a point where one is obliged to return backwards, whereas others generate new branches, and only one among them leads to the way out" (81). Without the Moondream mask, Tallis makes mistakes in a maze which is more difficult than most. As opposed to a spatial maze, a mythotopic maze allows for more than spatial choices, and the protean nature of the mythotopes means that backtracking does not return travelers to where they started. Impassable thickets, confusing mists, and variations in time and season confuse the travelers and turn them from the path. Only slowly are Tallis and Scathach drawn inwards along the one route that leads not outwards but to the center.

The Hollowing

With its starting-point in the multicursal structure of *Lavondyss*, the mythotopic structure in *The Hollowing* evolves into something more complex. Whereas the hollowings of the previous novel were created by people, here they are fixed structural components creating a net of possible routes to travel through the forest which makes it even easier to lose one's way. The protean nature of the mythotopes is more pronounced, but exploration and mapping are also brought into focus, suggesting that journeying in the forest can be safe. On the other hand, the mythogenetic process has a stronger, more immediate effect on the mythotopes, causing greater differences, especially as regards the passage of time and seasons. The individual unconscious is to a greater extent used as a source for mythogenesis.

When hollowings are introduced in *Lavondyss*, they are generally portrayed as the creation of people with special powers. Even the hollowings Tallis encounters before she enters the forest are interpreted as creations by herself or the masked mythago she calls "the Hollower." Only the book's coda describes a hollowing as part of its environment (387). In the third novel, hollowings as structural components of mythotopes are brought sharply into focus. Lytton explains to Richard that there are four ways to enter Ryhope Wood, and that two of them are hollowings which "run into different planes and different times, if we're not careful" (*The Hollowing* 106). One of these is, according to Lytton, the one through which Tallis entered, although she and Scathach are convinced that Tallis opened it herself with help from the mythago stag Broken Boy (*Lavondyss* 199). If Lytton is right, the permanent forest holds at least two hollowings. Deeper in the forest such portals abound, and many of them can be found in the area around the Old Stone Hollow Station. Since hollowings are part of the environment and not necessarily visible, it is possible to slip from one mythotope to another by mistake and end up far away in both time and space, especially as the forest is, as Lacan expresses it, "criss-crossed" with hollowings (*The Hollowing* 83). And since these gateways are not necessarily two-way structures, a traveler who accidentally walks through them might easily become lost. The hollowings that are components of mythotopes thus differ from those created by the hollowers of *Lavondyss*. In the former book, Wynne-Jones "sees the 'oolering man' as a guardian of the *way*" (*Lavondyss* 160), preventing him from walking through. In *The Hollowing*, on the other hand, these enigmatic portals are not guarded, and are thus a special peril to travelers.

Accidentally slipping through a hollowing can deposit a traveler anywhere (and anytime) in the forest, a forest which not only consists of numerous mythotopes next to one another but whose structure has evolved into increased spatiotemporal complexity through the addition of other "planes":

> The map showed five Ryhope "perimeters," one above the other in a
> staggered display, connected by thin tubes that curved down between
> them, some connecting adjacent planes, others running deeper and usu-
> ally ending in a question mark [*The Hollowing* 107].

The exact nature of these planes is not made clear, but the map implies
that while they somehow occupy the same position in space (that is, within
the boundaries of Ryhope Wood), they cannot be reached by moving "over
land" from one mythotope to its neighbor. Only through hollowings,
which allow travel between non-adjacent mythotopes, can different planes
be reached. The difficulties involved in finding one's way once lost now
appear to be insurmountable. Once on a different plane, only a hollowing
would return travelers to the "top" plane, allowing them to leave the forest.
This structure also has a temporal aspect: even if the travelers should find
their way out, hollowings could lead both backwards and forwards in time
(as is established in *Lavondyss*). It is apparently such a hollowing, possibly
created by a mythago, that leads to Helen's message being delivered eight
years too early.[2]

These complex woodlands are tackled logically and scientifically by
Lytton and the rest of the researchers at the Station. Already in *Mythago
Wood* it is made clear how the permanent forest can be mapped, and in
The Hollowing, mapping becomes even more precise. The map that Lytton
shows Richard not only displays the permanent forest inside the perimeter;
it also maps the various hollowings. "[A]ll we can hope to do," Lytton explains, "is establish safe routes down and back, so that later explorers can
at least have more than a hollowstick to guide them" (107). The Station researchers approach Ryhope Wood as cartographers, trying to gain control
of the protean forest by knowing their way around it. Apart from Lytton's
observation that the perimeter of the forest is the easy part to map (106),
this focus on mapping and exploration, as well as the ability to enter and
leave the forest at will, which the researchers appear to have gained, down-
plays the protean nature of the forest's mythotopes. This sense of permanency
is augmented by the precise descriptions of certain mythotopes: "the tundra
of an early Siberian myth-cycle" (118); "a dark lake-filled land, ... probably
from Slavonic legend" (107); and a number of water-related mythotopes
connected to the Wide-water Hollowing (87). The fact that the Station is
only one day's walk from Oak Lodge if one knows the way but it takes
Richard at least a week to return there on his own underscores the importance of knowing one's way about the forest (189). Although the difficulty

in penetrating the forest's defenses is not new to this book — the opposition between the researchers' quick route and Richard's tribulations echoes the ease with which Huxley, Wynne-Jones, and Christian slip into the forest as opposed to Steven and Harry's problems — it is much more pronounced in *The Hollowing*.

Whereas the permanent forest is more important in this novel, with all the comings and goings to the Station, the protean nature of mythotopes is still highly relevant to the plot. Lytton's main reason for wanting Alex out of the Mythago Wood is that the boy's unconscious "is like a tumor at the heart of the world, eroding, destroying the subtlety and the beauty of [the Mythago Wood]. His mind, roaming free, is like a fire, burning and charring" (*The Hollowing* 103). Rather than effecting subtle changes similar to those of Harry and Tallis, Alex wreaks havoc on the mythotopes. Instead of engendering the long-forgotten heroes of legend and their habitats, Alex's mind brings a mélange of mythagos into the forest. Evidence of the boy's mind permeates the mythotope where he is hiding:

> *Alex was everywhere, in the high hills, with its earth-works, ... in the crumbling fortresses that peered grayly through the matted greenwood, in the falls of water with their huge stone guardians.... In all of these things I recognized a reflection of the land around Shadoxhurst, of Alex's dream-castles, created from fairy tale and our family explorations, on holiday, of the wonderful Norman fortresses along the border between Wales and England. Alex had always seen faces in rocks, or bodies in the hills ...* [151].

Alex's mythotopes are not those of legends of old, but the creations of a child's imagination. To a scholar of myth and history such as Lytton, replacing the forgotten stories of ancient times with the fancies of the modern world is tantamount to the destruction of a priceless treasure. The above quotation also shows how changeable the mythogenic process is. In the two previous books, mythogenesis has been focused mainly on the creation of mythago characters, although the shaping of the land is discussed in *Lavondyss*. That kind of mythogenesis draws largely on the *collective* unconscious and the forgotten stories that lie hidden there. In this passage, however, there is an obvious shift to the stuff on which mythotopes are made by the *individual's* unconscious mind. Rather than having a subtle effect on a mythotope, such as Harry's scar recurring in the totem faces, Alex can easily be identified in the land that has sprung from him.

The changeability of the mythotopes is further emphasized when Alex starts killing his creations. The summer forest suddenly turns into winter, freezing the creatures and allowing them to merge back into the forest. Even the hollowings and the Old Stone Hollow rock itself are dismantled (*The Hollowing* 283–85). Alex has provided more than a seed for the forest to build upon in this case; his unconscious holds the mythotopes together. The switch from summer to winter, and the death of mythago creatures resulting from it, illustrate how the season is a central component — change it, and the mythotope changes. Without Alex, his creations change into other mythotopes, based on other myths, seeded by other minds. Thus, the wintry woodlands through which the group travels, for instance, soon contain new animals, more suitable to the forest vacated by the boy's mind.

The multitude of paths that the forest offers, on land and through hollowings, within and between the forest planes, take the forest beyond the multicursal maze of Lavondyss. This is close to the type of labyrinth that Eco calls a net, whose main feature is "that every point can be connected with every other point" (Eco 81).[3] In the forest in *The Hollowing*, every mythotope can be reached from any other mythotope by some route or other. These paths are, however, not necessarily short or obvious, and the possibility of losing one's way is ever present.

Eco also contends that "the abstract model of a net has neither a center nor an outside" (81), and whereas Ryhope Wood does have an outside, it is an outside that is impossibly small compared to the inner vastness. Furthermore, unlike the other three books, *The Hollowing* contains no quest for Lavondyss. The heart of the wood is Alex's hiding-place, located somewhere in the forest net, and any one of several routes leads there from Old Stone Hollow Station: through the hollowing in the cave, along Lytton's marked route, or on whatever pathway he used to reach the Mask Tree in the first place. As if the net of paths through the forest were not enough, this structure is further emphasized by the enigmatic and ubiquitous "rootweb" through which Alex can send his consciousness and see things all over the forest, a web underlying the net. And in the face of the enormous size and complexity of the net structure, the mapping and exploration becomes, at the end of the day, an exercise in futility.

Gate of Ivory, Gate of Horn

In the fourth novel of the cycle, the complex net structure of *The Hollowing* remains virtually unchanged. The mythotopes are made more protean, albeit with less reference to the individual unconscious, and the importance of hollowings is played down. The myths and mythotopic structures are broken up, however, by the host of mythago heroes called Legion. The path that the main characters take through the wood is no longer labyrinthine; the net structure no longer affects the characters' movement. Their path becomes a straightforward movement towards their goal, no longer influenced by the constraints of the spatiotemporal structure of the forest.

In the fourth book, very little happens to the complex net of protean mythotopes and the abundance of hollowings. The use of hollowings, however, as well as their implications for the spatiotemporal structure, is all but absent in *Gate of Ivory, Gate of Horn*: the portals are only briefly mentioned, together with the "oolerers" that can create them (134). There is also considerably less focus on the effects of the individual unconscious mind on mythogenesis (which places *Gate of Ivory, Gate of Horn* more on a par with *Lavondyss* in this respect), although the forest is portrayed as somewhat more protean. Having joined the Forlorn Hope, Christian quickly realizes how the mythotopes are prone to change without warning, as subtle changes to the paths cause him and Gwyr to lose their way when returning to camp (92). Other changes occur when boundaries between mythotopes are crossed, such as when the Forlorn Hope walk from midday into twilight outside Legion's defenses, or Christian rides from the day of Legion's march into the night of the Silent Towers (119–20, 143).

The mythotopic changes when entering and leaving the area of Legion suggest that the host of legendary heroes is something of a mythotope in its own right. In assembling it, Kylhuk constructs an entity that surpasses the individual myths and legends, breaks them apart, and subjugates them to his own story. He gathers countless mythagos, thus "transmuting their legend to his own quest" (123). The myths are dismantled and re-forged into something more powerful, something that can ignore the forest mythotopes just as it ignores the myths they belong to. It is through this re-forging of myth that Legion becomes its own mythotope, a setting for all the mythago heroes that are part of it. Unlike any other, however, this mythotope belongs to a myth sprung not from an outsider's unconscious or inherited memory, but from another mythago — from Kylhuk.

When Legion marches, it does not move consecutively through the mythotopes, nor does it move through the net of hollowings and planes. Instead, it breaks the structural components apart, piecing fractions of time and space together from numerous mythotopes into a new spatiotemporal structure. "Legion moved forward outside what you or I might think of as ordinary space and ordinary time," Christian explains, musing on the "strange effect" this might have on mythagos who would only see "Legion flow[ing] ... for a few seconds through their space and time" (139). The Legion mythotope has its own structure in relation to the rest of the woodlands, just as the latter have a structure dissimilar to that of the outside world. It moves through the forest like a bubble, but a bubble that has no need for following the structure through which its path leads.

In the previous three books, the various labyrinthine structures have all stressed how traveling in the Mythago Wood is indeed to travel in the *selva oscura*, the dark forest where any hope of a straightforward path is lost. Steven, Tallis, and Richard are all at the mercy of their respective labyrinths, and none of them escapes the forest. In *Gate of Ivory, Gate of Horn*, Christian is similarly at the mercy of the forest, but not because of its complex net structure. Instead, he is forced to become part of Kylhuk's quest and is brought into the mythotope of Legion. Christian's path takes him and his companions straight to the center on a route that suggests nothing of the circuitous inevitability of *Mythago Wood*. Rather, Kylhuk and Legion become an irresistible force, steadily marching towards their goal, sweeping Christian along — and then sending him out again.

Conclusion

The irresistible power of Kylhuk and Legion and their steady progress towards their goal in total disregard of the Wood's mythotopic complexity contrast sharply with how the previous three novels are structured to capture outsiders. Steven's path may twist and turn, but it takes him to the center of the forest as inevitably as he is subjugated to the myth of the Outsider and the Kinsman. Reaching the heart of the linear labyrinth means killing his brother regardless of his own wishes. Tallis is similarly drawn to the center of the forest, her attempts to navigate the protean and complex maze frustrated. She can do little but follow Scathach, whose myth moves him inexorably to his predestined death on the battlefield, and while she may set her brother free, she herself becomes trapped at the heart of the forest. Richard's struggles to find his way through the mythotopic net bring him to his son, the novel's central node of mythogenic activity. Richard's journey, with its false starts and many alternative routes, as well as the various fates of the other scientists at the Station similarly emphasize how the Wood traps not only the unwary but everyone drawn into it. Only Christian, seized by mythic forces powerful enough to dis-regard the mythotopic labyrinth, is returned to the outside, with as little volition as when he was pulled into the forest. In the Cycle, the complex mythotopic structures of Ryhope Wood and their interaction with those characters who wind up caught in them thus demonstrate the captivating power of myths while being integral parts of one of the most wonderful and engaging landscapes of the fantastic mode.

NOTES

1. Both myths and legends, as well as literary creations, are brought to life in the Mythago Cycle. Although to many these concepts refer to separate entities, I have used the words interchangeably here, since little if any difference is made between them in the novels. That the version, the time to which a legend's mythagos correspond, is highly relevant to the mythotopes may be seen from the example of Someone and Iss-abeau in *Gate of Ivory, Gate of Horn*. These two heroes belong to different versions of the same story. His is set in a Celtic land of pre–Roman northern Europe, whereas she comes from what corresponds to medieval France (242). Further discussions of myths and legends refer to certain versions of these myths and legends unless I have specified otherwise.

2. The temporal aspect is further complicated by inconstancy in the relative pas-sage of time. If the (approximate) 1:18 ratio suggested by Richard's two months to the Station's three years were constant, the three years of external time that the Station has been in operation would correspond to (approximately) fifty years of forest time, some-thing belied by the state of both the Station and researchers (compare *The Hollowing* 183, 89).

3. Although it is questionable whether a net as Eco describes it is in fact a labyrinth (compare Aarseth 6).

WORKS CITED

Aarseth, Espen J. *Cybertext: Perspectives on Ergodic Literature*. Baltimore: Johns Hopkins University Press, 1997.

"Biotope." *OED Online*. Oxford University Press. 14 January 2010 <dictionary.oed.com/entrance.dtl>.

Doob, Penelope Reed. *The Idea of the Labyrinth: From Classical Antiquity through the Middle Ages*. Ithaca, NY: Cornell University Press, 1992.

Eco, Umberto. *Semiotics and the Philosophy of Language (Advances in Semiotics)*. Bloom-ington, IN: Indiana University Press, 1986.

Holdstock, Robert. *Gate of Ivory, Gate of Horn*. 1997. London: Voyager-HarperCollins, 1998.

3. Exploring the Habitats of Myths (Ekman)

_____. *The Hollowing*. 1993. New York: ROC-Penguin, 1995.

_____. *Lavondyss: Journey to an Unknown Region*. 1988. New York: Avon, 1991.

_____. *Mythago Wood*. London: Gollancz, 1984.

Holloway, Lewis, and Phil Hubbard. *People and Place: The Extraordinary Geographies of Everyday Life*. Harlow, UK: Prentice Hall, 2001.

Tuan, Yi-Fu. "Space and Place." *Progress in Geography: International Reviews of Current Research*. Vol. 6. Ed. Christopher Board, et al. London: Edward Arnold, 1974. 211–52.

4

Time Winds:
Early Science Fiction

Andy Sawyer

Paul Kincaid writes that Holdstock's first three science-fiction novels "form a neat little trilogy of novels which detail anguished loss of humanity upon alien planets, gripped by an alien past which has generated alien forces" (8). *Eye Among the Blind* (1976), Holdstock's first novel, was well-received and attracted favorable comment from, among others, Ursula K. Le Guin, whose comment — "a serious, ambitious, fascinating first novel" — adorned the cover of the 1976 Pan paperback. Don D'Ammassa, summarizing Holdstock for the St. James Press *Science Fiction Writers* (449) calls *Earthwind* (1977) less successful, preferring *Where Time Winds Blow* (1981), while John Clute in *The Encyclopedia of Science Fiction* seems to concur, suggesting that Holdstock

> uneasily attempted to accommodate the compulsive mythologizing of his dark fantasies to "normal" sf worlds. The result was a series of books whose narrative energies seem hampered by decorum: the interplay between Aliens and alienation in *Eye Among the Blind* is effective but ponderously expressed; *Earthwind* utters slow-moving hints at the powers of a "chthonic" atavism; and *Where Time Winds Blow* (1981), the best of these early books, ornately but without much movement posits an environment suffering arbitrary transfigurations through time-shifts [578].

Looking back upon these novels, it seems clear that the language of science fiction, with its attention upon the physical world, its need for understanding and explanation, and its tendency to fall into action-adventure plots is not necessarily suited to the kind of symbolic fiction Holdstock was wanting to write, although Gene Wolfe was perhaps showing the way in *The Fifth Head of Cerberus* (1972). Nor, perhaps, was the horror mode of *Necromancer* (1978), which chronologically comes between *Earthwind* and *Where Time Winds Blow*. This essay, however, will concentrate on the three science-fiction novels as prefiguring, and to some extent wrestling with, the kind of fusion of science fiction and fantasy that Holdstock was to crystallize in *Mythago Wood*.

Eye Among the Blind is a novel that suggests unease with science fiction even as it embraces — rather too easily — some of its standard tropes. The beginning of *Eye Among the Blind* introduces us to three major images, seen through the experiences of Robert Zeitman, returning to Ree'hdworld where he had become estranged from his wife Kristina, and Susanna, a newcomer. First, there is Ree'hdworld itself, colonized, earthlike, but strange, inhabited by an enigmatic alien species. Secondly there is the Fear, a plague which has devastated a hundred worlds across the Galaxy, including, it is rumored, the Earth. Third, there is the vanishing, in full view of Susanna, of the blind man Maguire from the skimmer in which they are about to land upon Ree'hdworld.

In this universe, the Ree'hd are the only contemporary sentient aliens, although they share their world with the more primitive Rundii and seem to have a mythology about the Pianhmar, a kind of peripheral but superior culture which may have spread through the galaxy. (The Ree'hd themselves are a-technological, claiming to be "understanders" rather than "explorers" like the Pianhmar.) It is partly through the insights of Kristina, who has developed a relationship with the Ree'hd Urak and is rejecting her humanity, that we come to realize the true nature of Urak's statement that "Everything they [the Pianhmar] learned is with us. Everything they saw can be seen by us" (177). Kristina also claims that the Rundii, little more than animals, have become self-aware. While Holdstock creates a convincing alien world with an ecology and sense of place, there are elements of the "noble savage" cliché about the Ree'hd, with their habit of wandering to find inner peace and their complex kinship and religious customs, which sometimes undercuts their sense of difference. If our encounter with the Ree'hd is one of confrontation with Otherness, it is sometimes too familiar an Otherness to be thoroughly estranging. At other times, especially when Holdstock focuses upon Kristina's relationship with her Ree'hd "lover," this confrontation becomes truly unsettling, for Kristina's drive to *become* Ree'hd transcends simple sexual desire. It is difficult to articulate what motivates her, but Holdstock's point here seems to be to underline this difficulty. While Kristina can only "become Ree'hd" (whatever that means) by dying, her encounter with the alien is one of fulfillment rather than submission; following the Ree'hd into their evolutionary destiny rather than giving up humanity *per se*. This kind of transcendence through the alien can be apotheosis, as it is established in Stanley Kubrick and Arthur C. Clarke's film *2001: A Space Odyssey* (1968); or it can mirror the darker side of our obsession with Otherness, as in James Tiptree Jr.'s "And I Awoke and Found Me Here on the Cold Hill's Side" (1971). Holdstock's aliens are not the godlike beings that (in Clarke's fictions) represent science fiction's sometimes too easy aspirations for transcendence, nor are they the symbols (which Tiptree makes them) of our deeper obsessions with sex and death. Instead, they inhabit a universe which seems, in Holdstock's later fiction, to become its own symbol. It is a universe which seems resolutely secular, but which has religion's striving for an understanding beyond the physical.

It is a universe which, in *Eye Among the Blind*, is also being undermined. The aptly-named if sketchily-described Fear is driving refugees to Ree'hdworld, exacerbating the cultural divisions which already exist. The Ree'hd suffer from an illness which makes them appear drunk: "their 'blood' thinned, they lost weight and co-ordination, and their thinking processes faded. They were good, at this stage, for many routine jobs and not surprisingly were mercilessly exploited" (49). The apparent stone-age culture of the Ree'hd would make it easy for the refugees to claim "rights of survival," but Kristina, Zeitman, Maguire, and Susanna are increasingly sure, from different perspectives, that the Pianhmar still exist, particularly when a statue is discovered. What we have read as metaphor — "Everything they saw can be seen by us," Zeitman's "uncanny sensation that he was being watched" (183) on the small continent of Wooburren, the sense of design — turns out to be fact. The Pianhmar exist, but their evolutionary relationship with the Ree'hd is different from anything known elsewhere in the universe. "Fascinating, thought Robert Zeitman the scientist. An intelligent being with three physical forms, spread through time, and through which it must pass to evolve fully" (210).

While the Fear is disrupting civilization, another more existential disruption occurs in the discovery of the true nature of the Ree'hd and Kristina's embracing of Ree'hd, rather than human, nature. Maguire's disappearance — and reappearance — through teleportation is linked to his pilgrimage seven hundred years ago to discover the Pianhmar. His importance — his blindness is the reason the Pianhmar will receive him as they dislike being looked at, although his constant Pianhmar companion shares, telepathically, his own far more expansive visual sense — seems to be to literalize in a rather fuzzy way this metaphor of physical and moral blindness. It is Zeitman, the scientist, whose own interior and moral life is the shambolic opposite of his rational and analytic exterior, but Maguire's experiences are the key to our (the readers') understanding of the fictional universe we experience. He is, as Paul Kincaid points out, a catalyst rather than an actor (7). Between them, Zeitman, Kristina, and Maguire offer ways of transcending the gulf between Human and Ree'hd. The apparently paranormal powers given to Maguire are explained — or partly explained — towards the novel's close, but it is Zeitman who is left to be the "contact man" between the two species. What this means, though, in terms of future relationships between the two species, is unclear. Zeitman is alone with the Pianhmar who will be his "guardian" from then on; he is "no longer afraid" (218). But how, in terms of the politics of Holdstock's imagined universe, the tension between Humanity and Pianhmar/Ree'hd/Rundii is actually to be resolved is not figured unless we abandon the story as a colonial/political metaphor and return to its metaphysics.

All alien worlds are, of course, representations of inner rather than outer space, as J. G. Ballard suggested when asked, in his guest editorial in *New Worlds* May 1962, "Which Way to Inner Space?" But part of the science-fictional game is pretending that the imaginary is true, or at least plausible. An argument that the science-fictional alien is "only a metaphor" for something much more *fundamental* can be a sign that an author has neglected to engage with (or a critic to understand) science fiction's concern for plausible invention. We would wholeheartedly condemn a writer of realistic contemporary fiction whose novel set in Liverpool, say, shows no sign of the writer ever having been to, or imagined what it would be like to live in, the city, or whose description of the 1960s is full of anachronisms. Holdstock, I think, would never claim this excuse for carelessness, nor would he have claimed to be a hard–SF writer in the sense that we understand when Hal Clement devises a world that — if we comprehend the science correctly — could, or could at the time he published *Mission of Gravity* in *Astounding* (1953), exist in our universe. But, in using the "agreed" language of SF — the spaceships, the alien planet, the aliens themselves and how they live on their world, the relationship between this future and how it extrapolates from our present — Holdstock is walking in the science-fiction megastory that leads to a clash of symbols, which becomes more apparent as we work our ways through the subsequent novels.

The three science-fiction novels seem to be set in the same universe, sharing, as many SF sequences do, an imagined locale which serves as a metaphysical mindscape. There is a "Federation" in the first and third; in the second, we hear that the Federation has been replaced by the more repressive "Electra." We hear little about the political realities behind these, although the vivid backstory to *Earthwind* is one of the understated delights of the novel. The characters conveniently speak "Interling": a device for mutual understanding as obvious as any "universal translator." There are issues — as we have noted from the relationship between the Ree'hd and the humans of Ree'hdworld — of colonialism, but rather sketchily presented. (Think of the "drunken Indian" cliché in a Western film.) The worlds in this universe — Dominion, New Villefranche — seem almost random in their nomenclature. There is no *culture* in this future apart from the convenient "default future" that science fiction itself has pulled together out of its own images of spaceships, interstellar federations, and aliens. Holdstock, however, is, in these novels, developing his own sense of culture, and increasingly it is not part of this default future. The kind of science fiction which focuses upon the physical — the evocation of a world, like Frank Herbert's *Dune*; a technologically-advanced object, like Arthur C. Clarke's *Rama* or Larry Niven's *Ringworld*; or even the difference (and similarity) between human and alien, such as in much of Ursula K. Le Guin's fiction — is less and less the kind of SF that Holdstock appears to want to write.

The buffeting wind is perhaps the first thing we notice about Ree'hd-world. In these three novels, Wind is a major symbol, of time and interior archetypal mind-currents:

> here, where the Ree'hd had spent their evolutionary history, the great dawn wind was split, divided into lesser gales, each of which followed a branch of the spreading rivers as they wound in through steep banks and deep channels in the land. The mass of purple-green vegetation that swept in belts across the plain moved and writhed with the dawn, seeming sentient in its own right, but hiding the only real sentience on Ree'hdworld from aerial view [17].

The word "wind" appears in the title of the next two novels. It is associated in *Earthwind* with the "Earth-current," "the flow of earth-energy in the rock" (76), and the "interactions and the vital flow — be they gravitic, electromagnetic or quirk, that formed the great tao, the cosmic forces of the Universe at large" (117), and, in *Where Time Winds Blow*, with Time, the connection between self and other in past or future.

The Ree'hd greet the dawn-wind with song and communal bonding. In *Eye Among the Blind*, their telepathic communication moves beyond the limitations of physical culture to linking the living and the dead — "a mind web, an open channel" (208). As wind connects everything physical touched by it, so, in the subsequent novels, the idea of communication deepens to embody the idea of wind as psychic flow, connecting symbol and archetype. This exploration continues in *Earthwind*, where a survey ship lands upon a world whose colonists seem to be in touch with archetypal symbols.

Earthwind develops the tension between ways of considering the universe by means of figures like the ship's "rationalist" Peter Ashka, whose use of the *I Ching* (the Chinese oracle, which is another symbol of connection) to plot out courses of action makes him a combination of priest and diplomat. We understand the sense of conflict between him and the captain, Karl Gorstein, another (in the scientific sense) "rational" but flawed character. But before the ship landed, we have already met Elspeth Mueller on the world Aeran, where the colonists have developed a culture similar to that which may have centered on the Neolithic Boyne valley in Ireland, using similar spiral designs, one of which (a triple spiral) represents the "Earthwind." Her partner Austen perished on Aeran, mind apparently wiped. Resigned to a similar fate, Mueller is trying to find out why this culture has become so similar to one light-years away. Gorstein, meanwhile, has landed as part of a program by the new regime, the Electra,[1] to plant monitoring devices.

While D'Ammassa and Clute see this novel as less successful, *Earthwind* seems to me to be a more thorough-going attempt to engage with the symbolism associated with earth and time in a science-fiction mode. The neo–Neolithic culture Holdstock imagines seems to be based upon personal exposure to Irish megalithic remains interpreted through what sounds at times like Alfred Watkins's theory of ley-lines, popularized in *The Old Straight Track* (1925) and developed into a theory of "Earth Currents" in such "new age" works as *The View Over Atlantis* by John Michell (1969). Other symbolic elements include the *I Ching*, Taoism, (popularized in science fiction by Philip K. Dick and Ursula K. Le Guin), and Greek legend. Their fusion into a science-fiction mode of storytelling may sound awkward. In fact, Holdstock has integrated his symbolism with his narrative effectively: this is a universe which is much more solid than that of *Eye Among the Blind*. The adapted, furred human colonists and the details of their culture are vividly imagined. There is both teleportation and time, but here the "blackwings" and all life on Aeran seem to teleport. Nevertheless, while Maguire's teleportation in *Eye Among the Blind* is a startling event which receives a rather unconvincing explanation towards the end, here the "teleportation" is structurally part of the way the world *works*. Its explanation, as with so many explanations in science fiction, may convince only as far as we do not understand the mathematical model offered to us (160) and accept it as the kind of plausible game hard–SF plays with its readers, but Holdstock convinces us that it is not "magic" and by doing so confirms his universe where the plans of a highly technological civilization are guided in and through the *I Ching*. Indeed, this teleportation is the key to why the *I Ching* does not seem to work on Aeran. On Aeran time is *oscillatory* rather than sequential. It is a world "where at any one instant the past and the future were the same, held together in that past and pre-echo of the moment" (161). The oscillation is tiny, but like the point at the center of a spiral it has far-reaching effects. The image drawn from physics and the symbolic "wind" finds concrete meaning in the *tao*:

> [Ashka] broke off and stared at Iondai. "The tao is an ancient word ... for the energy and matter that flow around us and through us, every one of us."
>
> "Winds," said Iondai, "heat and cold, the forces that appear in our rock and stone, in the earth, the caught breath of time ... yes, I think I understand" [104].

Yet, while the universe of this book has shape, the essential link explaining why on Aeran the Neolithic symbols of Old Earth should be re-created remains less convincing compared to the potential richness of what drives the culture of the Electra: a society which, as its name suggests, seems to have combined the ruthlessness and numinous elements of the myth-time of Hellenic Greece.

Holdstock's characters are stronger, less representative of human drives. Phil Stephensen-Payne, reviewing *Eye Among the Blind* and *Earthwind* in *Vector*, calls Gorstein "a thoroughly detestable man" who nevertheless survives because of his determination and will. Elspeth is, perhaps, Holdstock's most interesting character until the Huxley family of *Mythago Wood*. Like Steven Huxley, she is attempting to uncover the secret of one of our most mysterious symbols, albeit less personified than Huxley's mythagos. She has been both damaged and—in the way those who undergo savage and complex rites of passage often are—*created* by the mutilation of her breasts. But, as Paul Kincaid argues, "there is little sense that what shapes the society [of the inhabitants of Aeran] is actually a deep-rooted part of people" (8). The wind that is blowing here is an exterior wind. One enjoys this as a science-fiction novel which plays with ideas, but the transposition of the symbolic language of the Megalithic cultures of pre–Celtic Ireland into another world does not quite convince us that it is a universal, human language.

The third science-fiction novel, *Where Time Winds Blow* (1981), is set upon a world where investigators from Earth are studying the streams of time-displacement which occasionally flow along the valleys of VanderZande's World, also known as Kamelios—the two names sign to us the ambiguity which pervades the novel. This doubling and ambiguity offers us greater opportunity to read *Where Time Winds Blow* both as science-fiction adventure and symbolic narrative. The time winds leave in their wake geological structures and artifacts from the planet's past or future, occasionally sweeping up individuals from the survey teams such as Mark Dojann, a former partner of the protagonist Leo Faulcon whose team has been joined by Mark's younger brother, Kris, believing that Mark may still be alive and contactable.

Both the world and its inhabitants—some of the human colonists, the "manchanged"—have abandoned the treasure-hunting to adapt themselves to the hostile environment—are, as we have come to expect, vividly, if enigmatically, described. There is debate about whether the *fiersig* (apparently an electrical/atmospheric phenomenon) might be intelligent life-forms (87). One of the leaders of the investigators believes that the time-winds are to do with time-traveling aliens with whom it is possible to make contact. One of Faulcon's colleagues, Leuwentok, describes what has been seen—aliens, lost friends, symbolic structures and shapes—in terms of a kind of Jungian desire for the numinous. There are no aliens, he says, but "something is dreaming ... we're not only chasing our own dreams on Kamelios, sometimes we're chasing something else's" (162).

Teleportation—that fundamental bridge in science fiction between the rational and irrational, for like "telepathy" (coined by F. W. Myers in 1882 as part of his engagement with the Society for Psychical Research) it simply offers a "scientific" word for a process which, even if it takes place, has no explanation within our scientific model of the world — is here a fact. We are told, with what might be an oblique reference to *Eye Among the Blind*, *Earthwind*, or both, that "certain planetary environments enhance that power, right?" (126). But thrown out in the same conversation is a concept which is worth a novel in itself and which may have been part of the process which led to *Mythago Wood*: the reference to "animal God creatures ... and ... communication with the creatures on Earth which live out of phase with humanity, the same beings who inspired all those legends and myths, right?" (126). The worlds of mythology and science are colliding, although it is unclear from this novel what such "animal God creatures" might actually be.

The metaphorical "readings" of the wind at the beginning of *Eye Among the Blind* have become "real" — the wind sends objects and people through time. And Time, for Holdstock, is a central image; *time* and *wind* are correlatives. It is time within which our culture exists. Just as the Ree'hd, Rundii, and Pianhmar *physically* exist in three different, yet unified, relationships through time, so a culture can only make sense if it is seen as an embodiment of time. But time, as Ballard argues in "Which Way to Inner Space?" is a much more complex thing than the science-fiction writers have made it. Instead of the default futures of the "Buck Rogers" enthusiasts for space travel,[2] Ballard calls for a kind of science fiction which is less old-fashioned and indebted to the tropes developed within the narrow contexts of the magazines: "science fiction should turn its back on space, on interstellar travel, extra-terrestrial life forms, galactic wars and the overlap of these ideas that spreads across the margins of nine-tenths of magazine s-f" (117). Central to the way science fiction should engage with the *real* concept of futurity as Ballard sees it is its treatment of *time*: "For example, instead of treating time like a sort of glorified scenic railway, I'd like to see it used for what it is, one of the perspectives of the personality, and the elaboration of concepts such as the time zone, deep time and archaeopsychic time" (118). It is precisely this treatment of time which Holdstock is attempting to engage with and develop a vocabulary for.

Towards the end of *Where Time Winds Blow*, Leo Faulcon confronts the "phantom" who has been seen, who may be one of the colonists picked up and driven through time by the winds, who Kris Dojaan has thought was his brother.

> Kris was convinced you were his brother; I thought you were Kris; later you became Lena, and Lena saw herself in you at the same time as I saw

Lena in you. We see what we want to see, or what our minds want to see. Isn't that right? ... [ellipsis added] You're a sort of mind's eye symbol, a deep-rooted image. Something archaic, archetypal ... the dead returned, the lost returned [239; ellipsis in the original].

All these elements — the "mind web," the "mind's eye symbol," and the Earth-wind oracle — combine later in the mythago, an idea which Holdstock seems to be looking for in his science-fiction novels but never quite crystallizes there. The notion is similar to that which infuses Jung's thinking about "flying saucers," and one might think that Holdstock's science fiction is an attempt to advance Jung's ideas, to use an essentially modern set of images to explore much older, more fluid archetypes. Holdstock refers to Jung in an interview with Catie Carey in *Vector* in a context which makes it clear that the symbols of place, words, earthworks, and markings in his works can be seen as Jungian signifiers of consciousness. Carroll Brown, writing about *Mythago Wood* as "a story of myth told in a scientific mode" (159), refers to the novel's intimate connection with Jungian archetype theory and the way Holdstock, early in the novel, emphasizes his deliberate use of these ideas.

Jung's explanation of UFOs or "flying saucers," to use the expression commonly employed at the time of the 1958 book on the subject collected in the *Civilization in Transition* volume of his *Collected Works*, as "psychically real" but not "physically real" ("Flying Saucers" 631) is not, perhaps, wholly satisfactory for science fiction. When we are concerned with what they represent, we can accept them as (to use Jung's term) "living myth" (322). In doing so, we have to eschew the claims of the ufologists at least to the point of strong agnosticism. If spacecraft from other worlds really *existed*, we would have to accept them as part of our mundane reality. We might go on to build symbolic images out of them, but this would be similar to the process in which we can create symbolic images out of real things in our world, such as a lion or a beehive to represent ideas of royalty or the State.[3] To adopt the (possibly apocryphal) comment by Jung's rival Freud, sometimes a cigar is just a cigar; sometimes an imaginary device in a work of fiction is an imaginary device. We want to believe in them, but not *really* believe: only for the story to make sense. We want to explore a plausible world. The Jungian explanation of "flying saucers" itself can become a good subject for a science-fiction story, as in Ian Watson's *Miracle Visitors* (1978), but for most science fiction the alien needs to exist within the parameters of the fiction. Science fiction needs our ability to hold a double viewpoint for it to be effective as literature. Its tropes are, of course, imaginary, plausible rather than possible, and not to be taken too seriously. But science fiction is built upon realist techniques. It is extrapolative rather than totally inventive.

Holdstock's science-fiction worlds are, paradoxically, too generic and too oblique to be truly plausible. If we compare them to those of Ursula Le Guin (whose words of praise, as I have noted previously, are printed upon the back cover of the 1976 Pan paperback of *Eye Among the Blind*), we see that Holdstock is struggling with his locales in the same way as she struggled in her first science-fiction novels, *Rocannon's World* (1966), *Planet of Exile* (1966), and *City of Illusion* (1967). The elements of Tolkienish fantasy which color the first novel are strong. *Rocannon's World* has the dwarfish Clayfolk, the Elvish Fiia, and a planetary culture similar to Andre Norton's Witchworld ("Hallan" compares to Norton's "High Hallack"). Not only do Le Guin's characters *speak* like characters out of fantasy novels, the initial tropes of the story are taken (possibly via J. R. R. Tolkien, but Le Guin would have been acquainted with many of these stories in the original) from the "cauldron of story" (as Tolkien puts it in his essay "On Fairy-Stories," 29) of European folklore. The story "Semley's Necklace," which provides a prologue for *Rocannon's World*, is a lightly disguised fantasy in which we may realize that these "legendary" characters are in fact "real" human or alien characters in a far future extrapolated from our universe. Or it could simply be that this fantasy mode provides a palatable way of entering into and understanding a science-fiction world.

Or it could be that Le Guin, who is known for her fantasy as much as her science fiction, is not as interested in defining boundaries as readers hooked upon a particular narrative style may want her to be. The question with which Le Guin begins the novel, "How can you tell the legend from the fact on these worlds that lie so many years away?" (*Rocannon's* 5), both provides an easy explanation for the mixture of modes and points towards the more sophisticated approach to viewpoint and interpretation in her later work such as Genly Ai's declaration that "I begin this report as if I told a story" (*The Left Hand of Darkness* 7) and the mixture of "reportage" and "fiction" styles in the stories collected in *The Birthday of the World*. Le Guin's early "Hainish cycle" is a future-history along the lines of Asimov's "Foundation" series: the story of a "Galactic Empire," rising and falling. As she became more assured in her ambitions and "discovered" more about her fictional space, it became a kind of laboratory in which anthropological "thought experiments" could be carried out. Le Guin stresses the importance of metaphor in *The Left Hand of Darkness* and, specifically, in the question-and-answer session following the delivery of her talk "Science Fiction and Mrs. Brown" at the Institute of Contemporary Arts in 1975, where she emphasizes the importance to her of the Tao, which appears in a different form in Holdstock's *Earthwind*.

Her worlds are vivid, part of a history which it is possible to chart. Compared to other writers of future-history or those science-fiction authors for whom the galaxy is a vast adventure-playground for the exploration of possibilities, her universe may be messy and chaotic. She sometimes forgets where she is: "the planet Werel in *Four Ways* is not the planet Werel in *Planet of Exile*. In between novels, I forget planets. Sorry" ("Answers" par. 5). Nevertheless, one can always speak of a Le Guin Universe, whereas, in the three novels under consideration here, one can only speak in the vaguest terms of a "Robert Holdstock Universe."

This kind of science fiction, the traditional future-historical depiction of alien worlds, with all the trappings — out of the Gernsback/Campbell magazine tradition — of humanity exploding into the galaxy and exploring what was to become famed in *Star Trek* as the "final frontier," is not what Holdstock came to be interested in. In *Eye Among the Blind, Earthwind,* and *Where Time Winds Blow*, we get the impression that the most intriguing events and aspects of Holdstock's imagined universe are often left offstage. This is partly true, but only in the sense that powerful stories can be constructed out of glimpses, asides, and half-understood allusions. The Fear in *Eye Among the Blind*, the fall of the Federation in *Where Time Winds Blow*, and the discovery of the "myth-creatures" in the same novel are all ideas which other writers, or Holdstock himself, could have devoted whole novels to, but they are essentially subordinate to what for him is the center: the Ballardian "inner space" of his protagonists. It is clear from his later works and his comments about them in interviews that the building-blocks of science fiction hold less interest for him than the far older vocabulary of myth and symbol which he discovered in the English landscape and carved on the walls of Neolithic tombs. It is as if Holdstock is circling — or spiraling? — around possible ways of telling their stories, trying to find the "real" location for his theme, which is essentially that of the relationship between the individual, the place, and the interior landscape of symbols.

Earthwind almost arrives there, but the science-fiction trappings of "time-displacement" get in the way. Paradoxically, it is too fertile, too imaginative a novel. It is only when Holdstock abandons "outer space" science fiction to return to 1940s Middle England and Ryhope Wood that the full richness of his symbolic approach can be let loose. Chapter 4 of *Mythago Wood*, where we read George Huxley's explanation of mythagos, is, of course, as science-fictional a piece of writing as Holdstock has ever done, but here the science is anthropology and psychology. We do not need the spaceships or alien worlds. Jung wrote that to him the unconscious was "a vast historical storehouse" ("Lecture IV" 127). One can see in Holdstock's first three science-fiction novels, perhaps, an attempt to find the key to unlocking this storehouse.

NOTES

1. We may recall that Electra was the daughter of Agamemnon and Clytemnestra, who helped her brother Orestes avenge their father's murder by their mother.
2. He begins his article with reference to the Russian-American space-race and the prospect of the successful landing of astronauts on the moon.
3. Medieval and renaissance emblem theory does embody "imaginary" beings such as the Phoenix, but this is a further step.

WORKS CITED

Ballard, J. G. "Which Way to Inner Space?" *New Worlds* 118 (May 1962): 2–3, 116–18.
Brown, Carroll. "The Flame in the Heart of the Wood: The Integration of Myth and Science in Robert Holdstock's *Mythago Wood*." *Extrapolation* 34.2 (1993): 158–71.
Cary, Catie. "Robert Holdstock Interviewed." *Vector* 175 (October–November 1993): 3–6.
Clute, John, and Peter Nicholls, eds. *The Encyclopedia of Science Fiction.* 2nd ed. London: Orbit, 1993.
D'Ammassa, Don. "Robert Holdstock." Jay P. Pederson, ed. *St. James Guide to Science Fiction Writers.* 4th ed. Detroit: St. James Press, 1996. 448–49.
Jung, Carl Gustav. "Flying Saucers: A Modern Myth of Things Seen in the Skies." *Civilization in Transition: Collected Works of C. G. Jung.* Vol. 10. 2nd ed. London: Routledge, 1970. 307–433.
_____. "Lecture IV." *The Symbolic Life: Miscellaneous Writings. Collected Works of C. G. Jung.* Vol. 18. London: Routledge and Kegan Paul, 1977. 102–34.
Holdstock, Robert. *Earthwind.* London: Faber, 1977.
_____. *Eye Among the Blind.* London: Faber, 1976.
_____. *Mythago Wood.* London: Gollancz, 1984.
_____. *Where Time Winds Blow.* London: Faber, 1981.
Kincaid, Paul. "Touching the Earth: The Fiction of Robert Holdstock." *Vector* 175 (October–November 1993): 7–9.
Le Guin, Ursula K. "Answers to a Questionnaire: FAQ." *Ursula K. Le Guin's Website.*

25 December 2009 <http://www.ursulakleguin.com/FAQ_Questionnaire5_01.
html>.

_____. *The Birthday of the World*. New York: HarperCollins, 2002.

_____. *The Dispossessed*. New York: Harper and Row, 1974.

_____. *The Left Hand of Darkness*. New York: Ace, 1969.

_____. *Rocannon's World*. New York: Ace, 1966.

_____. "Science Fiction and Mrs. Brown" [cassette tape of talk delivered at the Institute
of Contemporary Arts, January 1975]. Science Fiction Foundation, 1975.

Stephensen-Payne, Phil. "Civilization and Savagery: Two Novels by Robert Holdstock." *Vector* 175 (October–November 1993): 22–25.

Tiptree, James, Jr. "And I Awoke and Found Me Here on the Cold Hill's Side." *The
Thousand Light-Years from Home*. New York: Ace, 1978.

Tolkien, J. R. R. "On Fairy-Stories." *Tree and Leaf*. London: Unwin, 1964. 11–70.

Watkins, Alfred. *The Old Straight Track*. London: Methuen, 1925.

Watson, Ian. *Miracle Visitors*. London: Gollancz, 1978.

5

Profusion Sublime and the Fantastic: *Mythago Wood*

Marek Oziewicz

The greatest forces lie in the region of the uncomprehended.
(George MacDonald, *Dish of Orts* 232)

Robert Holdstock's *Mythago Wood* is a novel about visitations: the kind of visitations the protagonist does not expect, which he dreads and yet becomes increasingly fascinated with while being drawn into wanting them to recur. The obsessive nature of these visitations and the obsessive effects they have on characters stem from the nature of Holdstock's subject matter: the hypnotic allure and obscurity of the mystery encountered by the protagonist. According to the tradition established by Longinus, obscurity and mystery are two alternative sources of the sublime. Thus, while the most obvious readings Holdstock's novel lends itself to are Jungian, archetypal, and mythic, I propose to follow the trail of mystery and obscurity and examine *Mythago Wood* through the lens of the sublime.

Guy Sircello postulates a division between experiences of the sublime, sublime discourse, and talk about the sublime in "How Is a Theory of the Sublime Possible?" The first, he suggests, is the actual personal experience which "can and does occur in a large variety of personal, cultural, social, and historical contexts" (542); the second, sublime discourse, Sircello defines as "language that is or purports to be more or less immediately descriptive or expressive of sublime experience" (541); while, finally, talk about the sublime comprises "reflective or analytic discourse that takes as its subject matter primarily sublime experience or sublime discourse, but also itself and other talk about the sublime" (541). Although, as Sircello

81

admits, the distinction is "hard to maintain very rigorously" (541), its use nevertheless lies in embracing a recognition of sublime experience as distinct from its description or theorizing.

Although sublime experiences proper may not be limited to any particular culture or period, the modern understanding of the sublime comes from representations of the category "talk about the sublime." The concept itself has many faces: the sublime can be seen as Longinus's proud identification; Boileau's unusual exaltation of conception and style[1]; something that overpowers, overwhelms, even threatens, as in Burke; Kant's temporary failure and humiliation of the subject; Romantic-aesthetic rapture producing a correspondent overflow of feeling revealing the transcendent; Gothic or Freudian disintegration of identity; Rudolf Otto's encounter with the numinous; or Jean François Lyotard's presentation of the unpresentable.[2] Perhaps the sublime is all of these; perhaps, then, it is something yet different and impossible to be hemmed in by any talk of the sublime, by interpretations that merely theorize on sublime experience and sublime discourse.[3]

A Novel of "The Beyond"

Examining *Mythago Wood* as an instance of the fantastic sublime, a fictional narrative which reaches "beyond the actual, beyond what is known, or can be known" toward "the transcendent beyond" (Sandner 50), reveals that this grasping at the transcendent is fundamental to Holdstock's novel.[4] If Sircello is right in claiming that running through most versions of the sublime are themes of epistemological and ontological transcendence — namely, that "human mental powers ... have radically limited access to 'reality'" (543) and that there is "something on a level of being ... which transcends that of humankind and all of humankind's possible environments, natural and cultural" (545) — then Holdstock's novel deals with the sublime on this basic, irreducible level. Seen thus, the narrative of *Mythago Wood* contains sublime experiences, sublime discourse, and talk about the sublime. The proportions between those three are such that there are occasional sublime experiences "described" by the narrator or experiencing agents in sublime discourse, and this sublime discourse is, in turn, embedded in the talk of the sublime which makes up the bulk of the narrative.

If sublime experiences are personal encounters with the mystery, with beings, places, or presences out of the realm of the ordinary, then George Huxley, his sons Christian and Steven, and Harry Keeton must be seen as definitely having had experiences of the sublime. With the exception of Steven (the narrator of *Mythago Wood* whose sublime experiences the reader witnesses) these experiences are usually hinted at. George Huxley's encounter with the wood and its inhabitants is communicated to his sons and to the reader — in a very incomplete way — through his diary. Christian's experience is first hinted at in his letters to Steven and then, following their reunion, in Steven's awareness that his brother had changed radically as a result of experiences he is unwilling or unable to talk about. That Christian's encounters are similar to their father's is made clear when, rather than try to explain his strange behavior, Christian urges Steven to study their father's diary (34). Harry Keeton's sublime experience is also alluded to, first in a conversation when Steven asks Keeton to fly him over the wood, then on several other occasions, though the reader learns a bit more of Keeton's story, in his own words, by the end of the novel (306–08).

Steven's encounter and relationship with the mythago Guiwenneth illustrates this three-layered process of the sublime which, to an extent, is reflected in the tripartite division of the book. In Part One, Steven is being prepared for Guiwenneth by what he learns about mythagos from his father's diary and his conversation with Christian, as well as by his own discovery of Guiwenneth's, his father's mythago's, corpse. After Christian disappears into the woods to find the newly formed Guiwenneth, Steven is left alone in Oak Lodge where he's visited by the Late Bronze Age mythago of the hunter Cuchullain, and survives his first encounter with the mythago Urscumug. These episodes prepare Steven to acknowledge, though not to understand, the existence of a plane of being totally outside of his former experience. In Part Two, the visitations continue. First come the thick-smoke-shaped elementals (87), then the mythago of the first boatman Sorthalan (88–89), and two others, a neolith and a seventeenth-century Cavalier (94). None of them enter the house, though; Steven always steps outside to meet them. This changes when the young man becomes aware that he is having a visitor who walks about the house in his absence and watches him in his sleep. The narrator has an inkling of his mysterious guest's identity and his reaction is intense curiosity rather than apprehension (92). Thus, even before he actually meets her, Steven sees Guiwenneth's footprints, dirt and leaf litter she brought, notices objects she has moved, and begins to enjoy "the pungent smell of woodland female" (94) she would leave behind. "The house [appeared] ... haunted," Steven records, then adds a description of his feelings about the haunting, which reads quintessentially sublime, "one step removed ... [a] haunting, terrifying feeling" (96).

Already at this point Guiwenneth becomes, for Steven, indistinguishable from the sublime experience she is part of. And so it remains through the rest of Part Two, in which the mythago girl comes to live with Steven, the two establish a relationship and are finally separated when Christian and his mercenaries take Guiwenneth back to the Wood. Besides the meeting with Guiwenneth, this part of the novel recounts Steven's other sublime experiences — notably the episodes of the attempted flight over Ryhope Wood (106–09), the Wood taking over Oak Lodge (95, 150–51), and the meeting with Magidion and the Jaguth (167–73). The chapters are also packed with reflective and analytic discourse about these sublime experiences: Steven madly tries to figure out whose mythago Guiwenneth is — admitting at one place that he became obsessed with Guiwenneth's identity (126); he seeks the answer to how his father was able to penetrate the woodland and visits his father's colleague's daughter with the hope, rewarded, of retrieving some of his father's notes on that subject; he studies Guiwenneth, admitting to how uncanny it was "to watch and listen ... [to] Guiwenneth acquir[ing] English" (149); he wonders how Guiwenneth sees him (165), experiments on how far away from the Wood she can stray (176–77), and interviews her on her memories (182–87). "Why are you questioning me?" Guiwenneth asks. "Because I want answers," is Steven's response. "You fascinate me. You frighten me" (182). This need to know is not quenched. Steven's attempts at rationalizing the sublime turn out just as futile as his attempts to domesticate it.

Whereas in Part Two the sublime, in a way, reached out to Steven by entering his world, in Part Three it is Steven who quests after the sublime by entering Ryhope Wood in his search of Guiwenneth. Once inside the Wood, Steven finds himself in a different reality, "a psychomythic landscape, [where] normal Euclidean geometries of space, motion, and time are no longer applicable" (Brown 160). The inner is larger than the outer, and Steven's journey into the heartwood is long and arduous. It is also more episodic, which is structurally reflected in Holdstock's abandonment of numbered chapters — a feature of parts One and Two. From the moment

Steven and Harry enter Ryhope Wood they are literally thrown into the sublime: they move in a reality in which time and space are preternaturally flexible, they are filled with dread and awe of the Wood, and they encounter and interact with a number of mythagos. These mythagos, just like Guiwenneth and others that had appeared earlier in the plot, may be seen as what Steven Knapp calls "sublime personifications." They are abstract concepts — such as racial memory — transformed into animated beings, but in a way that erases "the boundaries between literal and figurative agency" (2). Sublime personifications, Knapp argues, are set apart from other fictional characters in that they evoke in a reader a simultaneous identification with and dissociation from themselves (3). In *Mythago Wood* this process is reflected in the characters' reactions to mythagos: a mythago is part of the protagonist's racial memory, yet it is also a mere projection of the mind. Each of these sublime personifications is characterized by "the virtually total saturation of its 'personality' by the thematic idea it represents" (3) and by "patent fictionality [which] reveals and in a sense enforces the inaccessibility of their self-originating power" (4). Beginning with Steven's encounter with the skeleton of the Bronze Age warrior (220), the *shamiga* (226–43), the medieval knight (249), the Saxon couple (254–60), the Urscumug (265, 328–30), Sorthalan (271–95), Spud Frampton (277–88), an early Scandinavian community (298), the Neolithic peoples (300–09), up to the final meeting with the wounded Guiwenneth, who is taken by the Urscumug to recover in the eternal Lavondyss, Part Three of the novel presents an impressive catalogue of sublime personifications.

If Steven's story contains sublime moments and references to the sublime, these are presented with specific textual markers suggestive of the four "types" of the sublime: the Burkean and Kantian sublime of "delightful horror," the Romantic "natural sublime," the religious sublime of Otto and Mircea Eliade, and the Lyotardian, postmodern sublime as "the unpresentable." Although most textual markers cannot be exclusively associated with one specific version of the sublime, a combination of them seems to point to the philosophical tradition they derive from.

Paths of the Sublime

The Burkean and Kantian sublime of "delightful horror" is the aesthetic reaction of the witnessing human subject to an event or idea which is awe-inspiring and may often be, unless removed from the observer, positively threatening to life.[5] Textual markers of this type of sublimity are visual, aural, tactile, and mental: a description of awesome sights, natural or human-constructed, including scenes of decay or ruins, of awe-inspiring or frightening sounds or silence, of intense odors, usually unpleasant, and of the feelings of dread associated with being alone, or being confronted with darkness, gloom, or obscurity.

Mythago Wood is replete with descriptions of awe-inspiring sights: Oak Lodge may be gloomy, but what Steven and Harry encounter in their march through Ryhope Wood surpasses, in its gloom, anything they had seen or experienced before. At one point they come across architectural mythagos, abandoned and ruined structures. These include the ruined stone tower (244); an Iron Age structure called the broch (246); a gabled house, a Tudor building, and a wooden house with a wolf guarding it (246); thatch, wicker, and daub structures and an overgrown fortress (247); a decaying brick roadway (251); and, finally, the ruins of a Roman villa (252).

Natural places and sights of awe-inspiring magnitude are there, too. Chasing after Christian, Steven and Harry encounter a ravine half a mile deep (263). When they descend it, Steven admits that climbing down to the river valley was the most terrifying experience so far; when they reach the bottom, he comments that seen from below the walls of the gorge seemed sinister (266). Later, they travel aboard Sorthalan's ship down the bleak gorge through dangerous rocky shallows, endless rapids, and white-water, frothed pools (293). A dangerous river, steep cliffs, vicious gorges, strange, decaying constructions built into the rock face — particularly a huge stone fortress, a man-shaped, rusting giant machine (292), and then an immense crumbling bridge (293) — do not exhaust awe-inspiring sights in the novel. There is also the wintry inner realm (294), classically sublime mountains of the timeless Lavondyss, and, finally, Peredur's stone. This wind-scoured megalith leaves Steven awestruck by its silent and commanding authority (313).

Solitude, silence, and intense, strange sounds are other markers of the Burkean and Kantian sublime in Holdstock's novel. The unrelieved gloom of Oak Lodge, its separateness, its environs with a muddy mill-pond, overgrown garden, all of it dominated by "the hidden gloom of the dense stand of oak woodland" (23) are mirrored in the characters of its inhabitants. George Huxley is unable or unwilling to communicate with his children or with his wife who eventually commits suicide. According to the narrator, old Huxley devoted his entire life to silent research of the oak woodland stretching behind the house (20). Christian and Steven are also presented as solitary characters. When Steven returns from war, the brothers are happy to see one another and yet uneasy with each other's company. Steven admits to having never before felt so distant from his own brother, and Christian soon disappears in the Wood (25). The protagonist's solitude, interrupted more by encounters with mythagos than with living humans, frequently entails dread associated with being alone or with being confronted with darkness, gloom, or obscurity. The whole area around the house was, as Steven says, "strangely quiet, uncannily still" (175). As he admits elsewhere, this stillness was rather chilling and quite frightening (88).

Much is also made of intense odors, usually unpleasant. In most cases the smell is associated with mythagos, although humans also acquire a peculiar aroma after they spend some time in the Wood. Upon his first return to Oak Lodge, Christian "reeked of sweat and vegetation as if he had spent ... days ... buried in compost" (42). Even more repulsive is the fetor of urine and rotten meat emanating from the mythago hunter Cuchullain (39–40), and the intense smell is dwelt upon whenever corpses are discovered (41). It is also part of descriptions of close encounters with mythagos, all of whom smell bad. Guiwenneth is the only exception, but that is only because the bad smell is associated with the woman's secretions and the aroma of sex (97). Whenever Steven comments on her overwhelming odor (115), he always treats Guiwenneth's smell in erotic categories (116).

Strong odors, silence, darkness, and a sense of dread are also components of the Romantic "natural sublime." In this type of the sublime, however, the most pronounced aspect is the apprehension of personalized force, or spirit in nature.[6] This spirit, or life-force, is felt as endowed with intentions, emotions, will, and memory, and it interacts with humans through natural artifacts: rocks, rivers, wind, temperature, and, of course, vegetation. In *Mythago Wood* the primary agent for the Romantic, natural sublime is Ryhope Wood. From the outset the Wood is spoken of as presence, superhuman yet involving humans and watching them. It is both protective and threatening, always enveloped in "mysterious darkness" (110). As the Romantic natural sublime it can be contemplated and it "implies the consubstantial world, the one life of the spirit" (Sandner 50). It is also "suggestive of infinity" (49), not least in containing the infinity of time, of human memories, and of landscapes which reach back across eons of natural history.

Not surprisingly, Holdstock makes Ryhope Wood a personalized presence, an active agent in its dealings with the humans. In this sense the Wood is the supreme sublime personification of the novel. It can allow humans in, but it can also defend itself: "the woodland defences were still a great nuisance," Steven records several days after they had entered the Wood. The outer defense is disorientation and impenetrable thickets. When the first zone is crossed, other defenses are deployed. "The wood began to haunt us," Steven says, with trees moving and branches falling off "in our mind's eyes, but not before we had reacted with exhausting shock" (217). Similarly, the ground appears to thrash about and crack open, with strange odors and the smell of fire reaching the adventurers (217). The Wood also watches the protagonists. When Steven says, "I felt a chill, an odd tingle, a sense of being watched" (63), he makes an assertion that recurs every few pages. This sense of being watched is just as strong when the protagonists stay on the fringes of the Wood as when they are inside it, although there the experience intensifies. Harry records in his journal that he senses a certain feature of the woods that "defies experience.... The whole wood breathes and sighs" (216). The Wood also changes depending on how deep into time and space the protagonists had moved (262).

The life of the Wood is represented not only by its conscious attention to human travelers. Perhaps nothing else speaks for it more than embodiments of the Wood's energies — mythagos and elementals. When Steven encounters the elementals of Sorthalan's entourage for the first time, he does wonder whether they are mythagos or not, but he has no doubts that they are the emanations of Ryhope Wood; they clearly reach toward him from the trees (87). Somewhat more difficult to believe is the fact that the flesh and bone mythagos are as much emanations of the Wood as the tendrils of smoke that the elementals are. And yet, this is exactly what Guiwenneth tells Steven after he had unsuccessfully tried to take her away from the Wood. "I am wood and rock, Steven, not flesh and bone" (179).

In many cases the Romantic natural sublime of superhuman presence blends with the Burkean and Kantian sublime of "delightful horror." The most extended example of this overlap is to be found in Part Two, chapter 3, in which Steven and Harry try to take aerial pictures of the Wood. The narrator's reassuring comments about wonderful visibility and peacefulness of the land below set a sharp contrast to what happens when the plane enters a billowing cloud of "eerie darkness" (107) that hangs over the Wood. Ebbing upwards from the trees, the cloud looks bizarre against the clear summery skies around it, appearing to Steven and Harry almost like a living entity. In the glimpses of the forest below, the Wood is presented with classical Burkean attributes of sublimity — stormy, threatening darkness: incomprehensible, impenetrable, and oppressive. Nonetheless, in the Romantic vein, it is at the same time not a passive agent of human contemplation, but rather a sublime personification of primary, raw, organic power hostile to human gaze, nagging at the mood of the human intruders and filling them "with something approaching dread" (107).

The active power of Ryhope Wood becomes even more apparent when, soon, Harry attempts to make a pass over it. As the narrator says, the forest seemed to lurch toward the human intruders, enveloping the plane in a storm wind accompanied by golden light and ghostly wailings (108). In the assault, the plane is struck and pushed away, while the two human characters witness a display of the Wood's threatening power. The fascination and fear recur moments later when Keeton turns the plane back for a second attempt to fly over the forest. Dumbfounded, the narrator sits stupefied with his gaze fixed on "*the wall of gloom*" ahead (108; emphasis added). As could be expected, the wind strikes again, sending the plane careening and spiraling out of control. The supernatural forces guarding the Wood will not tolerate a human gaze (108–09). With the howling wind and the ghastly, lightning-like illumination also comes mortal fear. Steven screams and cringes in his seat, while the angry and confused Harry desperately tries to hold the plane against the supernatural defenses. But the Wood wins, and the protagonists get away only with a ruptured tank. Harry does not attempt the third overpass, remembering how his plane was shot down by similar supernatural forces over a ghost wood in France (138).[7]

If this sounds like Holdstock is being transcendentalist about the Wood, as I think is the case, and if Kincaid's assertion about *Mythago Wood* as a "genuine exploration of the mystic imagination" (9) is to be taken seriously, as I think it ought to be, yet another possibility is to see Holdstock's novel as reflecting the religious sublime of Rudolf Otto and Mircea Eliade. In all fairness, Otto's and Eliade's ideas about the numinous and the holy, respectively, should be called spiritual rather than religious in that both argued for the spiritual component which underlies religion rather than about any religion specifically. The numinous and the holy are concepts which translate into the sublime quite well, although only Otto acknowledged the connection. Seen in Otto's perspective, *Mythago Wood* is a narrative account of an encounter with the numinous, with something that inspires dread or awe (Otto 15), and "shows itself as something uniquely attractive and fascinating" (31). Given this description, it is no wonder that Otto finds the closest analogy to the numinous in "the category and feeling of the sublime" (41).

In a sub-chapter entitled "Means by Which the Numinous is Expressed in Art," Otto acknowledges that art lacks direct methods of representing the numinous and the sublime and can best approach these in a negative way through darkness and silence (68). The third direct-yet-negative means is "*emptiness* and *empty distances*," which Otto calls "the sublime in the horizontal" and associates uniquely with oriental art (69). All these features — darkness, silence, emptiness, and distances, both in time and space — are prominent in Holdstock's novel. Considering emptiness and distances as textual markers of the religious sublime, each stage of Steven's journey toward the heart of the realm, Lavondyss, involves more empty spaces and larger distances. As he moves into the Ice Age landscape, trees become less significant, and windswept, snow-covered spaces take over as a primary presence. These spaces evoke in Steven the yearning for what is beyond them and what he can even glimpse: "[I]n the far distance ... was a stronger, widely diffuse glow..., the boundary between the encroaching forest and the clear land beyond.... A timeless zone that would be unexplorable" (303).

In its theme of the movement toward the "unexplorable," *Mythago Wood* resonates well as much with Otto's ideas about the sublime, or the numinous, as with Eliade's ideas about the holy. Seen in Eliade's perspective, *Mythago Wood* is an account of a chain of hierophanies which give the protagonist access to mythic, non-historical, or para-historical reality, literally *illud tempus*— Eliade's favorite term (55). A key feature of Eliade's interpretation of mythic time was that mythic believers actually become contemporaneous with characters described in their myths. *Mythago Wood* is an impressive illustration of this principle: by engaging in myth, Steven becomes a character in myth — the famed kinsman who will kill the murderous Outsider (257). This is also true of other characters: Christian becomes the Outsider, George Huxley turns into the Urscumug, Guiwenneth returns in another incarnation of her story. No character's story is finished; Steven, Christian, Harry, and other characters who enter the Wood will live on forever in a radically ahistorical, archetypal, reactualizable plane of existence. This idea mirrors Eliade's belief in "[t]he ahistorical character of popular memory, the inability of collective memory to retain historical events and individuals except insofar as it transforms them into archetypes" (46). On this principle, the nameless hunter described in the last chapter of *Mythago Wood* as waiting for a woman by the megalith tomb at the borders of Lavondyss must be identified with Steven. In other words, by engaging with the sublime, especially through repeated exposure, characters become absorbed into the sublime.

This absorption represents a version of Eliade's key concept of mythic renewal: a spiritual renewal achieved through the abolition of meaningless profane time and the immersion in sacred, mythic time. The novel offers multiple examples for Eliade's other key ideas, all of them related to what happens to humans exposed to the physical manifestations of the sacred (hierophanies), of power (cratophanies), and of being (ontophanies). For example, Steven's interaction with Ryhope Wood exemplifies what Eliade described as the dialectic of the sacred and the profane. In the words of Douglas Allen, in this paradoxical process "an ordinary, finite, historical thing, such as a tree or river or person, while remaining a natural thing, ... at the same time manifest[s] something that is infinite, transhistorical, and supernatural" and, on the other, "something transcendent, supernatural, infinite, and transhistorical limits itself by manifesting itself in stones, animals, or other relative, finite, natural, historical things" (80). This "foundational experience of the sacred" (82) is not unlike that of the sublime in which a human agent, through natural phenomena, is exposed to supernatural reality. In this sense *Mythago Wood* is also consistent with Eliade's theory of the fantastic. For Eliade, as Elaine L. Kleiner argues, "[t]he literary fantastic achieves its most typical effects ... when ordinary events begin to gather into mythic outlines, when myth begins to emerge from history" (15). This gathering of ordinary events into mythic outlines is exactly what happens in Steven Huxley's life.

This abandonment of the secure distance which makes the sublime an aesthetic category for Burke, Kant, and the Romantics, and its replacement with the immediate engagement with the transcendent Otherness that the sublime represents, is characteristic of both the religious and the postmodern sublime. In Lyotard's perspective, built on reformulated Kantian sublime as the presentation of the unpresentable, the postmodern sublime is what in a modern work of art bears witness to the fact that the unpresentable exists (78). The unpresentable, the unnamable is the difference which, for Lyotard, is irreducibly attached to reality as the Other and which makes any meditation on Otherness necessarily sublime. As he argues, there are concepts the presentation of which "appears to us as painfully inadequate" (78). In *Mythago Wood* these concepts include the infinitude of time, the infinitude of human and racial memory, and, in more general terms, the unpresentableness of Ryhope Wood itself. In this perspective all descriptions of Ryhope Wood, the Other of the primary reality of the novel, can be seen as allusions to the unpresentable, leading to it indirectly, with quite inadequate figural representation.

It is not insignificant that, as Steven realizes in his first conversation with Keeton, the Wood is uncharted and unmarked on any map, survey or otherwise (103). It defies mapping and measuring: at one point the narrator states that George Huxley was unsuccessful in his attempts to measure "earth energy" which supposedly runs below the ground, connecting "places of spiritual or ancient power" across England (53). But even Huxley's successful attempts at mapping the forest — his detailed maps of the woodland marked with strange circles and lines (53) — are quite unreadable to his sons. The Wood also defies naming and, like the mythagos, may be called by many names. The same sublime quality of the impossibility of verbally actualizing the experience of the Wood underlies all references to how time is felt there or in relation to it. For example, recalling his relationship with the first Guiwenneth, it appears to Christian that although he has just met her, "it seems like months" (58). On another occasion Steven wonders how long he had spent watching the woodland, for the experience may just as well have been hours, days, or even weeks (80).

In many descriptions of the Wood there is a recognizable shadow of doubt, distrust as to whether the character understands the experience or can express it. At one point, Steven asserts that they had not seen any mythagos, then adding almost with the same breath: "Or is that true?" (218). Comments occur frequently about how indescribable and how unknowable the Wood is (199). Also, Steven realizes that Ryhope Wood is "a world of mind and earth, ... outside [the] real laws of space and time" (223). As such it is also outside of the possibility of mimetic representation, a kind of sublime negativity which defies verbalization. The novel thus evokes the postmodern sublime in that, to use Lyotard's phrase, in its descriptions of the Wood it "puts forward the unpresentable in presentation itself" (81). The Wood is also suggestive of what Jean Luc Nancy in his "*L'Offrandre Sublime*" calls "a movement to the infinite or, more exactly, in the direction of illimitability ... which takes place by the side, on the edge of the limited and so on the edge of the presentation" (51). As an apprehension of illimitability, Ryhope Wood thus represents what Nancy identified as the essence of the sublime, "the infinity of beginnings" (51).

Given the evidence discussed, one must conclude that the fascinating mystery of Ryhope Wood and the experiences of the protagonists involve elements associated with at least four types of the sublime. Inasmuch as the Wood is a realm which transcends ordinary levels of reality, *Mythago Wood* may be seen as developing themes of ontological and epistemological transcendence which underlie all sublime discourse. In suggesting that reality is multilayered and that our access to reality, also to that of our unconscious minds, will always be limited, Holdstock's fiction is concerned with concrete imaginative experiences of the reality which is beyond rational understanding. As such it continues the tradition of the fantastic sublime, asserting George MacDonald's dictum that "the greatest forces lie in the region of the uncomprehended" (232).

NOTES

1. See the Greek Longinus's treatise on rhetoric, *Peri Hypsous* (first century CE), where the sublime is a rhetorical effect of certain distinction and excellence of expression: "the mind ... swells in transport and an inward pride" (Dorsch 68). In his 1672 translation of Longinus, *Traite du sublime et du marveilleux*, Nicolas Boileau-Despreaux reinterpreted the concept of the sublime and presented it as an "unusual exaltation of conception and style" rather than a rhetorical effect (Dorsch 24).

2. For other cogent theories in the history of the sublime, see notes 5 and 6.

3. One way to argue for the sublime in Holdstock's novel would be to see the book as a fictionalized record of his own sublime experience. Although I will not follow this track, Holdstock's professed interest in Earth Magic, his obsessive love of woodlands (Cary 4, 6), his weird writerly habits and meditations (Brown 7) do, indeed, allow one to see the book as a "genuine exploration of the mystic imagination, not just a simple story about it" (Kincaid 9).

4. As John Clute puts it: "A wind of sehnsucht blows from the heartwood and ultimately governs the actions of most of the sequence's protagonists, who obsessively try to gain access to that 'unknown region' where the human story begins to germinate and where the meaning of life is born" (Clute and Grant 475).

5. Edmund Burke associated the sublime with danger and saw it as a sensual, "scalable" category in close relationship to that of the beautiful. Whereas the beautiful was human in scale and susceptible to control, the sublime for Burke meant something that overpowers, overwhelms, even threatens us: "terror is in all cases whatsoever, either more latently or openly, the ruling principle of the sublime" (99). Of course, the source of danger evoked by fear and terror must be removed: "they are capable of producing delight; not pleasure, but a sort of delightful horror, a sort of tranquility tinged with terror; which, as it belongs to self-preservation, is one of the strongest of all the passions" (169). A similar dialectic may be seen in Kant, but, rather than terror, Kant's focus is on what Knapp calls "a temporary failure or humiliation of the subject" (74), and in

the *Critique of Judgment* (1790), he proposes the two major categories of the mathematical and the dynamic sublime.

6. Although they would quote Burke and Kant, Wordsworth and Coleridge championed a vision of the sublime which was neither Burkean terror nor Kantian humiliation, but rather a transcendental oneness, the feeling of being swept away into a larger cosmic unity. In *The Fantastic Sublime* (1996), the essence of the experience of the "natural sublime" was, as Sandner explains, "the apprehension of the spirit in nature," a quasi-religious experience in which "the contemplation of a natural object leads to an aesthetic rapture, which produces a correspondent overflow of feeling, revealing the transcendent" (49). This more explicit turn to transcendence led to the emergence of what Sandner calls "the fantastic sublime" (51), exemplified in the work of, among others, Mary Shelley, George MacDonald, and Kenneth Grahame, characterized by "a grasping beyond the actual, beyond what is known, or can be known" toward "the transcendent beyond" (50).

7. This, incidentally, implies that the Wood is alive in more than one country at the same time and that it is capable of issuing forth mythagos for different local cultures.

WORKS CITED

Allen, Douglas. *Myth and Religion in Mircea Eliade.* Routledge: New York, 2002.

Brown, Charles N. "Robert Holdstock: Lost Landscapes, Grand Obsessions." *Locus* 36 (April 1996): 6–7, 74.

Burke, Edmund. *A Philosophical Enquiry into the Origin of Our Ideas of the Sublime and Beautiful.* Boston, 1839.

Cary, Catie. "Robert Holdstock: Interview." *Vector* 175 (Oct.–Nov. 1993): 3–6.

Clute, John, and John Grant. *The Encyclopedia of Fantasy.* New York: St. Martin's Griffin, 1997.

Dorsch, T. S. *Classical Literary Criticism.* London: Penguin, 1984.

Eliade, Mircea. *The Myth of the Eternal Return: Or, Cosmos and History.* Trans. Willard R. Trask. Princeton: Princeton University Press, 1991.

Holdstock, Robert. *Mythago Wood.* 1984. New York: Orb, 2003.

Kant, Immanuel. *Critique of Judgment.* Trans. Werner S. Pluhar. Indianapolis: Hackett, 1987.

Kincaid, Paul. "Touching the Earth: The Fiction of Robert Holdstock." *Vector* 175 (Oct.–Nov. 1993): 7–9.

Kleiner, Elaine L. "Mircea Eliade's Theory of the Fantastic." Allienne R. Becker, ed. *Visions of the Fantastic: Selected Essays from the Fifteenth International Conference on the Fantastic in the Arts.* Westport, CT: Greenwood, 1996. 13–18.

Knapp, Steven. *Personification and the Sublime: Milton to Coleridge.* Cambridge: Harvard University Press, 1985.

Lyotard, Jean François. *The Postmodern Condition: A Report on Knowledge.* Manchester: Manchester University Press, 1994.

MacDonald, George. "The Fantastic Imagination." *A Dish of Orts.* Charleston, SC: BiblioBazaar, 2006 228–33.

Nancy, Jean-Luc. "*L'Offrandre Sublime.*" Michael Deguy, ed. *Du Sublime.* Berlin: Editions, 1988. 37–75.

5. Profusion Sublime and the Fantastic (Oziewicz)

Otto, Rudolf. *The Idea of the Holy An Inquiry into the Non-rational Factor in the Idea of the Divine and Its Relation to the Rational.* Trans. John W. Harvey. London: Oxford University Press, 1968.

Sandner, David. *The Fantastic Sublime: Romanticism and Transcendence in Nineteenth-Century Children's Fantasy Literature.* Westport, CT: Greenwood, 1996.

Sircello, Guy. "How Is a Theory of the Sublime Possible?" *The Journal of Aesthetics and Art Criticism* 51.4 (Fall 1993): 541–50.

6

Tallis, the Feminine Presence in Mythago Wood: *Lavondyss: Journey to an Unknown Region*

Elizabeth A. Whittingham

Robert Holdstock's books feature chiefly male protagonists: Steven Huxley in *Mythago Wood*, Richard Bradley in *The Hollowing*, Martin in *Merlin's Wood* (1994), Christian Huxley in *Gate of Ivory, Gate of Horn*, George Huxley in "The Bone Forest," and the mythago Caylen in "The Boy Who Jumped the Rapids." Even secondary perspectives are provided by males — sometimes through their writings and sometimes through the text's shift in viewpoint: Harry Keeton in *Mythago Wood*, Edward Wynne-Jones in *Lavondyss: Journey to an Unknown Region*, and Alex Bradley and James Keeton in *The Hollowing*. Furthermore, the contemporary history of Ryhope Wood begins with the explorations of George Huxley, and the men of the Huxley family dominate the series. Alexander Lytton credits George Huxley with being the one who "shaped" the wood (*The Hollowing* 117), and George's journal entries repeatedly appear throughout the series. In most of the books, the reader explores the Wood through male perspectives and reflections, and the Wood is perceived through male eyes. The most prominent exception is Tallis Keeton in *Lavondyss*. From the outset, Tallis is overtly female: in these tales of the mythic and mystical, her name is Tallis, not "talis*man*."

The Importance of Names

Lavondyss repeatedly emphasizes the significance of names. On the second page of the book, Owen Keeton, in his letter to his granddaughter,

96

declares, "*You will learn names*" (12). Two and a half pages later, the story having skipped ahead to when Tallis is thirteen, she explains to Mr. Williams about the "*secret* name," "*common* name," and "*private* name" (15, 16) of the places around her home, a distinction reiterated in another conversation between the two (138). In Granddad Owen's letter, he names her "Tallis" and "*Broken Boy's Fancy*" (64), and a few lines later he adds, "*Your own name has changed your life...*" (35), a comment that Holdstock emphasizes by repeating (64). The importance of her being named Tallis could not be clearer. In the same passage of the letter, her grandfather explains that everything has multiple names and that she will learn them from "[t]he whisperers" (64). His letter assures Tallis that her discovering and giving names to the meadows, hills, and trees around her home will uncover "*great truths*" (64). Because of her grandfather's teachings, Tallis appreciates the power of names. At one point, she realizes that to traverse a brook whose name she has not yet discerned will prevent her from returning (37). Part One, which comprises more than half the book, relates her search to discover names for the places around her and for the masks that she makes.

In sharing the story of "The Bone Forest" with Mr. Williams, Tallis recounts Cuwyn's naming of the woman who comes to his village. Because of the "ash twig" she carries and the "ash" to which she "will return" after death, he names her Ash (129). The female traveler later remarks favorably on Cuwyn's choice and states that he has comprehended the situation better than anyone else because how she is "called" determines who she is and how she will live her life (133), another affirmation of the power of names. Tallis's discovery of the secret name (176) for the Old Forbidden Place, Lavondyss, is what finally allows her to enter Ryhope Wood with Scathach. She realizes the name's resemblance to both Avalon and Lyonesse and the connection to "folklore and legend" (177). When she enters the Wood, seeking Harry, seeking Lavondyss, she is caught in the situation that she created when she changed the nature of the meadow (92), making it the scavengers' place of death, and discovers that the name of the place is Bird Spirit Land. Her thoughts, which are the source of her mythagos, her actions, and her naming, result in the journey that she travels. She eventually realizes the significance of the place's altered nature and name near the end of the book when discussing her experiences with the spirit of Wynne-Jones speaking through Tig. Names and naming remain significant matters in *Lavondyss*.

Tallis's name is a tribute to her grandfather, "a fine storyteller" (29), for the old man took great pleasure in being compared to "*Taliesin*, the legendary bard of Wales" (29). This explanation notwithstanding, her name does suggest the word "talisman" with its masculine ending, and the text strengthens the association in the statement, "there would be power in all her acts [and] words, all her talismans" (94). In contrast, the absence of those three letters, "man," at the end of her name emphasizes her gender. Furthermore, she is not given the actual name of the famous male bard Taliesin but a feminized form of it, and Tallis's interactions with Mr. Williams display her storytelling skills and confirm that she is aptly named.

Referring to her name as "lovely" and "unusual," Mr. Williams makes another connection. He notes, "A very fine man had that name once..." and exclaims about the quality of the music he wrote (106). Mr. Williams is referring to Thomas Tallis, an English composer of church music during the uncertain times of the sixteenth century. Though a curious allusion, the association with a musician is appropriate for this unusual girl. Despite the fact that she is primarily a storyteller, young Tallis also sings occasionally. She sings, "*A fire is burning in Bird Spirit Land...*" (*Lavondyss* 108) and then later tries to repeat it for Mr. Williams. Tallis is all that her name indicates: singer of songs, figure of great potency, and teller of stories.

Tallis as Protagonist

Although as a female protagonist she has contact with numerous male characters and is occasionally guided and aided by them — her grandfather, her father, Gaunt, and Scathach, for example — the story is her story, and her decisions and actions direct the plot. Events are perceived from her perspective. The one exception is the section told from the viewpoint of Wynne-Jones, which occupies some thirty-five out of 357 pages, and even that part of the tale primarily sets the scene for Tallis's reappearance. Wynne-Jones's importance becomes more apparent when the reader learns that he is the father of Scathach, Tallis's hero and lover. The old man also establishes a link with George Huxley since the two men had been friends and colleagues. The story's digression, moving away from the protagonist temporarily, also functions as a way of conveying the passage of time and building tension over the exact whereabouts of Tallis, who dominates the text like no other female character in the Mythago books.

6. Tallis, the Feminine Presence (Whittingham)

Other characters in Holdstock's series who are women often play interesting and significant roles. In *Mythago Wood*, Steven Huxley is the protagonist, but Guiwenneth motivates many of his actions. All three Huxley men desire and pursue her. Because of the nature of the mythagos in Ryhope Wood, the reader cannot always be sure which Guiwenneth is the product of whose mind. Evidently, the Guiwenneth whom Christian has married is created from Christian's "idealized" image (49), but as the reader later learns, apparently the Guiwenneth that Christian buries next to "the chicken huts" (37) is from George Huxley's mind (*Gate of Ivory, Gate of Horn* 40–42). Certainly, the Guiwenneth that stays at Oak Lodge with Steven (chapters seven through ten in Part Two of *Mythago Wood*) is from Steven's unconscious. As a mythago, Guiwenneth is marginalized and minimized, for she is not quite real. As Christian paradoxically explains, "she had no life, no real life. She's lived a thousand times, and she's never lived at all" (*Mythago Wood* 42). This description makes Guiwenneth a "thing" rather than a person, and the fact that this female character is repeatedly created by the minds of various men further places her in a subordinate role. Nevertheless, George, Christian, and Steven each love a Guiwenneth and their individual pursuits of her become the focus of their lives and a driving force behind the action in both *Mythago Wood* and *Gate of Ivory, Gate of Horn*.

In *The Hollowing*, the primary protagonist is Richard Bradley, while his son, Alex, plays a secondary role as the key character in the scenes in the Green Chapel. A number of women appear throughout the text — Alice Bradley, Margaret Huxley, Elizabeth Haylock, and Tallis in various forms — but the principle female character is Helen Silverlock. An American of Lakota-Sioux descent, Helen's mysterious arrival at the Bradleys' home begins a cycle of encounters between her and Richard that intrigues him and eventually draws him into Ryhope Wood. Helen is a member of the expeditionary team based at Old Stone Hollow Station deep in the Wood; she and Richard spend time together at the Station and then travel through the woods in search of Alex. When the two become separated, Richard is devastated: "Helen. I've lost you. Helen! What happened?" (*The Hollowing* 186). Though the primary force driving Richard remains his desire to find his son, he never forgets Helen and longs to be reunited with her: "She filled his waking dreams and occupied his thoughts obsessively..." (194). Their reunion takes mythic form and again they journey through the woods together. Ultimately, the tale resolves in the anticipated return to a home comprised of Richard, Alex, and Helen.

In *Gate of Ivory, Gate of Horn*, Christian Huxley, the protagonist, holds his mother, Jennifer, at the center of his thoughts. He repeatedly relives moments from his youth and in particular the moment when his mother seems to hang herself. At the end of the book, a shocking moment of climax involves his finally being able to remember the event clearly and realizing that both he, accidentally, and his father, purposefully, caused his mother's death. The devastating loss of his mother upends his life. Although not a sympathetic character in the first book of the series, in *Gate of Ivory, Gate of Horn*, Christian begins to appear sad and pitiable, becoming almost likable. Christian pursues Guiwenneth, another prominent female character, during repeated trips into the Wood and then travels with her and Kylhuk's Legion. As in all of the Mythago Wood series, these protagonists are men, and though the women play significant roles, they are often minor roles, for their importance lies in relationship to the male characters, which places the women in subordinate or marginalized positions. Tallis provides the only primary feminine perspective in the books.

The Significance of Three

Lavondyss contains many groups of threes, including the three types of names already mentioned. The most significant of these triplets involves Tallis's passing through three distinct stages of life: a girl of thirteen in the safety of her home, a young mother of twenty-one traveling through Ryhope Wood, and an old woman dying in a hut waiting for Harry. Though these stages suggest a chronology, her story is twisted by time. Her girlhood involves more than half the book, and although her growing understanding allows the reader to begin to comprehend what is happening along with Tallis, the tale's exposition is full of flashbacks and moments when she touches other places, times, and characters. From the branches of Strong against the Storm, the young girl looks down on Scathach, her future lover, just before his death. Twice in summer, she encounters a distant winter: once "smell[ing] winter" (53) and, on another occasion, gazing through a "slit between the worlds" (137) into a wintry storm. Outside the ruins of the Huxleys' home, the girl sees a boy that in the last days of her life she will know as Kyrdu, and he will call her Grandmother Tallis.

Later in the book when she first appears at the mortuary house of the Tuthanach, the story has jumped ahead eight years. She has no one with her, and the unfolding of her story continues to struggle against a chronological timeline. Only in retrospect does the reader learn that Tallis has had children: a son who survived no more than "five months" (247) and apparently "three" babies that died before birth (262). When Tallis returns from her long journey, she is an "old woman" (346), a description limited to the shortest section of the book. As a part of her journey and experiences as a young woman, she takes three forms: she becomes an oak tree, then a totem, and finally a coal from which hatches a bird within a holly-jack. During these transformations, centuries have passed, yet she is only beginning her life as a revered elder. While still at home, the young Tallis repeatedly sees "three ... cowled female figures" who seem to shadow her (51). These triplets surrounding her and comprising the stages of her life suggest the three forms of the goddess: maiden/virgin, mother/matron, and crone/wise woman.

Robert Graves, in his seminal work *The White Goddess* (1958), refers to the "all-powerful Threefold Goddess ... mother, bride and layer-out" (11). He traces the White Goddess back to ancient times, to "the early myths of the Hebrews, the Greeks and the Celts" (50).[1] *Lavondyss* portrays Tallis as a young maiden who, though only thirteen years of age, appears much older in other respects. When she tells Mr. Williams that she is "too young," he questions her assessment, and Tallis catches the "wry nature" of his response (17). Mr. Williams has seen much in her that belies her chronological age and reflects that her "language" is "quite sophisticated" (23), and though he occasionally glimpses "the child" in her, her customary appearance is that of a "young adult" (21). The text describes Tallis's actions as "precocious" (34), and though still a virgin, she presciently refers to Scathach as "[her] young love" (108) and her "lover," declaring her intention to become close to him when she is more mature (115). During one conversation, Mr. Williams sees something more in her expression that makes him picture an old woman, "the corpse in the child" (139). This passage reveals all three stages at once: the child in body, the adult woman within, and the crone to come.

Tallis as Maiden

As maiden, Tallis's two main activities involve discovering the names of the places around her home and carving masks and dolls. The repeated references to her dead grandfather and the letter he left her, the flashbacks to various stages of girlhood, and the interactions with other times and places complicate the telling of her story. Three of the masks she carves represent the three cowled and shadowy women that her grandfather had known and that follow her: the white mask is Gaberlungi, *"memory of the land"*; the white, green, and red one is Hollower; and the green one of hazel is Skogen *"shadow of the forest"* (52). These masks, however, are just the beginning.

By the summer she is twelve, the text identifies seven masks and ten dolls (53) in her collection. Then one day in July, Tallis smells "woodsmoke and winter" (60), and the idea comes to her for a new mask. The next May she carves Moondream, which allows her *"to see the woman in the land"* (80). After she fashions Moondream, Tallis first sees Scathach from the tree Strong against the Storm (85). Though she later protests that she is "too young" (17) and promises her father that she will not act impetuously, screaming "I'm not ready!" (169), she rides with Scathach into the woods when he comes for her. In the rush to enter the Hollowing, she loses Moondream, and her father picks it up as she disappears from his sight, a loss that has many repercussions in the Otherworld.

The moon, a prominent image in *Lavondyss*, traditionally has been coupled with the maiden figure or virgin. As Nor Hall asserts, "Women recognized their physical nature in moon cycles.... The moon has always been associated with (if not held responsible for) the menses: the blood flow and blood rest like the tide-pull-and-flow in every woman" (3). Linguistically, there is also a common source in Latin for "menses" and *mensis*, meaning "month," and in the Germanic languages between "month" and "moon" (*OED*). Besides the connection between the moon's influence and menses, Hall describes another correlation between women and the phases of the moon: "Imagine the new silvery moon crescent as the virgin or the nymph, the full moon as mother pregnant with life, and the old moon as old crone or withered woman descending into the darkness of death, only to rise again" (3). Linking these stages of life with other triple images in mythology and literature, Hall contends that the "three weird sisters, three fates, or three goddesses ... represent the life span of women from beginning to end" (3). One of the oldest representations of the goddess is Ishtar of Babylonian mythology, known as Inanna in Sumerian tales. In those cultures, Ishtar "was the giver of dreams, omens, revelations, and understandings of things that are hidden" (Hall 15). This description fits Tallis well except that initially Tallis receives, rather than gives, "dreams, omens, [and] revelations," though she later shares her "understanding of things ... hidden" with other people such as Mr. Williams and her father.

The presence of the moon in *Lavondyss* begins with the third word of the book: "The bright moon" lights the surrounding countryside (11). Correspondingly, the first chapter, "White Mask," refers to "the hooded figure" that waits for Owen Keeton, Tallis's grandfather, to come outside (13), and parallels the round, white face of the moon. In Chapter 1, Owen begs White Mask to leave the infant Tallis with her parents for a while, to let them enjoy their daughter before carrying her away (14). Many years later, Tallis learns that White Mask and her two companions are actually her brother Harry's mythago with "a little of [her] grandfather and of [herself]" (276). Despite not being her own mythago, this white face becomes an integral part of her childhood. At the age of eight, Tallis sees White Mask herself for the first time, but the mask Gaberlungi she subsequently carves and that represents the mythago White Mask is not her moon mask, but one inducing "memory of the land" (52). Moondream with its white countenance allows her "to see the woman in the land" (80) and, like the figure White Mask, is a part of her maidenhood. Appropriately, the Moondream mask is left behind with her father when Tallis enters Ryhope Wood, the mask being lost to her shortly before she loses her virginity. When Tallis next appears in the story, eight years have passed, and she has become a bereaved mother carrying the bones of her son.

Tallis as Mother

The loss of the Moondream mask remains important to Tallis those many years later. She believes that she has been unable to achieve her task because she does not possess the mask. Wynne-Jones confirms the seriousness of this loss. He asserts that the masks are various aspects "of an oracle," which she will be unable to access unless she has all of them (264). All of Tallis's endeavors, all of her struggles have, therefore, been hampered because she does not have Moondream. She tries to amend the situation by carving a new Moondream mask, which she realizes will be different, as she is a changed person and the mask representing that "deep unconscious" part of herself is gone (240). Furthermore, without the mask, Tallis has "lost ... that particular link with the female in the land" (240). Her efforts are interrupted by the girl, Morthen, half-sister to Scathach, and though she does not complete the mask, she makes a connection to this girl, this female in the woods. Disappointed that her carving is disrupted, Tallis believes that if she had had just a little more time she could have completed it.

When Tallis is able finally to make a new Moondream mask, it contains many images. First and foremost, the "white moon" shines forth, but despite the moon and "blood," it is not the mask of a virgin, for it also contains all of her experiences as a woman: reflections of touching her beloved in sexual intimacy, being a mother, losing a child, watching her lover burn on his pyre (270). As Tallis creates the figures, carves each feature, and adds color, "the dead wood beg[ins] to live and breathe" (271). When she at last possesses all ten masks again, Wynne-Jones tells her that she has to set off on her journey (273). It is, perhaps, a journey that she could not have taken — or at least completed — without the full complement of masks. She is a mother, but a mother without children, and Scathach's leaving when she finishes the mask suggests she may become a woman without a mate, though she has not yet lost him forever.

On the early part of the journey, when accompanied by Scathach and Wynne-Jones, her youthfulness appears reconfirmed, and the chronology of her life is again thwarted. Tallis has thought of herself as aging, and in contrast to Morthen, she is described as "older" (240, 255), but when the threesome are approached by the Daurog, Wynne-Jones refers to Tallis as "young" and explains that the Daurog is attracted because "it smells [her] blood" (290), a connection to the moon and the virgin. Wynne-Jones insists that she is "creating life" (290) and elucidates by telling her the Daurog's creation myth in which she is taking a part. Later that same night, Tallis watches the Holly-jack astride the male Willow-jack, copulating in the moonlight. As with humans, this act precedes a life-giving one, though in the case of the Daurog, the penetration seems to allow Holly-jack to release the birds within her. Tallis senses that the Holly-jack's having released the birds in some way granted her freedom (297). The Holly-jack's youth has returned because she has given birth. Wynne-Jones recognizes that the Daurog are attracted to Tallis and seem to "trust her" (297), which he accounts for by surmising that they are her mythagos, and the narrative refers to Holly-jack as "the oddest of primitive heroines" (298), another association with the protagonist. Tallis's connection to the Holly-jack, however, is far greater than the twenty-one-year-old woman can imagine at this point in her journey, for the Holly-jack is a later form of herself.

6. *Tallis, the Feminine Presence* (Whittingham)

Tallis, no longer the worn and tired figure that first appeared before Wynne-Jones, becomes reinvigorated during this journey. Though she had been losing "her soul" to "the forest" through being depleted by it (238), she feels young again. In this time of renewal, there are moments of intimacy between Tallis and Scathach, yet she does not fulfill her promise to return and give him "a proper farewell" (308). She appears almost virginal. With Wynne-Jones's having turned back to his home among the Tuthanach and Scathach's having traveled ahead to meet his fate at the Battle of Bavduin, Tallis rides alone. As she nears the battle, she almost reverts to the girl who watched the wounded Scathach from the branches of Strong against the Storm, loving him from afar. Wondering about the woman who had ridden around his pyre and about how she might rescue Scathach, she remembers that in the distant past of her childhood she had yet to fashion Moondream, so she could not have seen "the woman in the land." This belief is the first clue that her memory is tricking her, for she *had* made Moondream before she saw Scathach on his pyre. She believes that the screaming figure with the white features she saw in that long-ago past is herself (318) and that peering through Moondream would possibly have helped her to better understand what was happening and to be more discerning about the individuals and their roles.

Coloring "her face and ... hair" with "white clay" (318), Tallis takes on the appearance of Moondream by using the very same clay she had used in making the mask. She colors her skin and hair immediately after remembering Wynne-Jones' admonition: "*Let the child ride with you. Watch and hear with a child's senses*" (318), as though that act was her response to the old man's advice. Despite her thoughts about the Moondream mask and Wynne-Jones's words, she does not look ahead through either Moondream or Sinisalo, the mask for "*seeing the child in the land*" (94). When Tallis finally reaches the battlefield and the pyre with the body of Scathach, she is confused; she does not feel like expressing her pain and grief by shrieking and cannot understand why she does not feel the ardor and anguish that she remembered seeing herself portray (321). Instead, she merely feels detached acknowledgment of Scathach's death. When Morthen appears screaming to rescue her brother, Tallis realizes that she has always been mistaken about the identity of the grieving woman — she has forgotten this "female in the land" and has not imagined someone else loving Scathach as much as she herself.

Heartache and anger transform Morthen from maiden to woman to crone, completing the alteration begun by the erratic movement of time in the woods. She has already aged while traveling; then, seeing Tallis standing near Scathach on the pyre, Morthen's anger and hatred age her further, removing all traces of youth from her features (322). Tallis is also altered. No stranger to defending herself over the years, she is helpless before Morthen and, on reflection, realizes that she might have died at the hands of her opponent. Tallis makes one last attempt to recover her past and her youthful vision. She travels to the ancient oak and climbs its branches as she had as a girl, trying to assume the role of the child as Wynne-Jones has advised, but nothing is the same. When she tries to remember, her memory fails her. She persists, knowing that her younger self is nearby, but when she jumps from the tree, she is not returned to that distant summer of her girlhood. She is cold and wounded, and Scathach is lying on the ground.

As a one-time mother whose children are dead and whose lover has fallen in battle as she has always known he would, Tallis hides her masks (326) before she goes into the castle to begin another journey, another transformation. In the castle's topmost room she rests, and as time passes a hornbeam — appropriately — penetrates her, spreads throughout her body, splits her open, and she becomes fully tree without any human organs (327). She flourishes, ages, and then her "oak trunk opened" (329), releasing hundreds of black birds (330). Like a virgin, she has been painfully penetrated, and like a mother, she has given birth (330). She ages further, apparently over many decades, and finally falls only to be taken by a young boy and carved into a totem placed over the body of the family's deceased grandmother (332). Desiring help and wisdom, the family members summon Grandmother Asha by speaking to "the oak statue that was Tallis" (333), both women functioning as crones and the latter fulfilling her name by becoming a talisman.

Tallis-totem by watching the family gains understanding. The dreamer, the boy who carved Tallis-tree into a totem, speaks to her and reveals his desire to find a warm land. He laments that he lacks the birds that might bear him away (338). Reminding Tallis-totem that once, as a tree, she held many birds, he prays for "a winged dreamer" (338). The boy Dreamer, having asked for wisdom, finds an answer. He addresses the totem again, saying that she has the power to release him, and he burns her on a fire until she is only a tiny piece of coal (341–42). Tallis later realizes that when she wove the spells to banish the carrion birds from Bird

Spirit Land to protect the dying Scathach, she had affected her long-lost half-brother, Harry.

When Dreamer comes to Tallis the final time, she recognizes the voice as Harry's. Finally, the brother whom Tallis has long sought and had promised to free from the land where he was confined comes and speaks to the spirit of his little sister, explaining that the journey from "the first forest" differs for each person (342). Tallis learns that though she had ensnared him, her acts have finally freed him (342). Harry assures her that she has not reached the end of her life but is only traveling, and he promises to return to her. The spirit of man–Harry has been healed of his burns and freed from the body of the Dreamer: as crow–Harry, he escapes (342). Tallis has fulfilled her promise by following the path laid before her by Harry's mythagos, the three women who had spoken to her grandfather, waited, and then taken Tallis.

Tallis, however, still has one more journey to complete. In transition from coal to woman, she briefly becomes a holly tree, for "[t]he first tree in the wood had been holly..." (344). Just as Holdstock has developed his world around myth and legend, he also draws on traditional English lyrics. The chorus of "Sans Day Carol" begins, "And Mary bore Jesus our Saviour for to be, / And the first tree in the greenwood, it was the holly." The verses enumerate the ways in which the holly's berry resembles Mary, including one verse that declares, "Now the holly bears a berry as black as the coal, / And Mary bore Jesus, who died for us all..." ("Sans Day Carol"). The association of the holly and the coal with Tallis establishes a connection between Tallis and Mary, further emphasizing the protagonist's role as maiden and increasing her significance. The well-known carol "The Holly and the Ivy" furthers this glorification by asserting, "Of all the trees that are in the wood, / The holly bears the crown." As in the previous carol, the verses compare various aspects of the holly tree to Mary, highlighting Tallis's preeminence as well as her maidenhood and motherhood.

As the Holly-jack, Tallis places the coal from the fire millennia earlier within herself (*Lavondyss* 344), a seed for new creation. When she meets up with the Daurog shaman, they copulate, the act that Tallis had witnessed many lifetimes ago, and he nourishes the life within her (344). After Holly-Tallis releases those birds, a life-giving act, she eventually reaches the castle, rests next to Tallis's decaying corpse (345), and upon waking finds that she is human once more. She is, as Geoffrey Ashe describes the goddess, "the universal life-bestower" (12, 14). Tallis has traveled down a terrible and painful path to reach "the first forest," and, as Wynne-Jones had fore-told, her journey was complicated and arduous (*Lavondyss* 346), a journey through time that has come full circle. Dismayed at the wrinkles she dis-covers, Tallis faces the fact that she has truly become an old woman (346). She has reached the final stage of her life journey: she is crone.

Tallis as Crone

The description of Tallis's time as crone is the briefest of the three stages in *Lavondyss*, but in some ways it is the most important. It encom-passes one chapter and the concise "Coda," only twenty pages, but within this section, the story comes to its resolution, and all of Tallis's quests are fulfilled. According to Barbara G. Walker, the crone is a figure of "power [and] wisdom" (174). In ancient times, "semen was not yet recognized as the vehicle of 'seed,'" so "life-giving powers were attributed only to blood, after the manner of the female uterine blood bond" (Walker 47). Specifi-cally, the power was in the blood of menses, the woman's "moon-blood" (48). The connection was explained by what was observed: "pregnant women ... ceased to menstruate, presumably because their magic blood was otherwise occupied in the manufacture of the female miracle, a new life" (49). Post-menopausal women, "old women ... described as the wisest of mortals" were revered, and "retained menstrual blood was often regarded as the source of their wisdom" (49). Furthermore, women possess "intel-ligence," the result of their being mothers and, by necessity, "quick learners and keen observers" (177). As Walker argues, "With the cumulative expe-rience of many years of living, observing, and relating to others, women may routinely achieve higher levels of understanding the human condition than most men dream of" (177). Wisdom accompanies increasing age, and the crone is a figure to be valued and esteemed.

Throughout *Lavondyss*, Tallis has been growing and accumulating knowledge and understanding. Her grandfather and the three cowled women give her knowledge beyond her years, and her experiences in the woods have exceeded those of a lifetime of learning. In the first forest, she lives uncounted years as a tree and then totem. She also gathers the wisdom of the archetypal old man, Wynne-Jones, the Wyn-rajathuk, originally as they live and travel together and then as he speaks through the youth, Tig. She learns that Elethandian, the daughter of her brother Harry, is Scathach's mother, and she is, therefore, Scathach's aunt as well as his lover (356). The text suggests nothing immoral about these relationships because in the woods, without a stable social context, a nebulous amorality prevails. In *The Virgin and the Bride* (1996), Kate Cooper writes of the sexual morality inherent in ancient societies where "private life" reflected on "public duty" and of the importance to one's "reputation" of "modesty" in defining the "chaste woman" of a family (13). In contrast, such distinctions as "private" and "public" become meaningless and such institutions as marriage and political office appear nonexistent in Ryhope Wood. Although Tallis is raised in post–World War II England, where centuries of Christian influence shape contemporary mores, Ryhope Wood's wildly fluctuating temporal settings and characters from incompatible times and cultures negate many social constructs.

As Tallis listens to the voice of Wynne-Jones speaking through Tig, she gains insight and grows in wisdom. In the midst of these realizations, she comprehends that Scathach was with her on her journey as he found his way back from Lavondyss "in the woodland form of Ghost of the Tree" (*Lavondyss* 356). Tallis goes back to the woods and finally finds Scathach, her brother's grandson as a result of the convoluted passage of time in Ryhope, and completes one quest. "Only briefly described, their years together apparently are gratifying," and Tallis becomes "the old-woman-who-was-oracle" (361) and "Grandmother Tallis" (362). Eventually, the time comes when the people with whom she has lived are fearful because the wise woman, the crone, a figure of wisdom and power among them, is near death (361). The remarkably short overview of Tallis's last years as crone lacks detail, de-emphasizing her years of understanding and authority in contrast to the carefully developed description of her complicated and time-twisted progress through the first two stages of her life.

Finally, in the moment of her death, she and Harry are reunited, and though her quest was to save Harry, it is her brother who rescues her (364). Cheerfully he tells her, "That's the way it goes," and he explains that he is taking her home (364). With Harry's help, she completes her final quest, to get back to her father. In a scene that is mirrored in *The Hollowing*, in the moment of James Keeton's death, father and daughter are reunited. In death, the dream of both their lives is fulfilled, and new journeys begin, which is appropriate for the crone, for the underworld is "not a place of punishment" but, as Walker argues, "the dark womb, symbolized by the cave, cauldron, pit, well, or mountain interior, to which the dead returned, and from which they could be regenerated" (85). Tallis is virgin, mother, and crone and exemplifies the wholeness and cyclical nature of women described by Walker: "As the birth-giving Virgin and death-dealing Crone were part of one another, death and life together were like the new seed within the withered fruit..." (29). Life, death, and rebirth are also the three stages of womanhood.

When Tallis's body is burned on a "pyre," Kyrdu, the young boy who called her "Grandmother," watches the smoke being blown westward and remembers that Grandmother Tallis had told him that "her *real* home lay" in that direction (*Lavondyss* 366). Traditionally and especially in Celtic belief, the underworld lies to the west: "Ancient people often believed their honored dead became stars ... in heaven, immortal because the Mother gave them daily rebirth as they passed from her Western gate under the earth to the East. This gate of the dead was located, naturally, in the West" (Walker 77). Similarly, Ashe notes that the goddess leads the "dead" into "the afterlife" and is the focus of "belief in that future rebirth" (15). The smoke of Tallis's funeral pyre travels to the west, the underworld, but also toward her home where her renewed life with her father and Harry begins.

Lavondyss ends with Kyrdu sitting in the cave, the place of the hollowing, "wonder[ing] how to journey there" (367), to Tallis's "*real* home," but the reader knows that this is not fruitless daydreaming, for early in the book, the story is told of his encounter with young Tallis near Oak Lodge. Kyrdu's journey is not the only one that begins with the death of the Crone. In *The Hollowing*, the connection between Tallis and Alex Bradley is firmly established, and he is the one who identifies the Moon-dream mask. Richard and Alex Bradley are present when James Keeton dies, and they hear him call out to Tallis as well as his final words, "Well. Thank God for that" (41)—words first heard at the reunion of father and daughter at the end of *Lavondyss*. From that moment, the boy Alex is changed, and in due course his journey takes him into Ryhope Wood where his father later follows in hope of finding his son. The journeys of father and son are spurred by the experiences of Tallis and James Keeton.

E. A. Wallis Budge observes, "As among the gods, so among the mortals was death everywhere women's business.... Women cradle the infant and the corpse, each to its particular new life" (qtd. in Walker 76). From death comes rebirth, for every death is another beginning. Not only is rebirth associated with the crone, but also with Lavondyss: Lavondyss is created "out of memory ... the first stories ... the deeds that *generate* the myths..." (*Lavondyss* 354). From the killing of a man grew "the legend" (354) that is at the heart of the book, the legend that Tallis changes and follows and in which she lives. Within these myth-generating woods, Tallis-mother carries her children and watches them die; Tallis-crone spends her last years with Scathach until his death, overseeing birth, death, and rebirth.

"The Holly Bears the Crown"

At first glance, Holdstock's Mythago Wood series seems dominated by men. All the protagonists — except Tallis — are men, and even most of the secondary perspectives in journals and letters are from the viewpoint of men. In *The Hollowing*, Alexander Lytton attributes what Ryhope Wood has become to George Huxley. Lytton tells Richard Bradley, "Everything you *see* is Huxley. The wood was here from the first seed after the ice, yes, of course. And people came and went and seeded the wood with the products of their myths. Yes. *Yes*. But not until Huxley was it *shaped*.... We are living *in* the man, in the mind of Huxley himself" (117). Lytton, as is clear throughout the text, is obsessed with George Huxley and is not without prejudice. In contrast to Lytton's assertion, the evidence suggests that Ryhope Wood is feminine. Wynne-Jones indicates that the trees around him and Tallis are her mythagos, and that "the living earth" is her creation (*Lavondyss* 275). When Tallis travels to the first forest, the text reveals that the holly was "[t]he first tree in the wood" and then one holly tree, Tallis, transforms, becoming "a woman" (344). The Holly-jack places "the petrified wood ... the heart of the forest," the surviving piece of Tallis-totem, within herself and becomes Tallis-Holly (344). The first tree is the Holly; the Holly is a woman, and the woman is Tallis. Ryhope Wood is feminine, and the Moondream mask enables Tallis to see "the female in the land," not the male. Moreover, the forest is repeatedly penetrated by men. Tallis is unable to enter the Wood until she is escorted by a man, and the few women who enter the Wood seem usually to do so in the company of men. In this aspect, the feminine nature of the wood is further underscored.

The male protagonists are driven by a curiosity about, and even an obsession with, the Wood, but most of them desire to find and be united with a woman. The Huxleys each seek their own version of Guiwenneth,

111

and Christian is haunted by the death of his mother; Richard Bradley seeks Helen Silverlock; James Keeton follows his daughter, Tallis, into the woods, and his return impels the events in *The Hollowing*. Though marginalized, these women take prominent roles, and likewise in *Lavondyss*, Tallis is not alone. The male characters — Owen Bradley, her father, Mr. Williams, Gaunt, Scathach, Edward Wynne-Jones, and Tig — provide guidance and understanding. Without them, she could not have completed her quest. Despite their marginalization, examination of the various texts in the series brings to light the prominence of women, but not even that shared status embodies the whole picture. The Mythago cycle portrays men and women together. As in the Legion and at Old Stone Hollow Station where men and women work together to accomplish their goals, they protect and nurture one another, and together they find their way through the woods.

The paths through Ryhope Wood are as confusing and convoluted as the passage of time there. They are intricately interwoven, and the relationship of the characters to one another and Tallis's connection to the woods are no less complex. Lytton minimizes the fact that the Wood existed before George Huxley molded it; nevertheless, that remains an essential fact: Tallis-totem is hidden within Tallis-Holly, and the Holly is the first tree of the first forest. Tallis Keeton grows up with the Wood in her life, and the threefold goddess haunts the edges of her life until she herself becomes the threefold goddess: virgin of the moon, mother of the dead, and crone who turns into child and, in her reunion with Harry and her father, completes the cycle of renewal. Her love for Scathach changes Harry's story, and only through her own journey is she able to bring about her brother's freedom. Through Harry, her father, and Scathach, Tallis's tale is interwoven with all the other stories of Mythago Wood, and she is the feminine presence in the woods.

NOTE

1. Graves's book focuses on the lengthy work *Câd Goddeu*, translated as "The Battle of the Trees," which is part of *The Romance of Taliesin* (19). The name Taliesin and the trees in the poem, which include Ash, Oak, and Holly — trees significant in Tallis's story — are closely associated with the White Goddess. The Battle of the Trees was fought between the man Bran and "a woman called Achren," meaning "trees" (Graves 35), and Graves affirms that this woman is the White Goddess. He alternately refers to her as "the Universal Mother" (108), "the White Moon Goddess" (108), "the Queen of the Woods" (125), "the quickening Triple Muse" (171), and "the Triple Goddess" (196).

6. *Tallis, the Feminine Presence* (Whittingham)

The goddess figure and aspects of maiden/mother/crone are present throughout ancient and medieval literature.

Works Cited

Anderson, Douglas D., ed. *The Hymns and Carols of Christmas.* 1 September 2008 <http://www.hymnsandcarolsofchristmas.com>.

Ashe, Geoffrey. *The Virgin.* London: Routledge and Kegan Paul, 1976.

Cooper, Kate. *The Virgin and the Bride.* Cambridge: Harvard University Press, 1996.

Graves, Robert. *The White Goddess.* 1948. New York: Vintage, 1958.

Hall, Nor. *The Moon and the Virgin.* New York: Harper, 1980.

Holdstock, Robert. *The Bone Forest.* New York: Avon, 1991.

_____. *Gate of Ivory, Gate of Horn.* New York: ROC-Penguin Putnam, 1997.

_____. *The Hollowing.* New York: Doherty, 1993.

_____. *Lavondyss: Journey to an Unknown Region.* New York: Morrow, 1988.

_____. *Merlin's Wood.* London: HarperCollins, 1994.

_____. *Mythago Wood.* London: HarperCollins, 1984.

"The Holly and the Ivy." Anderson. 1 September 2008 <http://www.hymnsandcarolsofchristmas.com/Hymns_and_Carols/holly_and_the_ivy.htm>.

Oxford English Dictionary. Oxford University Press, 2008. Drake Memorial Library, Brockport, NY. 26 January 2008 <http://ezproxy2.drake.brockport.edu>.

"Sans Day Carol." Anderson. 24 August 2008<http://www.hymnsandcarolsofchristmas.com/Hymns_and_Carols/ sans_day_carol.htm>.

Walker, Barbara G. *The Crone: Woman of Age, Wisdom, and Power.* New York: HarperSanFrancisco–HarperCollins, 1988.

7

Embedded Narratives in *Lavondyss* and Ursula K. Le Guin's *The Left Hand of Darkness*

Vera Benczik

I'll make my report as if I told a story, for I was taught as a child on my homeworld that Truth is a matter of the imagination. (Le Guin, *The Left Hand of Darkness* 1)

Introduction

Narratives often feature other narratives within their body. William Nelles points out that such stories within a story are "so widespread among the narrative literature of all cultures and periods as to approach universality" (339). Tzvetan Todorov poses the then relevant question "why does the embedded narrative need to be included within another narrative?" and answers duly that "each narrative seems to have something excessive, a supplement which remains outside the closed form produced by the development of the plot" (76). Thus, embedded narratives basically serve as sources of information excluded from the body of text, complementing or supplementing the development of the main plotline. Yet sometimes their function is more complex: they may subvert the plot, subtly or more directly undermining the structure of the main narrative.

It is this complex use of the embedded narratives that makes worthwhile a side-by-side examination of Ursula K. Le Guin's *The Left Hand of Darkness* (1969) and Robert Holdstock's *Lavondyss: Journey to an Unknown Region* (1988), two novels far apart in the space and time of fiction. Both

114

draw heavily upon mythology, but *The Left Hand of Darkness* uses an anthropological approach while *Lavondyss* relies on the Jungian system of archetypes and ancestral memory as its structuring principle. Despite inherent differences the two narratives exhibit significant similarities in the use of their embeddings: these stories within the story transgress the "simple" uses of embedded narratives and are simultaneously constructed as both discourses of disambiguation and originators of ambiguity. While on one level they serve to clarify certain elements and gaps in the narratives, they inconveniently blur other areas of the plot.

The Left Hand of Darkness is essentially divisible into three sub-narratives: first, there is Genly Ai's account of his journeys on Gethen (Chapters 1, 3, 5, 8, 10, 13, 15, 18, 19, and 20), which is counterbalanced by excerpts from Estraven's journal (Chapters 6, 11, 14, and 16). Then there are the interspersed embedded narratives, all fragments of Gethenian mythology or religious texts (Chapters 2, 4, 9, 12, and 17), excluding a scientific report of previous off-world visitors to Gethen (Chapter 7). The frame unifying these texts is the "catalogue card" identifying the novel as a manuscript in the "archives of Hain" (1), shifting the narrative from the realm of present reality into the realm of past mythology immediately at the outset, thus constructing the text as a sub-narrative embedded in the post-colonial "grand narrative" of Hainish exploration.

This framework identifies and validates the narrative as a scientific text, a trait echoed and reinforced in the presentation of the embedded narratives as either scientific discourses or the results of scientific research. Yet the objectivity and inherent truth value implied by the scientific labels on the frames and sub-frames stands in stark contrast with the high level of subjectivity in both the main and the embedded narratives: the emphasis on the relationship between Genly Ai and Estraven gradually gains prominence over the initial public/political focus — Gethen's advent into the Ekumen — and moves from subtext to foreground in the main narratives, while the embeddings are highly charged by the subjective symbolism of their mythological and religious contents. This objectivity implied by the form also contrasts the inconsistencies, contradictions, and significant narrative lacunae contained in the narrative itself. The short chapter on "The Gethenian Calendar and Clock" (302–04) consummates the frame at the end, reinforcing the notion that the narrative is an edited text from the past, analeptic by the sheer fact of its archival position. Again the reader experiences the contrast between the removed, scientific closure of the frame, and the highly personal note of the ending of the narrative per se.

While the frame constructs Ai's and Estraven's narratives as embeddings themselves, these concern the events of the same temporal and physical plane, the "now" of the novel, and thus may be regarded as the two dominant, parallel narratives, the backbone of the novel, intertwined and juxtaposed in the Taoist sense to supply the reader with a harmonious whole: darkness and light, self and Other. The mythological inserts and the scientific report are distinctly set apart and presented as subtexts, serving as both supplements and counterpoints to the main narrative, and will, therefore, be regarded and analyzed as the embedded narratives proper within the text.

Lavondyss, on the contrary, exhibits an apparently more conservative approach to the plot: a master narrative runs through the book, interspersed with frequent examples of slightly metamorphosed Anglo-Saxon and Celtic myths that appear in various forms — the printed book of myths given to Tallis by her grandfather, the stories channeled through Tallis by her masked teachers, stories related to Ryhope Wood collected in the scientific journals of Wynne-Jones and George Huxley, and so forth. The mythagos, the protagonists of these embedded narratives, are a fusion of their mythological originals and the particular characteristics their creator imprinted on their personality. Thus, while complying with the general flow of the narrative they originate from, they are also altered by the mind that produces them, exemplifying how a reader may take an active part in the creative process of constructing the story.

The novel's master narrative is divided into two distinct parts. One is set in what we might call a consensus, albeit parallel, reality, one of post–World War II Britain, called "Old Forbidden Place" in anticipation of entering the mythological realm. The other, entitled "In the Unknown Region" and introduced after crossing the threshold in the Campbellian sense (see Campbell, *Hero* 71), is set in Ryhope Wood, the ancient forest around Shadoxhurst, whose existence is rooted in both consensus reality and mythology and whose ontology is overlaid with the image of the enchanted forest of the human unconscious.

It is only more than halfway through the book, wandering through this forest of the mind, that the reader realizes that part of what previously appeared as analeptic metadiegetic embeddings (see Genette, *Revisited* 93)—that is, separate embedded narratives referring to past events or myths — are, in fact, proleptic diegetic embeddings: flash forwards to later events of the master narrative looping back upon and interacting with itself at various points in the text.

The Left Hand of Darkness

There is no such ambiguity regarding the embeddings within *The Left Hand of Darkness*, which, from a narratological point of view, may all be regarded as simple metadiegetic embeddings. Both the embedded mythological excerpts and the field report are emphatically set apart from the main narrative, their authorial slot either specifically filled — with Ong Tot Oppong in "The Question of Sex" (89) — or left vacant on purpose, in order to validate their mythological and thus unauthored nature.

When reading the novel we have to bear in mind that *The Left Hand of Darkness* is an edited text: Genly's account, the excerpts from Estraven's journal, and the embedded narratives have all been chosen and compiled by the "structuring consciousness" behind the novel, Genly Ai himself (Bickman 43). Thus his decision determines what is included — and, sometimes more importantly, what is left out — just as he oversees the arrangement of the various embedded narratives, supplying the rhythm of the book. As in the case of *Lavondyss*, the embeddings of *The Left Hand of Darkness* fulfill a dual role: while on one level they complement the narrative by supplying missing information, they also serve as subversive and contrastive subtexts to the main narratives. Their ambiguity, furthermore, lies not in the (mis)communication of what they are, as is the case with *Lavondyss*, but partly in the intentions behind the editing process, since they operate on different levels depending on the intended audience, the reader, on the one hand, and Genly Ai, on the other.

For the extradiegetic reader, which I will call the extroverted level of the embedded narratives, these embeddings provide information missing from and highlight issues not elucidated in the main plotline, following or preceding chapters in which certain issues are left vague and need further explanation, and rather than including long, descriptive parts in the story, Le Guin opts for interspersed texts to bridge the gaps. In what could be called the motto of the novel, Genly Ai tells us:

> The story is not all mine, nor told by me alone. Indeed I am not sure whose story it is; you can judge better. But it is all one, and if at

117

moments the facts seem to alter with an altered voice, why then you can choose the fact you like best; yet none of them are false, and it is all one story [1–2].

Thus, the embeddings, although presented as independent tales, often seem to duplicate the narrative, either in issues, in plotline, or in details — the correspondence of names and fates in "Estraven the Traitor" (124–29) to the events of the main narratives, for example, or the parallels to the episode of the central journey over the Gobrin Ice in "The Place inside the Blizzard" (22–26) — which adds an extra emphasis to their explanatory and supplementary nature.

On the reflexive, introverted level, the same embeddings may be read as devices aiding Genly in his re-evaluation of his journey on Gethen, both physical and mental, and his re-enactment and processing of the deeply personal trauma of loving and losing Estraven. The comfortable distance these embedded narratives provide help Genly verbalize issues kept vague or only mentioned in passing in the main narrative. The two levels are, of course, intertwined, yet each relates to different instances of the main narratives: while "Estraven the Traitor" provides to the extra-diegetic reader information about both the rules of the Gethenian clan-system and Estraven's effort to work towards the integration of Gethen into the Ekumen, even at the cost of personal prestige, the introverted level focuses most on the relationship between the mortal enemies, whose inevitable attraction to each other proves fatal for one of them. It is this instance where we glimpse Genly's possible guilt, as Estraven's death may be read as a direct result of the personal feelings he harbored for his friend.

The contrastive-subversive aspect of the embeddings in my reading focuses on the topos of love and sexuality prevalent in all the embedded narratives — except perhaps in "On Time and Darkness" (162–64) — undermining the main narratives' relative silence on the same issues. Genly and Estraven's relationship is not verbalized extensively within the main narratives; the undeniable sexual tension is perhaps most articulately, albeit briefly, examined in the central episode on the Gobrin Plateau (200–60), only to conclude that their love could never, would never, be consummated (248–49) and their relationship is conveniently moved from the physical plane to the mental plane (252), a comfortable alternative to physical inter-racial intimacy. It is this first *kemmer* of Estraven that is followed by what for me proves to be one of the most intriguing gaps in the novel: the narratives are both explicitly silent about Estraven's two additional *kemmers* made possible by the duration of the journey over the Ice. The evident explanation is, of course, that after the climax in the sexual tension between them, the verbalization of the mutual feelings and the decision to abstain from bodily contact, the conflict is resolved, and any further reference to it would prove superfluous.

Yet the explicit absence of any reference to sexual tension later on, the restrained yet looming presence of the theme in the main narratives contrasted with the verbosity of the embedded narratives on the same topoi, raises doubts about the credibility of the main narratives and the reliability of Genly as author/editor. "The story is well-known in various versions" (124), Genly Ai remarks on "Estraven the Traitor" (124–29), yet this may well be applied to the novel as a whole. The significant narrative gaps in the main storyline and the ambiguity inherent in the embeddings allow the reader to construct numerous possible "truths."

Half the stories are highly personal narratives of fatal love: the tragedy of lovers separated by taboo and suicide in "The Place inside the Blizzard" (22–26) supplies the reader with background information on the taboos of full siblings vowing *kemmer*, on the deep Gethenian cultural resentment of suicide, and on the ill-fated love of Estraven and his sibling Arek. It also shows a glimpse of the unyielding harshness of the Gobrin Ice, the background for the central episode of the narrative. "The Nineteenth Day" (43–46) reminds one of the Oracle at Delphi whose ambiguous answers sometimes prompted ill-fated actions on behalf of the askers. It not only highlights the paraphernalia of *foretelling*, but also demonstrates how the process itself becomes part of self-fulfilling prophecy. "Estraven the Traitor" (124–29) tells of political stability and economic wealth resulting from the personal tragedy of mortal enemies falling in love against the odds of their social and ethical backgrounds.

These subjective micro-histories of love, betrayal, and death are counterbalanced by the other triad of the embedded narratives, more removed from personal involvement: the strictly scientific account of "The Question of Sex" (89–97) observes the peculiarities Gethenian sexual physiology, "On Time and Darkness" (162–64) grants insight into the Yomeshta cult with special regard to the center of time, and "An Orgota Creation Myth" (237–39) is a version of how beginnings were imagined in this place of ice and cold.

While these embeddings serve as convenient narrative devices of conveying information, they also help Genly cope with his personal taboos and his personal trauma: the recurring theme of suicide echoes Estraven's quasi-suicide at the end of the novel (286), yet not by applying the disdainful label of cultural taboo to a seemingly avoidable turn in the plot, but through reverbalizing the act of voluntary death in order to understand Estraven's choice and to come to terms with the frustration and anger at feeling desolate and betrayed.

But the overbearing theme pervading the embedded narratives remains love and sexuality. Instituting Genly in the slot of reader, this insistence on obsessive verbalization sheds light on the emotional chaos that reigns beneath the seemingly calm surface of Genly's personality. It is not only the doubt concerning the rightness of a choice made — the restraint from sexual contact, or, in a parallel reading, the fulfillment thereof— and the sorrow over the loss of love that have to be dealt with, but a much more complex set of dilemmas: the instinctive rejection of interspecies love and possible homophobia all push this theme out of the main narratives into the embeddings. Genly seems only comfortable with (interracial) sexual intimacy if confined either to a scientific report or to accounts of another species, as both the interspecies barrier and the controlled language of scientific discourse provide safe distancing.

We may observe that the embeddings falling in the personal category may be found in the first half of the novel, while the distanced/scientific narratives are featured in the second half. The shift from personal to public complements the shift in the opposite direction in the main narratives, as themes of prior importance for Genly in the first half— political-diplomatic endeavors to bring Gethen into the Ekumen — lose prominence, and his private sphere, the relationship to Estraven, gains in importance until it totally eclipses the diplomatic concerns. The personal issues before the journey over the Ice are marred by disharmony and misunderstanding. With the shift in priority the tone and themes of Genly's narrative become more personal and less avoiding when talking about deeply private issues of love, sexuality, and loss. Misunderstanding gives way to interpersonal harmony, and this is paralleled not only by the shift in registers within the embeddings, but also by a thinning in their frequency, having become superfluous as both the vehicle for suppressed information and as emotional crutches for Genly in coping with his trauma. The narratives at that point have arrived at the trauma proper.

The last embedded narrative, "An Orgota Creation Myth," a story about beginnings on the Ice, beautifully counterbalances the climax of

Genly's narrative, which from a certain viewpoint ends on the Gobrin Ice, rendering it the private Center of Time for the envoy.

Lavondyss

While in *The Left Hand of Darkness* the embeddings focus on the communication of information concerning the gaps in the narrative — and thus either supplement the narrative or further the re-enactment of personal trauma — and their inherent ambiguity results from the intended reader-ship, the main themes explored by and through the embedded narratives in *Lavondyss* concern misreading and miscommunication, the passivity/activity of the "reader" of a story, as well as the multi-layeredness of the stories and the constant transformation they undergo in the course of their evolution.

Misreading in *Lavondyss* results in part from the faulty assignment of authorship to the embedded narratives and their perception as occupying a separate diegetic plane instead of a different diegetic time. Tallis mistak-enly supposes that all instances of embedding originate from the same metadiegetic level (see Genette, *Narrative Discourse* 234–36), authored by persons other than her trying to communicate vital messages about Harry's whereabouts in the realm of the subconscious, left as a "trail" for her to follow (*Lavondyss* 288). This assumption is correct in some cases, and the book of myths, the teachings of Gaberlungi, and the scientific journals are all the creations of others. But "time is out of joint" (*Hamlet* 1.5.197), and part of the embeddings Tallis interprets as messages from the past are in reality the main narrative embedded in itself.

These are the embeddings attached to the fragments of the narrative of the fallen warrior Scathach, glimpsed through the branches of the oak tree where Tallis's grandfather died (82–83, 83–84, 87–88, and 95, respec-tively) which Tallis believes to be a story from the past or outside her time-line altogether. This episode is subject to multiple misreadings by Tallis. Assigning external authorship is her first mistake, as it is her own future narrative she witnesses, the course of events triggered by her decision to become an active participant instead of remaining a passive spectator: instead of witnessing and mourning the death of the hero, she desperately tries to save Scathach from the women she interprets as corpse robbers (95). This is another significant misinterpretation, as in truth the women are there to save the warrior's soul by providing the proper funeral rites for his body. By this time she is so infatuated with Scathach that she is unable to glimpse the dual nature of the narrative. Since it is situated in the world of Harry's making, Scathach's fate mirrors Harry's entrapment in Lavondyss, and presents — because of the warped nature of time — the way to his freedom.

Another misconception is that "time, for her wounded hero, existed only when she was watching" (89), which is proven wrong when Tallis witnesses the flow of the narrative from the "other side" (321–41), filling in the gaps in between her sightings from the tree. When already aware of the proleptic nature of the embedding, she assumes that the female warrior emerging from the trees to mourn her fallen lover is none other than herself (334), but this is later revealed to be Morthen, Scathach's half-sister, as one of the rules governing these proleptic embeddings appears to be that Tallis does not meet herself, at least not in her unaltered human form: in the episode with the *Daurogs* (302–13) Tallis travels parallel with her tree-self, Holly-Tallis, yet her metamorphosed, disguised form here prevents her from recognizing this part as a psuedo-embedded narrative.

The Battle of Bavduin seems to function as the center-point for the misreadings in the narrative. In this instance Tallis chooses to interfere in the course of events and transforms from reader into actor-author. The activity/passivity of the reader is the second theme explored through the embedded narratives. The novel does not only play with the role of author-ship, but also with the role of reader. It seems that reading is safe as long as the reader remains outside the narrative, but events take a wrong turn when passive absorption becomes active participation and the reader becomes an author. Things go wrong because Tallis "had *interfered* with a process which only should have been *watched*" (103).

Harry is the shaping consciousness of Tallis's world, and when the girl meets Wynne-Jones in the Forest the scholar tells her that she has been in her "brother's skull for years" (287). He further informs her that all mythagos in the realm of reality had been fragments of Harry's soul (288), and that her whole life, all her actions and thoughts, were not in compli-ance with an inner drive but an external force — Harry — drawing Tallis to himself "like a fish on a line" (289). This scenario may be translated as a narrative authored by Harry Keeton in which Tallis is only assigned the dual role of protagonist/reader. Her function is basically passive: to read and interpret the messages of her brother and to follow his instructions to set him free. Her becoming a co-author is not part of Harry's design, and it is possible to read the long learning process with the three cowled and masked women as Harry's attempt to superimpose his narrative on her own: by the tedious process of renaming the territory around her — where the place names appear to spring into her mind from nowhere — Tallis works herself into her brother's narrative and thus allows him authorship over her own self, giving up her own independent narrative to the task of freeing Harry.

Thus intervention is one of the taboos in this world created by Harry, as is frequently alluded to: Tallis argues with Mr. Williams that changing a story makes it unreal (136–37), and Wynne-Jones later tells her that "if we interfere we become involved[,] ... become trapped" (277), echoing exactly what had happened to Harry. Tallis's self surfaces at the wrong moment, and her intervention not only bars Scathach's soul from being set free, but due to the scrambled nature of time and the interwoven mental planes of the narrative, her appearance also traps Harry in Lavondyss, presenting us with the neat paradox that Tallis's intervention from the present into future events is at the same time the initiator of events in the past, prior even to her birth. This one instance of breaking the taboo of authorship serves as the main driving force behind the plot.

This same dilemma between activity/passivity is revisited and re-enacted on a small scale during the embedded narrative of the Shadox Dance (117–23), where Tallis starts out as a spectator but becomes involved in the narrative, this time not of her own free will, but drawn into it by Thorn, one of the dancers, mirroring Scathach and his power over the girl. First a participant, she then becomes actor when she creates a *hollowing* (120), a tear in the space-time fabric dividing consensus reality and the realm of fantasy, and summons the birds that in the seemingly parallel narrative become the flock of Bird Spirit Land. Just like her saving Scathach made the two planes of existence touch, her action causes the disruption of the narrative, and she stands in the void between reality and fantasy, without being able to repair the torn fabric of reality.

The third theme explored through the embeddings is the transformation and development of stories in the course of their history. *Lavondyss* is built upon the idea that there exist archetypal core myths, rudimentary stories which have gone through so many metamorphoses that the narrative "debris" that attached itself to their original form effaced the initial plot beyond recognition. Thus the whole magical/Jungian/mythological realm in *Lavondyss*, and by deduction, all of Anglo-Saxon and Celtic mythology in the book, is built upon a pre–Ice Age family tragedy of filicide and patricide in the wake of the coming of the Cold. Hence the image of unbearable eternal winter that pervades the glimpses of Lavondyss.

The simplified plot of the novel thus might read as a sequence of narrative metalepses, "the move by means of which a character, frequently a narrator, moves from one diegetic level to another" (Nelles 350), as Tallis encounters and enters one version after another of the same myth — embeds herself deeper and deeper in the narrative — moving gradually back in time, peeling away layers of mythological residue to get to the archetypal core, the First Forest and the tribal trauma of murder (361); and by reaching to the pre-human origins of mythology becomes ready to free her brother's soul, or what remains of it, in the symbolic act of giving birth to a flock of birds. This act then sends ripples through the surface of the narrative, both forward and backward, which embed themselves in the form of the recurring flock of birds: the creatures seen in Bird Spirit Land (95), the birds that exit the tree during the shadox dance (120), Tallis-Holly's "burden of birds" (311), the flock of birds Tallis sees from the windows of the castle (327), and the birthing of the birds narrated from Tallis-Holly's point of view (363), just to mention a few.

Setting Harry free from the prison of his own mind at the same time grants her release from Harry's narrative and freedom to author her own life. After fulfilling her quest, still in the core of the mythological realm, Tallis witnesses the tribal murder which is the other shaping force behind the winter-narrative (361) and begins her copious journey home, withdrawing from the embedded layers towards the world of reality.

Traveling against the current of the stories' evolution, Tallis herself undergoes a series of transformations: the girl becomes woman after she enters the Forest, then lover and mother, later widow, and, in the end, relinquishes all human form to metamorphose into a tree of the First Forest: the human core acquires a mythological coating, and thus Tallis the human and Tallis the creature of Harry's world melt into one in a symbolic unification of the two realms, a moment of fulfillment and peace (347). It is in this form that she witnesses the archetypal myth in its making and with the knowledge that transpires sets out homeward. Withdrawing from the embeddings, her transformations — indicating her movement away from the core — take her closer to her original human form: she first changes into a *daurog*, a creature between tree and human, half-aware of her humanity, half still lost in treeness. It is this form which re-enacts the setting free of Harry, which we encounter twice in the narrative: told from both human–Tallis's (312) and Tallis-Holly's point of view (363). She then becomes human once again only to find that the quest has drained her of her life energy and left her an old woman, still trapped within the world that Harry left behind.

She finds Scathach alive, although an old man, and they are able to spend their remaining years together before he dies, leaving her alone again in the duality that is Ryhope Wood. Besides being unable to complete the circle home, and thus completely withdraw from the mythological realm, Tallis is denied certainty whether her act of giving birth to the birds has granted Harry — and thus her — the desired freedom. When she dies, her consciousness or her spirit — it is left undecided — revisits the point when she emerged from the Wood into the arms of her worried father, now embedding consensus reality in the mythological realm. It is also ambiguous whether this finally frees her from Harry's narrative and allows her to continue her life liberated from having to comply with authorial demands other than her own, or whether it is just the fantasy of a failing mind. The funeral rites and, therefore, the continued existence of her timeline in the woods indicate a possibility for both narratives existing parallel to each other in this world of warped space and time.

When analyzing the embeddings, there is a difference in their behavior in the two distinct — pre-threshold and post-threshold — parts of the main narrative. The real embeddings, incursions of the mythic realm — Harry's mind — into reality, cease to exist once the narrative moves to the post-threshold part, into that selfsame realm. Here Tallis's hollowing potential establishes her as co-author, capable of changing Harry's narrative and thus altering the version of the Forest created by him, yet unable to free herself from it. While the landscape changes, as Wynne-Jones remarks when looking upon the transformation of the rajathuks (205), the changes are superficial, and the basic structure lies undisturbed.

The pseudo-embeddings, also part of the post-threshold world, remain intact due to their temporal dislocation but become hidden because their distinguishing features, the paraphernalia that identify them as mythic in opposition to what is real, do not upset post-threshold reality. The journey with the *daurogs* (302–13) is only revealed to be a non-parallel narrative, and thus an embedding, when the same episode is replayed from Tallis-Holly's point-of-view.

The objectified narratives, the written texts that are assigned physical form, however, act similarly in both the realms of reality and of myth: the book on Celtic and Anglo-Saxon mythology with Owen Keeton's letter embedded in the margins and the scientific journals of Huxley and Wynne-Jones are present in both spheres as "sacred" texts, codified and canonized keys to the mythic realm. The fragmentary nature of these texts, either concerning their physical condition or their disjointed and incomplete appearance in the narrative, is a significant common feature: the book of myths is frequently alluded to, yet we only get partial glimpses, almost nothing of its actual content is known aside from identifying it as containing stories from the Anglo-Saxon mythological cycle. The embedded narrative, the letter of Tallis's grandfather, is cited in full, but this full citation is arrived at after various circles which, as Tallis ages and gains more and more expertise in reading, reveal more and more of its contents. This gradual exposure may be read as an initiation rite, in which the aspiring *hollower* is given only as much information as she can process.

The fragmented nature of text extends to both scientific journals. The de(con)structive force of the forest had rendered Huxley's scientific narrative a collection of lacunae by the time Tallis finds it (152), with only parts decipherable, and the reading of Wynne-Jones's journal is at first delayed by mythic events (Tig's attack on his father [239], the invasion of the barbarian tribe [294–300]), and later, after Wynne-Jones's death, it is destroyed by his mythic child who by eating his father ingests the knowledge he and his journals carry, and just as the forest altered, fragmented, and "spit out" Huxley's journal, shards of Wynne-Jones's diary exit from Tig, the personified forest. The destructive effect the mythic realm has on these intended maps may be read as myth subverting science/reality, oral tradition prevailing over the written texts, and the prevalence of flexible orality over the rigidity of fixed written accounts. The "sacred" texts provide little or no help in mapping the realm; their existence, therefore, stands in stark contrast with the highlighting function embeddings are traditionally meant for.

Another set of embedded narratives of utmost importance, which are not present in the pre-threshold realm, refer to the events of the eight-year gap in Tallis's narrative following the crossing of the threshold. This period is crucial as it concerns Tallis's various metamorphoses while traveling deeper into the realm: her coming-of-age, the consummation of her relationship to Scathach, the birth of her dead children, and her affair with

Gyonval, one of the riders in whose company and in whose narrative she tries to find the way to Lavondyss.

This crucial period is only revealed in hints, and has to be reconstructed from analeptic embeddings later on. As the events concern Tallis's rite of passage into womanhood, this lacuna may be explained by the loss of the mask Moondream — "The Woman in the Land" (201) — which serves as the mediator of the female aspect of the narrative, and due to its absence this part is rendered illegible and may only be recovered after the tool for reading it has been refashioned within the narrative (281–87).

Conclusion

The Left Hand of Darkness and *Lavondyss* make extended use of embedded narratives, with certain similarities but with significant differences. In both works, one of the basic functions of the embedded narratives is the communication of messages to the readers, with the assumption that "reader" here may imply any person — real or fictitious — who comes into contact with the story and tries to interpret it. While bridging the gaps in the narratives by supplying relevant information, the embeddings themselves are the source of uncertainty and miscommunication.

Both works employ mythology as the vehicle for communication. The embedded mythological excerpts serve as metaphorical maps to explain and highlight certain points of the main narratives. A notable difference is that *Lavondyss* relies on extant Anglo-Saxon and Celtic lore, while in *The Left Hand of Darkness* Le Guin makes use of an imagined mythology (as is often the case in both her science fiction and fantasy): the folklore of Gethen.

Winter functions as the ultimate mythic realm in both works. In *The Left Hand of Darkness* the icy setting serves both to counterpoint the personal warmth of Genly Ai and Estraven's relationship and as a background that helps eradicate all life beyond the two main characters in the central episode on the Gobrin Ice. This device finally eliminates the Alien/Other opposition, rendering the two poles interchangeable and hence meaningless when reduced to two organic entities. In *Lavondyss* the mythic winter realm reaches back across time into the pre-historic era of Ice-Age Europe, where the climatic catastrophe of the world plunging into winter and the deeply personal trauma of familial murder becomes the origin of all stories to follow. Winter means death but at the same time also functions as the wellspring of all narratives and, hence, of life.

Authorship of the embeddings works differently in the two novels. In *Lavondyss*, faulty assignment of authorship is the main cause for misreading and the main drive of the narrative. In *The Left Hand of Darkness*, authorship is always clear; the inherent ambiguity of the main narratives as well as the embeddings stems from the superimposition of Genly Ai as editor over the authors and the vague motifs that lie behind his structuring of the text.

While *The Left Hand of Darkness* provides no evidence that the world "outside" does not exist independently of Genly Ai, *Lavondyss* in my reading emanates a degree of uncertainty in this respect; the garbled time-line of a mythic realm that makes the appearance of Harry's mythagos — Broken Boy, for one — possible long before Harry's entrapment in Lavondyss arouses suspicion as to whether the linear "reality" of the narrative is at least partially independent of its author or whether the contemporary "reality" of the novel and all its prior events somehow have their origin in the trapped mind of Harry. Should this be the case, all chance is lost for Tallis to somehow reach the desired freedom from her brother's narrative, as she herself is only a figment of his imagination, an embedding in his narrative.

WORKS CITED

Bickman, Martin. "Le Guin's *Left Hand of Darkness*: Form and Content." *Science Fiction Studies* 4.1 (March 1977): 42–47.

Campbell, Joseph. *Hero with a Thousand Faces*. Bollingen commemorative ed. Princeton: Princeton University Press, 2004.

Genette, Gérard. *Narrative Discourse*. Ithaca: Cornell University Press, 1983.

_____. *Narrative Discourse Revisited*. Ithaca: Cornell University Press, 1988.

Holdstock, Robert. *Lavondyss*. New York: Avon, 1988.

Le Guin, Ursula K. *The Left Hand of Darkness*. 1969. New York: Ace, 1976.

Nelles, William. "Stories within Stories: Narrative Levels and Embedded Narrative." Richardson 339–53.

Richardson, Brian, ed. *Narrative Dynamics: Essays on Time, Plot, Closure, and Frames*. Columbus: Ohio State University Press, 2002.

Shakespeare, William. *Hamlet*. Ed. David Bevington. New York: Bantam, 1988.

Torodov, Tzvetan. *The Poetics of Prose*. Ithaca: Cornell University Press, 1977.

8

Stories to Illuminate Truth and Lies to Hide Pain: *Gate of Ivory, Gate of Horn*

Donald E. Morse

> We create stories to illuinate truth. We create lies to hide pain.
> (*Gate of Ivory, Gate of Horn* 301)

Robert Holdstock's *Gate of Ivory, Gate of Horn* remains one of the most psychologically complex novels within the mode of contemporary fantasy. If Antoine Saint-Exupéry in *The Little Prince* "succeeded in doing that which few writers have been able to do — he captured the innocence of childhood" through fantasy, as James Higgins rightly claims (16) — then surely Holdstock has also succeeded in doing that which few writers have been able to do: he captured the trauma of childhood through fantasy. Confronted by the necessary but impossible task of trying to understand his mother's suicide that occurred when he was a young boy, the main character, Christian Huxley triggers a strange sequence of events in Ryhope Wood through his overwhelming psychological need: "from my deep unconsciousness my most secret dream" (139). "I was being called inward," he says using words that describe both his trip into the woods as well as his trip into his own traumatic past (59). A character in an earlier Holdstock novel discussing the power of the unknown might well have been describing Christian when he remarks: "deep down, ... we can't run out on our need to see those images, to visualize our dreams, or our fears" (*Where Time Winds Blow* 137). Each of the male members of the Huxley family in various novels visualizes his dreams and fears. In *Gate of Ivory, Gate of Horn* Christian through his mythagos gives form to his dream of

129

saving his mother while also having to face his fear that he was responsible for her death. Again and again he will be told: here is "[s]omething for you to see. To understand" (104). "You must think about it" (107). But thinking about his mother is painful and understanding comes only slowly upon him. When asked, "What do you seek?" he answers: "I seek my Mother." "What is served by finding her?" "The Truth," he replies confidently if naïvely (284–85), for truth often proves terribly complex.

Kay Redfield Jamison contends in her authoritative study *Night Falls Fast: Understanding Suicide* that "[s]uicide is a death like no other, and those who are left behind to struggle with it must confront a pain like no other" (292). While the death of a parent always proves difficult for surviving children of whatever age because of their now being left as the exposed link in their family's chain, those whose parent dies from suicide face additional difficulties. From Christian's youthful perspective and with his partial knowledge, his mother's violent death is completely unexpected and "compounded by a denial of the nature of the death" (Jamison 293). What he witnesses his young mind and immature emotions cannot process, for everything he sees proves far too threatening. The event itself is intensely brutal, while the part he played in it appears ambiguous at best. Like most close relatives of a suicide he blames himself, for, as Jamison further argues, "guilt is a usual and corrosive presence after suicide" (294), and the closer the relation, the more corrosive the guilt. For a young son such as Christian, who blames himself—at least in part—for the event itself, things may become complicated since no previous happening leading to this most traumatic event helps account for or begins to explain what happened. Instead, his mother's death occurs, like "most suicides ... in an already highly stressed and fragile personal world, a world fraught with anxiety, frayed tempers, ... and ill will" (Jamison 294). Jamison's description of the "likely" emotional circumstances surrounding or leading up to a suicide fits exactly Christian and his mother's situation: "However great the love may have been for the person who commits suicide, it is likely that the most sustaining relationships were, at the time of death, frazzled, drained, or severed entirely" (294). His mother's deep depression results in her transformation that first leaves Christian puzzled, then frustrated, and, finally, impatient. Again, Jamison describes his predicament precisely:

> The absolute hopelessness of suicidal depression is, by its nature, contagious, and it renders those who would help impotent to do so. By the time the suicide occurs, those who kill themselves may resemble only

slightly children or spouses once greatly loved and enjoyed for their company [294].

This drastic, appalling change is surely true of Christian's mother's last days, the bizarre behavior exemplified in her "bottling unscalded tomatoes; they would go rotten in a matter of days" (12). That action coupled with her neglecting to wear an apron creates a portrait of her in a "green tweed suit ... splashed with juice." She becomes "increasingly drenched in the red juices" (12), and Christian's attempts to rectify the situation are soundly rebuffed. He senses the hopelessness of the situation both for her and for him: "She was doing nothing right and Chris felt like crying" (12).

Those traumatic events of his mother's last days remain for Christian intellectually and emotionally as he experienced them then and remembers them now. Nevertheless, they may not have happened in exactly the way he believes they happened, for the child's vision is necessarily influenced both by his circumscribed experience and his immature emotional state. An adult's perspective, although also limited, may be constricted in ways quite different from that of a child's and it is this contrast between Christian's perspective on his mother's suicide as a child and his perspective on it as an adult that lies at the heart of *Gate of Ivory, Gate of Horn*.

"What a little of all we know is said," wisely remarked Ralph Waldo Emerson, and in the case of childhood trauma, such as occurs when a mother commits suicide, what a little of all that happens do we know — much less are able to say. For Christian, the events surrounding his mother's suicide as well as the central event itself continue to be as inexplicable as they are painful to recall. As an adult he first seeks to allay the pain by undoing that string of painful events from childhood, but, unfortunately, he cannot — for the Heraclitean river of time flows in one direction only. But in attempting to overturn what he recalls as her untimely, traumatic, and unnecessary death he learns to see his mother anew, to look through her eyes empathetically, and this process results in his reconsidering his old memory and, possibly, replacing it with a new one.

To explore this psychologically complex and emotionally rich situation, Holdstock in *Gate of Ivory, Gate of Horn* draws upon the eclectic English fantasy tradition that begins with Shakespeare's *A Midsummer Night's Dream* and *The Tempest*. This distinctive heritage became unique to England, because, as Ursula K. Le Guin argues, "[n]owhere else in Europe did folk tale, legend, medieval romance, travelers' tales and individual genius coalesce in such works of the imagination as those plays" (1). And it is from these same Shakespearean sources that Holdstock draws his characters, plots, and symbols in this novel. As a result, he, too, "find[s] an inexplicit but radically vivid imagery with which to explore the intersections of reality and dream" (Le Guin 2) as encapsulated in the mythagos of Ryhope Wood.[1]

The mythago concept in itself gives the varied and various materials in *Gate of Ivory, Gate of Horn* coherence, as all the characters, settings, and events of Christian's adventure in Ryhope Wood derive from his psychological need as he calls them into existence and they coalesce around the primal issue of his mother's death. For instance, a major unanswered question for Christian that is explored through his mythagos is: What role, if any, did his father play in his mother's death? Was he, perhaps, in part responsible for her suicide? Within Mythago Wood Christian confronts his father under a number of guises resulting in a series of strong emotional responses. In the process he himself shifts emotionally from the dutiful son obeying the wishes of his father to the puzzled son fearing his father to the appalled son confronting his father "who ... turned on me like a wild creature" (39). More cogently, he realizes that he has become his father's rival and that leads in turn to his nadir vision of his father as the despised progenitor — the Saturn who eats his children. By this harsh light Huxley as father appears as a truly despicable human being, who "called by his own obsession" (22) abandoned his roles as husband and father to spend all his time in Ryhope Wood. Turning completely inward, away from his life in the world and his role within his family, he follows his mythago: that dream of an ideal woman found in the archetypal setting of dreams, the primeval wood.

Holdstock found a model for this pursuit of the fantastic, ideal woman — Huxley's mythago — in W. B. Yeats's "The Song of Wandering Ængus," the poem he alludes to when dedicating the novel to his late sister ("our glimmering girl"). In "The Song of Wandering Ængus," Yeats daringly attributes such a search for an ideal magical woman not to a mortal but to a god, Ængus Og, the Celtic god of love. At the magical time of night between the dark and dawn, an enchanted "silver trout" becomes transformed:

> It has become a glimmering girl
> With apple blossoms in her hair
> Who called me by my names and ran
> And faded through the brightening air [lines 13–16].

And so the god of love himself pursues his ideal "glimmering girl" in a search for timeless love, vowing "I will find out where she has gone" (line 19) as he wanders the world — much as Huxley roams Ryhope Wood searching in his turn for his "glimmering girl." At the end of *Gate of Ivory, Gate of Horn*, Christian vows that he, having made peace with the memory of his mother, will now return to hunt for the girl. Thus, in Holdstock's ironic twist on this story of a love-sick ancient god searching for an enchanted and enchanting girl, both father and son pursue this "glimmering girl." Rather than the Oedipal myth of the son killing the father and marrying the mother, in Holdstock's novel the son appears to kill the mother and then to follow after the father supplanting him as lover of the glimmering-girl.

The girl, identified as a centuries' old warrior, near the beginning of the novel lies dead in the snow where Christian finds and buries her, only to find her again in the Wood and to experience her dying again near the end of his adventure. Father and son both pursue this prehistoric warrior, a mythago that each creates out of his own need but one which both share. A vast difference separates the two men, however, in the way each relates to this mythago. Huxley pursues his "idealized vision" of what he calls "a life force" (46) — at the expense of everything and everyone else. He abandons his wife and family for long periods to pursue his dream. Upon returning home from the Wood he attacks his son with a shotgun. According to his wife, he then first helps precipitate then aids in her suicide. However that may be, the suicide leaves Christian coping with a horrendous psychological heritage of conflicted feelings: jealousy, confusion, guilt, and abandonment. As he comes of age and moves through adolescence into adulthood, he must, therefore, deal not simply with the death of a parent, but, more specifically and terribly, with the breakdown of his parent's marriage, the ambiguity of his father alternately neglecting and violently threatening him, and his mother's suicide together with his father's possible implication in it. The child may be "father to the man," but it remains the man's, the adult's, job to assess and assimilate the child's experience. The process for Christian proves lengthy, traumatic, and extremely difficult as well as fraught with violence. His initial attempts to deal with these psychological issues are unsuccessful and it is only after he matures into a man that he becomes at long last able to face those issues left unsettled from his boyhood. Having fought in the Second World War, he returns home ready at last to confront and finish the unfinished business of childhood.

The imaginative device of mythagos and the Mythago Wood produce an admirable set of parallel images for such a psychological confrontation. Out of his trauma Christian summons his mythagos: "I had called them to mark me," he realizes in retrospect as he recounts events long after they have happened in an effort to preserve their memory (81). The Wood presents him with a mixture of legend "and my dreams" (80–81). As is true of every element in our dreams, every element in the Wood — every character, incident, and even the setting itself— derives from Christian's life, reading, thoughts, and emotions. And in this sense, as well as others, he has "indeed called them to mark [him]."

The title, *Gate of Ivory, Gate of Horn*, refers to the familiar distinction drawn in book 19 of Homer's *Odyssey*, which Holdstock quotes as his epigraph to the novel:

> ... there are two gates through which dreams reach us. Those that come through the Ivory Gate cheat us with empty promises that never see fulfillment. Those that issue from the Gate of Horn inform the dreamer of the Truth.

This dichotomy of the false versus the true dream is in turn mirrored in the novel by Huxley's false dreams of the ideal woman that leads to his trail of destroyed lives. Similarly, Christian's false dream, his Forlorn Hope of rescuing his mother from death — a death that he is repeatedly told "was not as you think" (195), is one impossible to fulfill but, given the circumstances surrounding her death, one equally almost impossible to abandon.[2] Eventually his false dream of bringing her back to life becomes supplanted by his true dream of laying her ghost to rest and getting on with his own life, which leads, in its turn, to a mature deed of self-sacrifice. But before that may happen, Christian must learn several difficult, basic lessons that he often hears in the form of gnomic pronouncements — "We have the time we have" (218), "all stories" are necessarily "incomplete" (224)— along with opaque proclamations, such as when he is told that it was his mother who made him forget (313). Sometimes such sayings appear as psychological clichés: "you can't create the love you need" (302) and — most difficult of all to accept when told to him by his mother with the noose in her hand —"you cannot help me — only yourself" (304). Forgetting enabled him to survive from early adolescence into adulthood. Only as an adult who has gone through the World War, experiencing its many attendant horrors, is Christian ready and able to face the terrible truth of his mother's suicide. And that truth must include her belief that it was his father who actively precipitated it and then participated in it — a participation that, if factually true, amounts to accessory to murder (311). If the event was for Christian "not as you think," its reality for his mother lies beyond most imagining, as she experiences his father roaring at her, "his mouth twisted into a grimace of hate. 'Why don't you do it? [kill yourself],'" he taunts (306). The nightmare climaxes for his mother in her image of Huxley leaping onto the tree:

> Like the wild animal he had become, this boar, this man, this Huxley leapt to the bough, pulled hard on the rope and wound it round the branch, knotting it. My mother screeched, then gasped...
> My father, legs splayed, urinated on the woman below him, leaping like a wild man on the bough, making it bend and buckle, making the woman dance below him [307].

This nightmare vision that Christian sees through his mother's eyes lies far beyond most young people's ability or, perhaps, any child's ability to accept and survive psychologically: only an adult could begin to be able to understand that the basis of this scene lies in his mother's belief as may also be true of the ensuing vision of his farther seeking her death. It, too, may or may not have happened — there is simply no way for Christian to know. What he does come to realize is that his own life has been shaped "by a *lie* she was led to believe in" (322). As an adult he is able to face the truth: what his mother saw and experienced, like her subsequent action, was a consequence of her deep clinical depression — depression that continually overwhelmed her. Her cry "I must end the pain!" (305) is one echoed again and again by victims of deep depression. More tragic still is the fact that much of his mother's motivation for ending her life came from her certain but mistaken belief in another dream out of the Gate of Ivory of Christian murdering his brother Steven by hanging him: "her eldest son kill[ed] her youngest son," she believed through-and-through as he understands to his dismay when he sees through her eyes (303–04). William Cowper writing centuries earlier captured succinctly the resulting horror his mother felt:

> No voice divine the storm allay'd,
> No light propitious shone;
> When, snatch'd from all effectual aid,
> We perished, each alone:
> But I beneath a rougher sea,

And whelm'd in deeper gulphs than he
["The Castaway" lines 61–66].

Her depression is so fierce that she feels more isolated and helpless than even someone cast away on a storm-tossed sea — the boat from which he fell having disappeared in the dark.

Part of the full, extended nightmare for Christian lies in his father's role in his mother's suicide acted out vividly in primal detail as man and as boar (his totem animal form) and his subsequent attacking Christian because of what he witnessed as a boy. But what of all this is true? Or in what sense are these fantastic details true? In order to survive this living nightmare Christian creates his own version of events that enables him to go on. Like the dreams that issue from those two opposite gates, "We create stories to illuminate truth. We create lies to hide pain" (301). And the underlying painful truth from which Christian hides by creating a just bearable story of his parents is that he "can't create the love [he] need[s]" (302). Such nurturing love arrives as a gift from others to others, but not to Christian, whose parents were in thrall to the Gate of Ivory and their individual false dreams: his father "had written away his life and [his] mind" (303) in pursuit of an impossible dream of a "glimmering girl" (302–03) and his mother's mind was controlled and warped by a false dream of fratricide. Thus does the Gate of Ivory turn truth into lies (301).

But the novel complicates any such single reading. While Huxley's pursuit of the glimmering girl proves a false dream out of the Gate of Ivory, he appears unable to learn from it and at the same time appears powerless to abandon it. Does Christian's similar vow of finding the girl after all he has been through issue from that same gate or, perhaps, from the Gate of Horn? Is this his true dream or his false dream? Within the novel, the father's dream is false and leads, at least, in part, to death, destruction of a family, suicide, and much else besides. Christian's dream of rescuing his mother appears blameless, almost altruistic, but it, too, proves mistaken. When he at last meets his mother, he later reports: "I was twelve years old again" (109). It is his mother who reveals the truth to him — a truth so understandably difficult for him to accept that only the combination of his preparatory adventure in Ryhope Wood and her admonition "I was dead and in a wonderful place" allow him to accept it. What he comes to understand is that the peace of death was and is her desire —

not the torture of life. She cautions Christian against becoming preoccupied exclusively with her condition, rather than getting on with his own life. She describes him as "alive and behaving like a dead man." Her criticism may appear harsh, given his preoccupation with her predicament, but proves salutary: "You have wasted your life. There were better things for you to do. You have one life only..." (336). The Scottish poet, Douglas Dunn, echoed this advice of Christian's mother to her son, when he wrote, "Look to the living, love them, and hold on" ("Disenchantments" qtd. in Jamison 311).

Gate of Ivory, Gate of Horn ends when Christian, like Orpheus, is given the opportunity to bring his mother back from the Underworld; that is, his greatest wish to save her from death is granted. But unlike Euridice his mother has no wish to return to the land of the living, that terrible place that was for her only continual and incomprehensible pain and agony. The choice of death was for her a positive choice and in that she went further than many typical suicides, such as the Japanese writer Ryunosuke Akutagawa, who found that "[t]he world I am living in now is the icily transparent universe of sickly nerves...." He concludes: "Of course, I do not want to die, but it is suffering to live" (qtd. in Iga 82–83). Christian's mother's situation appears somewhat different and, from her perspective, far clearer, since she does not want to live but wants to die. Events surrounding her death when seen from deep in Ryhope Wood suggest that her choice was positive, for death has saved her from an impossible situation in an intolerable life. Now she is at rest (109). Her situation and attitude parallel exactly one of the most famous psychological case studies in existential psychoanalysis, "The Case of Ellen West," discussed at length by Ludwig Binswanger. Ellen West found nothing in life that made her want to live; all avenues of hope appeared blocked. So severe was her situation that her psychoanalyst concluded that suicide remained for her the only viable, authentic act. Hence for Ellen West to die rather than to live became a positive act. When Christian goes into Ryhope Wood wanting to bring his mother back to life, he laments, "I had been too young when she died" (110). Focusing solely on himself and his loss, he neglects to ask himself if his mother's choice might have been in some way a positive choice — terrible though it was. Hence his shock when she tells him she has no desire to return to life and the living. Death is the desired end of life for her, and death, as Walter Benjamin wisely noted, "is the sanction of everything that the story-teller can tell"

(94). It authenticates the teller and the tale; Christian's mother and her tale, in this instance.

Disabused of his myopia, Christian brings back from his adventure not his mother but a gift of love for his friend and a memory of his positive encounter with his mother. Since all memories exist only in the present, all future memories of his mother will from now on include his meeting with her in Ryhope Wood, along with her assurance that she is at rest and at peace with herself, her life, and her death. With such a promise Christian may now reclaim those good years he had with her before dark depression conquered all: his mother has blessed him (333). Laying her ghost to rest, the Child of the Land has grown up and will now heed his Shadow-guide's warning: "you must not question your decision" (331), or you will lead a life of regret — the most wasteful of all human emotions.

Christian's memory of his mother changed significantly; the mythagos he called into being from his need (314) provided the occasion for him to do the hard work of accepting events that happened by seeing them not solely through his eyes as a child but also empathetically through his mother's eyes. The result is his new terrible vision and new reassuring memory. Going into Ryhope Wood he hoped to reverse time and overcome death — clearly a false dream. But as Wallace Stevens famously intoned, "Death is the mother of beauty," as death is the mother of love and all that is precious to human beings. Mortality confers blessing. To deny mortality is to wish to return to Eden with its everlasting spring where the ripe fruit hangs forever on the trees.[3] *Gate of Ivory, Gate of Horn* opposes to the Edenic myth the Parable of the Land of Flowers (104–07), which makes the point that life and death exist together in balance — one needs the other. Another parable, this one of the river known as the Long Person, similarly emphasizes the yin and yang nature of life and death, although the acceptance of death's place may be difficult.

> I glimpsed for the first time the extraordinary flow of life that was erupting at the river's source; and of the death that it was drawing back, against the stream, as if the impulse to life was the easiest, that to death the hardest ... [249].

While it is true that "[f]ew of us lose a parent without regret and some self-reproach, some sense of things undone or injustices unredressed; it is a natural component of grief" (Johnson and Murray 4), children of suicides have a particularly difficult time dealing with such feelings. Thanks to his mythagos, Christian has, to a large extent, lost the feeling of self-reproach, begun the process of accepting what he cannot change, and is getting on with his life. In sum: the novel traces his becoming an adult.

Erik H. Erikson, the developmental psychologist, defined the passage between adulthood and maturity as choosing between the acceptance of life as lived that leads to serenity or the rejection of life as lived that leads to disgust and despair. Christian has made a good start on what Erikson describes as the task of maturity, the state of mind that reflects

> the acceptance of one's own and only life cycle and of the people who have become significant to it as something that had to be and that, by necessity, permitted of no substitutions. It thus means a new different love of one's parents, free of the wish that they should have been different, and an acceptance of the fact that one's life is one's own responsibility. It is a sense of comradeship with men and women of distant times and of different pursuits, who have created orders and objects and sayings conveying human dignity and love [104].

Much of this kind of far-reaching acceptance Christian has accomplished — however tentatively. At the end of the novel, he has achieved, in Erikson's phrase, a "healthy personality." Yet his father predicts that he, too, will end in despair, if not in disgust because of being enthralled by his adventure in Ryhope Wood: "like me, you will pursue a dream. We pursue the same dream, Chris. That dream will become your life" (344). But Huxley may be speaking more of himself than for his son. Clearly, Huxley sees Christian as a rival — one to be disposed of, if necessary (138). His father also suggests that Chris will spend his "one life" in pursuit of his glimmering girl through the woods as he, his father, has chosen to do and as Wandering Ængus did before both of them. An incident early in the novel suggests exactly how false the dream was for the father and how dangerous it could be for the son. Before he goes into Ryhope Wood for the first time, Christian discovers the girl's dead body in the snow beside his home and buries her. Once in the Wood, he appears to forget this significant fact until the warrior-girl, Guiwenneth herself, reminds him of it. She describes herself as his dream and tasks him to "dream ... [her] well. Dream [her] beautiful, ... happy, and with a heart that can fulfill all your own needs and love" (336). Christian maintains that he will "dream ... [her] well," that he will find her. He has then adopted his father's dream as his own, an often dangerous proposition. But whether this dream issues from the Gate of Ivory or the Gate of Horn remains to be seen.

NOTES

1. Holdstock has said he prefers to mix legends and myths drawn from several times and places, yet his sources remain predominantly Celtic.

2. Holdstock captures Christian's dilemma in the image of the river of life opposed to the tenacious current of death "as if the impulse to life was the easiest, that to death the hardest, all notion of entropy ignored" (249). This modification of Heraclitus's river of time captures the psychological reality of Christian unable to accept death, even death by suicide as the end of life, hence "the impulse of life was the easiest." The rest of the novel focuses on his eventual acceptance of his mother's choice to end her life. He is indeed "on a river journey to the heart of the world" (264); that is, to the very heart of the human experience of mortality.

3. Stevens's poem "Sunday Morning" also rhetorically asks: "Does ripe fruit never fall [in Paradise]?" (6.1–2). In the ancient Hebrew myth in Genesis, the ripe fruit does fall to feed the inhabitants of Paradise who in their turn are also mortal but accept death as the natural end of life.

WORKS CITED

Binswanger, Ludwig. "Ellen West." *Being-in-the-World: Selected Papers of Ludwig Binswanger.* Trans. Jacob Needleman. New York: Basic Books, 1963.

Cowper, William. "The Castaway." *The Penguin Book of English Verse.* 1956. Ed. John Hayward. Harmondsworth: Penguin, 1973. 236–37.

Erikson, Erik H. *Identity and the Life Cycle.* 1959. New York: Norton, 1980.

Higgins, James E. *Beyond Words: Mystical Fancy in Children's Literature.* New York: Teachers College Press, 1970.

Holdstock, Robert. *Gate of Ivory, Gate of Horn.* 1997. London: HarperCollins, 1998.

_____. *Where Time Winds Blow.* New York: Pocket Books, 1981.

Iga, M. *The Thorn in the Chrysanthemum: Suicide and Economic Success in Japan.* Berkeley: University of California Press, 1986.

Jamison, Kay Redfield. *Night Falls Fast: Understanding Suicide.* 1999. New York: Vintage, 2000.

Johnson, Diane, and John F. Murray. "Will to Live." Review of *Swimming in a Sea of Death: A Son's Memoir* by David Rieff. *New York Review of Books* 55.2 (14 February 2008): 4, 6, 8.

Roethke, Theodore. "The Waking." *The Collected Poems of Theodore Roethke.* Garden City: Anchor, 1975. 104.

Stevens, Wallace. "Sunday Morning Service." *The Palm at the End of the Mind: Selected Poems and a Play.* Ed. Holly Stevens. New York: Vintage, 1972. 5–8.

9

"A Heap of Broken Images" — The Mythological Wasteland of the Mind: *The Hollowing* and *Ancient Echoes*

Ildikó Limpár

The Road to the Mental Landscape

The created world of imagination, a defining feature of all fantasy works, can manifest itself in so many forms that the possibilities of variation appear limitless. Limits, however, do play an extremely important role in where the author places the locus of fantastic actions. Depending on where the writer feels the limits of the real world are, the fantasy realm may surface at various distances from our contemporary environment. For Shakespeare a simple (brain)storm was enough to bring his magician Prospero to an island which Ariel and Caliban, two of the best-known fantastic creatures of world literature, inhabited and which was situated, as it turned out, not very far from Milan. The world then was known to be not fully known; there were islands waiting to be discovered, but while on the white map of the expanding world, they could be populated by the fantastic as long as reality failed to reach them. By the time geography was crystallized and we ran out of undiscovered islands, new strategies for finding room for new worlds had had to be invented. After the white spots disappeared from the maps of our own world, the still-expanding universe offered a new way to face the fantastic first in faraway planets, then in faraway galaxies. And by the time imagination bumped into limits again, Einstein's theories of relativity had opened up new doors for the new experimenters who could send their heroes back to the past or ahead to the future, as they (we) fancied. Yet, as could be expected, both space and time soon reached their limits: simultaneously to the wide use of parallel universes, an attempt at returning to the contemporary world of reality was observable when writers realized it is the very place we inhabit that had not been thoroughly investigated from the respect of the fantastic. Thus, having seen our world successfully re-mythologized by now, authors may justly think that they have searched near and far both spatially and temporally and there is no other place or time left to visit. Or is there?

After reaching as far as imagination could, the way back led to the reality that surrounds us. Is it possible to approximate the marrow of life any more closely? Certainly it is, Robert Holdstock argues, and demonstrates with *The Hollowing* and *Ancient Echoes* (1996). Both novels opt to get so close to the self that we actually end up *within* the self—or, more precisely, within the self's psyche, which functions as a classic otherworld known from fantasy literature yet also operates according to the rules of reality.[1] For modern authors, the perfect site for the unknown is not to be found in another galaxy but within the unconscious, which, as Brightmore explains to Jack in *Ancient Echoes* (146), serves as a well of inspiration for all innovative writers: that is, the place where all good fantasy stories originate. This source gets different treatment in Holdstock's two novels: *The Hollowing* presents a psychic landscape as a magical otherworld within the real one, which is capable of giving life to what the mind projects onto it and thus manifests the fusion of many psyches, whereas *Ancient Echoes* opens up the channel to the deep regions of one specific mind. Despite the difference in location, the novels use the psychic landscapes for the same purpose: the hero must enter in order to fulfill his personal quest, that is, to reclaim his child. The condition of the hero's life in contemporary reality is bound to the condition of the psychic landscape; therefore, the hero's quest lies in restoring the otherworld as only by this act can he restore his own life, the token of which is his child, or, to be more exact, his child's completeness.

Holdstock's approach results in the combination of two types of fantasy otherworlds. On the one hand, the psychic landscape may be considered as an independent world that is different and detached from the real environs of the hero. On the other hand, since the site of the fantastic adventures is situated within the hero's psyche in *Ancient Echoes* and is inherently connected to the psyches of the characters entering the magical Ryhope Wood in *The Hollowing,* these specific otherworlds may be thought of as manifestations of the transmythologized real world. It is all the more so since what makes these sites fantastic is the presence and workings of various mythologies, which, according to Carl Gustav Jung's theory, reside in our unconscious in the forms of archetypes ("Structure" 39–46; "Concept" 59–60). As a consequence, the quest becomes the modern person's wanderings among the ancient bits that are echoes of mythologies, signifying the other, the unknown, while the aim of the quest is to make out some meaning in order to save the world — both inside and outside.

Holdstock's characters, similarly to T. S. Eliot's in *The Waste Land,* cover vast stretches of time and space in a distorted world of mythologies, seeking regeneration. The parallel may appear at first sight arbitrary and far-fetched, but Holdstock's books are based on the workings of the unconscious as described by Jung, and these novels, especially *The Hollowing,* echo the world of *The Waste Land.*[2]

The first of the two epigraphs to *Ancient Echoes* is taken from Eliot's *The Hollow Men* (a poem strongly connected to *The Waste Land),* repeated at the beginning of chapter 16 (145) and, finally, used as an explanation of the nature of the psychic journey that awaits the protagonist. A direct reference to *The Waste Land* in the same novel also reveals Holdstock's depth of learning in interpreting Eliot's masterpiece: when his William of the Ice Age speaks of the spring encouraging dances, Holdstock's protagonist, Jack, immediately associates the ritual with what he has read about it: "I felt like saying to him that in the libraries of my own land his story was listed in a thousand different ways — The Wasteland, most notably" (198).

Although these examples all come from *Ancient Echoes,* a fantasy work written three years after *The Hollowing,* the earlier piece already clearly reflects the Eliotian concept of the modern world, and it is not too great a leap to suggest that Holdstock used the poem in constructing his Ryhope Wood.

The Mental Landscapes

The Hollowing and *Ancient Echoes* share certain characteristics that allow readers to formulate a composite picture of how the mind as a possible landscape — the "mental landscape," to use Helen Silverlock's terminology from *The Hollowing* (153) — works in Holdstock's scheme. Although the two novels seem to present us with two different fantastic worlds, a closer investigation reveals that the dissimilarity actually comes from focus-ing on diverse aspects of the same world, which is the human mind itself. Nevertheless, an additional comparison of the two works may shed light on parallels as well. The analogous components of the plots contribute to making the functions of the human mind more comprehensible for us as readers, who, not unlike the protagonists of the novels, are also to be ini-tiated — by experiencing their adventures in *our* own minds.

In *The Hollowing*, Richard Bradley's long magical journey in the Wood, which, by means of the so-called hollowings, expands much further into space and time than he could ever have imagined, produces mythagos. Richard must interpret Alex's mythagos as well as his own — not to mention fighting several dangerous ones generated by various other psyches — in order to track down his son and gain the opportunity to release him from the shackles of his own mind; to bring him home healthily, or, in other words, *completely.* His success at doing so becomes, at the same time, an act that restores the magical Ryhope Wood more or less to its original state. In addition, the adventure presents Richard with a new partner, Helen, who, being his helper in the Wood, manages to replace the wife whom he divorced after the tragedy of losing their son. The subplots reveal various people's quests in the Wood, which, although very disparate con-cerning their details, share the common aspect of functioning as life-healers which allow the characters to solve the greatest problems of their respective lives.

Ancient Echoes also features a father, Jack Chatwin, and his daughter, whose completeness becomes endangered when Jack's mind starts to act as a gate between the "real" and the fantastic (his mental) world and this gate gets opened up by one of his mythagos, Grayface/Baalgor, whose sister-wife, Greenface/Nemet chooses to stay within the psychic world, most unfortunately for the male mythago. The brother subverts the health of Jack's daughter to persuade Jack, it appears, to undertake adventures within his own mind in order to find Greenface and bring her to him (Grayface) in the outside world. Jack's participation in the scientific exper-iment allows him to take on these adventures and to enter deeper and deeper regions of his mind, searching through various layers of space and time to fulfill his quest. In addition to resetting the original balance between the two worlds, by forcing Grayface back to the fate that inevitably waits for the man for his past wrongdoing, he manages to regain his daugh-ter, Natalie, in her original state, and — thanks to the adventures acted out in the inner realm — he gains a new partner in the person (or, rather, in the mythago) of Greenface, replacing his estranged wife.

The key concepts and keywords that run parallel in the two novels — mythagos, time and space of the mind, the quest of restoring and healing both the inner and the outer worlds, family and other emotional bonds; all of which are to be connected to the working of the psyche — provide a guide to the labyrinths of the mind. Holdstock relies primarily on Jung's psychological observations, and, unsurprisingly, in *Ancient Echoes* Brightmore, the leader of Richard's psychological experiment, explains the essence of Richard's mental experiences using Jungian ideas and terminology: "when you dream — images and fears, moods, emotions, and the energetic psychic manifestation Carl Gustav Jung labeled *archetypes*—all of them flow *up* to the preconscious, and partly penetrate to awareness" (146).

Richard in *The Hollowing* gets a similar introduction to Jungian psychology by the expert Lacan, who explains the phenomenon of mythagos by way of archetypes and who, interestingly enough, studied Jung for some years (64–65). Holdstock adds to this theory an ancient philosophical problem, that of the dream-butterfly and the dreamer,[3] which is the basis of much postmodern literature that aims at presenting the blurred boundary between the real and the imagined: he gives "Form! Shape! And Story!" (*Ancient Echoes* 146) to these archetypes, turning them into mythagos, and ensuring interactions between them and his human characters so that the borderline between the two worlds may disappear at least for a while.

Ancient Echoes demonstrates the way in which entities Jung calls the personal and the collective unconscious ("Relations" 70–83) relate to one another: the deeper Jack journeys into his own mind, the more ancient images dominate his "dream," while, at the same time, the images he is emotionally connected to resurface in all times and become modified if circumstances demand so. The beginning of his mental journey shows signs of "real" dreaming, reflecting mostly on his external emotions, as he himself notices (*Ancient Echoes* 139), and thus is perfectly suitable for the Jungian dream interpretation.[4] In the deeper regions, however, the direct effect of the outside world appears to lose its significance, and there is a clear emotional separation between the two worlds for Jack, who begins to prefer his inner world. It is no surprise, then, that at the end of the experiment he is found in need of uniting the two worlds: not only does he keep returning to his psyche, but he also founds his new family there after separating from his former wife in the outside world.

In *The Hollowing*, time does not function in the same way as in the outside world. The hollowings themselves are time and space channels, similarly to the various paths present in Jack's mental landscape. Here the magical Ryhope Wood provides the kind of space that Jack has found in his own psyche. Nevertheless, instead of focusing on the aspect of change in the forms of mythagos generated by the hero's entering deeper regions, Holdstock gives us a most complex survey on how one's archetypes/mythagos are created, and thus lays special emphasis on the *nature* of these mind-projections made possible by a significant deviation between the mental landscapes of the two novels: Ryhope Wood shows more or less the form that was created by the mind of one person, George Huxley. This, however, is a form in fluctuation, as anyone entering the Wood may modify its content by his/her own mythagos, a characteristic which enhances the sensation that we are in one and several minds at the same time. Jung argues that the personal unconscious supplies our mind with a unique feature that makes it diverge from all other psyches, while the collective unconscious is a kind of store-house of archetypes produced by innumerable minds throughout human history ("Concept" 59–60). Ryhope Wood, as a mental landscape, performs both aspects of the unconscious: the mythagos strongly connect to their "owners," who, thanks to Holdstock's careful design, are of various ethnicities of the world, and, as a consequence of that, the variety of their mythagos reflects humanity's history as well as its diverse cultures, making the Wood indeed this store-house of archetypes.

Quests in the Mental Landscapes

Although the plot of *The Hollowing* centers on Richard's son being mentally imprisoned in the Wood, and it is his mythagos that do serious damage to the "original" state of this magical landscape, it is the father and not the son who can be considered the protagonist. Alex's activity is limited to dreaming, which functions as self-defense in the Wood; his aim becomes to re-connect with his father somehow when he senses Richard approaching. Presented mostly as a passive character, the "object" of the quest his father is performing, Alex, nevertheless, proves not altogether passive, as his dreaming actively helps those searching for him. Still, he does not have explicitly conscious goals but acts merely on the level of instinct.

9. *"A Heap of Broken Images"* (Limpár)

Richard, conversely, knows very clearly what — or rather whom — he wants and subordinates everything to that objective. He becomes obsessed with the idea that his life might be restored by regaining his son, but after joining the scientific team that works in Ryhope Wood he must realize that he is surrounded by people equally obsessed by their own quests: team leader Lytton's personal mission is to meet Huxley and to preserve as much of Huxley's mind-projections in the Wood as possible; Lacan is in search of his own death, meaning his magical wife; and Helen wants to meet and take revenge on the trickster Coyote, thus undoing the curse her family has been suffering from for generations.

Although the quest is different for each character, its purpose remains the same: to restore the world for the self. Ryhope Wood offers a tiny ray — indeed, a "rye" — of hope for everyone entering it. The Wood in *The Hollowing* functions as a kind of Waste Land, where people having lost their hopes and beliefs — their lives — are granted an opportunity to find that which would make their lives meaningful or complete again. This, in our world, is no less than magic — but magic is made real in Ryhope Wood. At first sight, it appears here as the Wood's ability to produce the solid forms of the archetypes. There is, however, a different kind of magic at work, too — a magic that may bring us closer to understanding the relationship between Holdstock's *The Hollowing* and Eliot's *The Waste Land*.

The magic Eliot writes about in his poem constitutes spiritual regeneration, inevitable for the restoration of the world. The major part of the poem presents the spiritual waste land, inhabited by spiritually and emotionally empty people from various nations and ages. These "hollow men," people whose lives is meaningless, experience a continuous sense of misplacement. They are the pieces of the jigsaw-world that has fallen apart and appears impossible to put together; their world is dead, for its pieces do not connect: "I can connect / Nothing with nothing," declares Eliot in "The Fire Sermon." For Cleanth Brooks this sentence is uttered by a hopeless voice from the Inferno (75), but to my mind it is Eliot's magic which he intended to enforce through his attempt at putting this poem together from the "heap of broken images" he had collected and stored in his mind, while, as I imagine, he tried to convince himself of the use of his efforts, repeating to himself: "I *can* connect [even] nothing with nothing." For that is where real magic lies. The kind of magic Prospero was capable of on his fantastic island.

The types of magic that Shakespeare–Prospero, Eliot, and Holdstock

147

are after partake of the very same nature. The magicians bring characters that experience a serious lack in their lives to a miraculous world, create circumstances that allow these characters to lose their selves — literally in some cases, owing to, for instance, the hollowings in Ryhope Wood — and thus enable them to find their selves again. Magic may turn loss into gain; it may create life out of death. "[D]eath which is a portal into a realm of the rich and strange — a death which becomes a sort of birth" (Brooks 69) — is only remembered in *The Waste Land* through the fragment of the song from *The Tempest:* "Those are pearls that were his eyes" (1.2.401). What was once lost is found and better appreciated than ever in Shakespeare's play; what was lost a long time ago and has kept getting lost ever since is hoped to be found by following what the thunder said; while, finally, Holdstock presents the restoration of the characters and the world, combining the Shakespearean and the Eliotian methods. In *The Hollowing*, Alex's life is regained and Richard's life is completed through reuniting with his son and finding a new partner in love, while the common quest of finding Alex offers fulfillment for Lytton, too, who is at last given the opportunity to meet Huxley and who will see his precious Ryhope Wood as a manifestation of Huxley's mind, restored more or less after Alex the "tumor" (103) has been removed from the forest. Lacan's life shows signs of healing, as well, although his case is the most problematic because what he desires and gains has never been real. Finally, Helen's emotional life is restored by Richard's love, and the novel — somewhat mysteriously — ends with "the sound of a wolf triumphant ... cut off" (314), while readers realize that Helen has eventually gone to hunt down her Coyote.

The magic Ryhope Wood is imbued with, therefore, proves surprisingly manifold. Most importantly, it gives an opportunity for everyone who enters the Wood to fulfill their personal quests, however different in nature these may be. The hollowings provide a spatial and temporal labyrinth for these wandering persons, mysteriously enlarging the scope of their adventures. Time thus becomes relative, and the past strongly interacts with the present. This feature of the woodlands again throws light on how the human mind works: the co-existence of the personal and the collective unconscious is, at the same time, a co-existence of various time dimensions, where the past — unconsciously, of course — significantly influences the present. Another manifestation of the same mental function may be observed in the mythagos themselves, which are combined projections of one's personal and collective imagination. As Helen puts it when speaking of Alex's collosi-mythagos, "[w]hen Alex created these monstrosities, he drew on several parts of his unconscious: personal imagination was just the model; forgotten folk-lore was the shape" (147). In addition, the collective unconscious is shown to be indeed common to the various minds: no wonder that, for instance, "[t]here are hundreds of them in the wood, the stereotyped Robin Hood. It's a combination of race memory and enriched imagination" (132).

Ryhope Wood, as a mental landscape of humanity, so to speak, presents a fusion of mythology, turning one's personal quest into an imitation of mankind's wanderings. Holdstock presents characters from various nations, even if some of them — the Finns for one — have only a minor role in the story. As everyone is searching for mythagos connected to their own pasts, the presentation of diverse ethnicities already promises the variety of myths to be encountered in the Wood: Helen's Coyote is as much a personal enemy as a mythological character of the Indian tribe she comes from; Lacan's mythical wife belongs to the Biblical Babel story familiar throughout the Judeo-Christian world; and the Finlanders' quest centers on Tuonela, the otherworld of Finnish mythology, and the hero Vainamoinen (118), protagonist of the Kalevala.

Not only does the diversity of nationalities serve to create an image of mankind, but Holdstock also carefully selects his characters to provide various *types* of people so as to reach his desired effect. Lytton — true follower of *Mythago Wood*'s Huxley — represents the obsessed scientist type, someone who understands and treats even magic as science. He builds machines to keep away mythagos and to locate a person's protogenomorph, a scientific term for something most people would not acknowledge as a scientifically identified phenomenon, for it is defined as one's "free spirit" or "first consciousness" or "the first dreaming form of the dreaming mind" (*The Hollowing* 184–85).

Lacan, on the other hand, is a person not of the mind but of the heart: embodying the romantic lover, he is in love with the ideal he desires and which has never existed in the real world: the most important part of his life, Matilde was only his "dream ... made real" (281). There is nothing new under the sun: Prospero (to return to Shakespeare's magical island) has already articulated this problem: "We are such stuff / As dreams are made on, and our little life / Is rounded with a sleep" (4.1.156–58). Magic, for Lacan, was as real as it is for Lytton — the disparity, however, is striking. Lytton does not *want* to differentiate between magic and reality, because that is the way he can fulfill his dream. Lacan, in contrast, *could not* differentiate between charm and real life, which caused his destruction; therefore, he forces himself to tell the two worlds apart even when he finds a chance to "resurrect" his Matilde for a while through the figure, or, as he says, the "shadow of the shadow" (281), of Sarin.

Helen's attitude to life and magic stands, in a way, in between that of her two colleagues. If we have Lytton of the mind and Lacan of the heart, we could see Helen as someone of the blood — the natural, instinctive woman. She, accordingly, considers magic as an integral part of her life — thanks to her Native American roots. Magical thinking is part of her cultural heritage, and even her personal quest is based on the fact that what is taken as magical for others shapes reality for the Native Americans. In a peculiar way, her drive can be perceived as just the opposite of Lacan's: she wants to "undo" magic that has been so negatively influencing her life, while the Frenchman seeks to re-establish the magic that ruined his life, hoping that this would restore his happiness. He starts hesitating doing so only when he is given a real opportunity to do so. His hesitation has roots in his recognition that magic and reality are incompatible and reality may not, in fact, influence magic, which has a life of its own — as a result, he is afraid to love Sarin because he envisions the very same loss that he suffered when Matilde "died." Helen's determination, on the other hand, stems from her natural belief that magic is as real as any other part of life, so a person may change its effects if she wishes.

Because of the obsessions Lytton, Lacan, and Helen respectively have, it is much more difficult to identify ourselves with them than with Richard, who fulfils the role of Everyman in the novel. Since his starting point is as "normal" as our own lives (we hope) are, and since we follow him as he gradually grows from a total skeptic into a believer, we may recognize ourselves in his behavior. He stands for the average, and his desire is the easiest to understand for another person, since all he wants is to get his normal life back: first his son; then a partner to fill in the gap left by his wife's departure.

Finally, Alex as a type assumes as much importance as all the other characters in the team of explorers. Emblematically, the entrance to his world is guarded by the effigies of Jesus and Saint Sebastian (150), two symbolic characters of agony — for Alex is the suffering son, the lost child, who waits to be redeemed by the father. His character strongly connects to Richard's and thus becomes inseparable from the everyman image.

Although pictured as someone mentally incomplete and mentally-physically imprisoned, he takes journeys as adventurous as those who are looking for him — the difference being that he mind-travels, dreams; but as Jung observed, dreams interact with reality ("Relations" 75–76). As a consequence, he becomes an active figure in the plot, directing the other characters via his dreaming. Nevertheless, his impotence is central in this complex presentation of humanity's quest for rebirth: while all the members of Lytton's team appear active, determined to change their own fates and ready to act for this sacred goal, they get trapped by the Wood even if this is not so evident when contrasted to Alex's position. The boy, however, reminds the reader of the fact that whoever enters this enchanted wood becomes entrapped: there's no real escape until the quest is completed. The quest itself binds the character, no matter how much room they are given to move about physically. The quest takes place *inside*— for Ryhope Wood, after all, is a mental landscape.

The Quest for Meaning

Holdstock keeps his reader imprisoned in his fantastic wood — and if we enter deep enough, we find Alex in his Green Chapel, driving us even further into our minds to find the green chapel we know of and to encounter the myths connected to it in our collective unconscious. For what Alex experiences in the Wood is given a logical, or, rather, psychological, explanation: not only was he familiar with the legend of Sir Gawain and the Green Knight, but it was one of his most vivid memories from the past that he was able to recall with a clear consciousness, and thus the ruined cathedral he created for himself as a hiding and healing place gives the impression of being solely the product of his personal unconscious. However, the Green Chapel resides in our collective unconscious, too; therefore, Alex's shelter has a strong symbolic content in the novel.

The Green Chapel in the Arthurian cycle — and thus in the European cultural understanding — is a symbol of mankind's quest and, at the same time, human fallibility: Gawain, who as the youngest of Arthur's knights neatly matches Alex's position in the novel, does complete his quest by finding the chapel and meeting the Green Knight to answer his challenge, but he also has to learn that even the most virtuous are to fall in face of the threat of mortality. The great quest (which is also a great test) — the desire to be virtuous and worthy of the prize — and mankind's wish to avoid mortality are coded in Western culture as another mythical quest from Arthurian legend, the quest for the Holy Grail (versions of which include the legend of the Fisher King), and provide the basis for Eliot's *The Waste Land*.

The Grail's shape and its etymology vary from myth to myth. The uncertainty about exactly what the Grail is forms an inevitable part of the idea: the Grail is a secret that has become taboo, proves invisible to the unworthy, and appears in various forms even to the worthy, unveiling its secret to a diverse extent for the questers (Hoppál 337). Meaning is, then, a central problem of these myths, as the legend of the Fisher King demonstrates. As Hugh Kenner asserts, the Chapel Perilous is the place where the quester needs to search for meaning: when he asks the right question about the meaning of the things shown to him, the objects gain meaning and the king's wound becomes healed (190), which emphasizes the importance of the *search* for meaning. In a broken world, one that Eliot presents in *The Waste Land,* one has to ask for meaning, as Kenner argues (190).

The Waste Land Eliot conjured up from so many fragments, similarly to Jack's mind in *Ancient Echoes* or to Ryhope Wood in *The Hollowing*, is a mental landscape meant to be that of the world if we consider Eliot's artistic purpose, but, factually speaking, it must be that of Eliot himself. As Conrad Aiken suggests:

> We are invited into a mind, a world, which is a "broken bundle of mirrors," a "heap of broken images." Isn't it that Mr. Eliot, finding it "impossible to say just what he means"— to recapitulate, to enumerate all the events and discoveries and memories that make a consciousness — has emulated the "magic lantern" that throws "the nerves in pattern on a screen?" [97].

The pattern (which is fully emotional, as Aiken argues [98], yet is terribly intellectual, as Eliot hints through his ever-disputed footnotes) is for us to detect. The task is not easy, as we wander in a waste land of mythologies, and accordingly, what we find there is a heap of fragments. In the mind of modern man myths appear in a distorted form, and the restoration of the world is possible through identifying and completing these fragments. Holdstock presents a similar experience: in *Ancient Echoes*, Jack must find the missing component of something that first appears as a personal myth but later, through many steps of identification, turns out to be a collective myth, while the questers in Ryhope Wood regularly come across the distorted shapes of mythagos, representing the deterioration that has taken place in our understanding of myths. Holdstock's novels, along the lines of *The Waste Land,* heavily express the sense of being lost in a world mostly unfamiliar to those roaming it. This feeling of misplacement and incomprehension manifests itself through a two-way channel. Not only is modern man puzzled by the inexplicable nature of the world composed of broken myths, but representatives of forgotten myths are equally perplexed when facing the modern world: Tiresias, Baalgor, and Sarin share the same fate to a certain extent.

The questers, however, prove successful as there is either a clear triumph (Jack, Richard, Alex) or a promise of accomplishment (Lytton, Helen, Lacan); similarly, Eliot's quest promises success — both for himself as regenerator of the world in artistic terms and for his poetic characters through his guidance. Since success has been defined as perceiving meaning, the question is what kind of meaning can be achieved through the various quests. On the level of the individual, the character, obviously, must find the meaning of his life in order to restore his own world, his own completeness. On a larger scale, however, these quests embody the important warning that ignorance is, in the long run, lethal. For Jack it is highly dangerous not to understand the relationship between Greenface and Grayface. Ryhope Wood is equally perilous for the scientific team because of their own productions of distorted mythagos, let alone Alex's, which are even more deformed by the boy's wild imagination. Eliot's *Waste Land* characters are mostly so ignorant that they do not even recognize the peril they live with. Thus all these texts emphasize that distorted myths *are* hazardous.

To restore the world is to remember the myths with their original meaning and content; what defines our psyche is a series of interrelated myths. Eliot's *Waste Land* relies upon the poet's enlightenment about a striking similarity "between vegetation myths of the rebirth of the year, the fertility myths of the rebirth of the potency of man, the Christian story of Resurrection, and the Grail legend of purification," as drawn from Jessie Weston's *From Ritual to Romance* (Matthiessen 110). Sacrifice is in the center of these myths, but an emptied sacrifice, having been deprived of its original meaning, cannot bring salvation or regeneration: it will issue death, without the magical quality of being able to turn it into new life.

This is exactly why every attempt at making humans conscious of the knowledge long-forgotten myths and rituals or even gods carry is to be called back to life. This quality has made *The Waste Land* one of the twentieth century's most important poems. This is the very quality, I suggest, that makes Holdstock's fantasy world so attractive and precious. Eliot made an attempt at collecting the pieces scattered about his mind and put them together to recreate cohesion within an utterly collapsed world. Holdstock, more than seventy years later, turned to another genre in order to succeed in the same attempt: he, too, collected fragments and used the magic of imagination to complete the missing parts and to recreate — where impossible to restore — the myths we all carry somewhere in the back of our minds. By completing and reinterpreting the myths, Holdstock not only asks for meaning to heal the wounds of the world, but also provides meaning that renews the dying myths, the dying world. For death is inevitable, but we do not have to live "in the waste land of modern life" where "even death is sterile" (Brooks 69): as the protagonist of *The Waste Land* could remember the magic of *The Tempest* connected to the transforming power of death, so Holdstock's characters may experience the power of reminiscence in restoring the world — personal and universal alike.

The miraculous transformation, the sea-change, turns the lifeless reality into a work of art, providing for it new meaning, new interpretation. Deprived of meaning, Eliot points out in *The Waste Land,* religion, myth and literature — culture — are dead and in need of regeneration. Thus it is understandable that Eliot turned to Shakespeare and conjured up Prospero's magic while trying to regenerate the human world centuries later. And now, reading Holdstock's fiction, we may connect Holdstock to Shakespeare (instead of nothing to nothing), and the path leads through a modern waste land. Those who are ready for this journey will experience themselves that *The Hollowing* and *Ancient Echoes* are real pearls in today's fantasy literature — rich and strange in their inherent power of regeneration.

NOTES

1. Provided that we can speak of reality at all when discussing the workings of the brain, relying on the shaky science of psychology, which, in the present case, is Jungian.

2. Whether this connection was established consciously by Holdstock is questionable; however, the author would not object to acknowledging the effect a poem had, arising out of his unconscious after having read it once in his life: When Garth wonders how Jack could be familiar with the faces he sees in his daydreaming, he asks if the boy had seen those anywhere in town before. Holdstock provides us here with an introduction to how the mind works: "Jack understood the point of the question:

if this savage painting of his dream-hunters was represented elsewhere in Exburgh, then he might have seen the faces, registered them subliminally, used them to form his hallucinatory encounters with the running couple" [*Ancient Echoes* 47–48].

3. "Once Zhuangzi dreamt he was a butterfly, a butterfly flitting and fluttering around, happy with himself and doing as he pleased. He didn't know he was Zhuangzi. Suddenly he woke up and there he was, solid and unmistakable Zhuangzi. But he didn't know if he was Zhuangzi who had dreamt he was a butterfly, or a butterfly dreaming he was Zhuangzi. Between Zhuangzi and a butterfly there must be *some* distinction! This is called the Transformation of Things" (Watson 49).

4. On Jungian dream interpretation, see Jung, "Relations," especially 75–83.

Works Cited

Aiken, Conrad. "An Anatomy of Melancholy." Cox and Hinchliffe 91–99.

Brooks, Cleanth. "*The Waste Land:* Critique of the Myth." Jay Martin, ed. *A Collection of Critical Essays on "The Waste Land."* Englewood Cliffs, NJ: Prentice Hall, 1968. 59–86.

Cox, C. B., and Arnold P. Hinchliffe, eds. *T. S. Eliot: The Waste Land.* Houndmills: Macmillan, 1968.

Holdstock, Robert. *Ancient Echoes.* 1996. New York: ROC, 1997.

_____. *The Hollowing.* 1993. New York: ROC, 1995.

Hoppál, Mihály, ed. *Mitológiai Enciklopédia.* Vols. 1–2. Budapest: Gondolat, 1988.

Jung, Carl Gustav. "The Concept of the Collective Unconscious." *The Portable Jung* 59–69.

_____. *The Portable Jung.* Ed. Joseph Campbell. Transl. R. F. C. Hull. New York: Penguin, 1980.

_____. "The Relations Between the Ego and the Unconscious." *The Portable Jung* 70–138.

_____. "The Structure of the Psyche." *The Portable Jung* 23–46.

Kenner, Hugh. "The Invisible Poet." Cox and Hinchliffe 168–99.

Watson, Burton, trans. *The Complete Works of Chuang Tzu.* New York: Columbia University Press, 1968.

10

"So many names in so many tongues...": Allusive Mythology in *Celtika*

C. W. Sullivan III

A first-time reader of Robert Holdstock's *Celtika: Book One of the Merlin Codex*[1] can certainly be pardoned if, after reading the prologue and the first chapter, he or she closes the book to wonder whether or not the cover and the text belong together. The title on the cover, containing the words "Celtika" and "Merlin," seems to promise an Arthurian novel or series, but the prologue takes place in the Greece of Jason, some 20 years after the *Argo's* famous voyage, and the first chapter is set, some 700 years later, in a Finland containing echoes of the *Kalevala*. But as he proved with the publication of *Mythago Wood*, Holdstock is no mere borrower of mythic names; he is an author who understands that it is necessary to use mythic and legendary materials conscientiously such that the nature of the original character or story is reflected in the new one.[2] Moreover, Holdstock understands how mythology works, or in Joseph Campbell's language, how mythology "functions."[3] As a result, *Celtika* contains not only original treatments of the stories of Merlin and Jason, treatments which are conscientious and do not violate the natures of the original characters, but also combines these obvious myths and legends with less well-known materials and allusive references to still others to create a beautifully woven narrative tapestry of myth, legend, history, and culture.

Merlin

Holdstock's Merlin is an enchanter, a young enchanter when *Celtika* opens, living in a time or times long before the reign of King Arthur. When a fantasy writer uses a well-known figure, such as Merlin or Arthur or a dragon, he or she knows that the character already exists in the reader's mind having come there from earlier narratives. The good writers take such well-known figures and make them their own; the writer's creative originality making this Merlin or this Arthur or this dragon different in some (usually important) way from previous Merlins, Arthurs, and dragons. But the writer has to do this, has to add to the original, without violating the essential nature of that original. Holdstock's Merlin has been alive for centuries, but that is not the creatively original part; what is interesting about this Merlin is that he ages only when and if he uses his magical powers.

Merlin, it seems (especially in this first book), is on, or has wandered a bit from, a "long path" and he is not alone (more about that later). He is curious, has wandered the world studying magic, and has had many adventures. More than 700 years before the story told in this book, he sailed with Jason aboard the *Argo*; more recently, he has become aware of two things: Jason may not be dead, and Jason's sons were not slain by Medea. As a result, when the reader meets Merlin in this novel, he is on a journey to a frozen lake in Finland where, he rightly believes, the *Argo* had taken Jason some 20 years after the Golden Fleece adventure. There, Merlin will spend some of his magic and, therefore, some of his life, to raise the *Argo* and Jason and to begin the adventure that will structure the books: the search for Jason's sons. It is only near the end of this first book that Merlin's future with Arthur is even mentioned.

Jason

The Jason of the prologue has aged in the 20 years since the Golden Fleece adventure, has lost the favor of Hera, has spent the intervening years looking for the bodies of his sons, and is now alone aboard the *Argo* in a Greek harbor. At the end of the prologue, the *Argo* sails away under some power other than human, even though not Hera's, and carries Jason with her — as Merlin rightly surmises — to that lake in Finland. Throughout the course of this novel, however, the reader hears in flashbacks the story of Jason that accords with the accounts in Bulfinch's and Hamilton's mythologies: the building of the *Argo*, the recruiting of the crew (including Merlin, known then as Antiokus), the relationship with and desertion of Medea for Glauce, and Medea's (supposed) killing of their two sons.

Here, as with the character and story of Merlin, Holdstock builds on the story that even a general reading public should know. But in Holdstock's novel, the *Argo* has preserved a spark of Jason's life as well as the integrity of his physical body in this icy lake. Merlin braves the local spirits, calls to the *Argo*, and watches as she rises from the depths. Jason comes back to life and, with Merlin's help and the help of Finnish shipwrights, rebuilds the *Argo*, placing a new and icy Finnish spirit, Mielikki, in the heart of the ship. Hera has long been gone, but there is a more ancient and unnamed spirit in the *Argo* as well. Jason and Merlin recruit a crew from the various locals and from other "pilgrims" to the lake, including some Celtic Britons, and sail south in search of Jason's sons, whom Medea (who, like Merlin, has also wandered the "long path") had only pretended to slay and had then sent to a different time/place so that Jason would never find them. This last element, the pretended slaying, is Holdstock's significant departure from the original story, and it is the departure that makes *Celtika* possible.

History

In addition to adapting the legendary story of Merlin and the legendary or mythological story of Jason, Holdstock also draws the actual, if little-known, history of the Celtic tribes that invaded Greece (and many other places) in the third century BCE. It is a matter of historical record that the Celts invaded Greece as the empire of Alexander the Great began to fall apart. The first invasion was made by a band of wandering Celts, led by Bolgios, who descended into Macedonia from the Danube, fought at least one decisive battle, and "overran and plundered the country ... before disappearing with their booty" (Herm 36).

The second wave of Celts, led by Brennus, was larger and more organized. The army may have numbered 30,000 men and was sufficient to sweep aside defenders at the Pass of Thermopylae and advance on and destroy Delphi and its oracular priestess, Pytheia, in about the year 279 BCE. Brennus was slain shortly thereafter, and the remnants of his army retreated north and disappeared, never reaching home. A third invasion was less successful, but many of the survivors continued east and settled in, among other regions, Galatia (36–41).

In Holdstock's *Celtika*, there is a "great quest" (60) of Celtic tribes led by a chieftain named Brennos and two lesser chieftains, Bolgios and Achichoros — the last also a tribal leader from the historical invasions (Herm 37). The names of the tribes involved are also accurately Celtic: among them the Biturges, the Avernii, the Senones, the Ambarii, the Carnutes, and the Trocmii (Holdstock 195). Moreover, if I have calculated Holdstock's chronology correctly, his Celtic invasion of Greece occurs in the third century BCE; also, the geographical route of the invaders that Holdstock describes is similar to that of the second historical invasion. Brennos's huge army invades from the north, sees little significant action until their victorious battle at Thermopylae, and moves on south to sack several shrines, including Pythia's at Delphi. Brennos's army then begins to fragment, the other leaders splitting their forces off and going their own way, and Holdstock leaves the Celtic forces at that point to follow Merlin and Jason in Jason's quest for his sons in the final chapter of this first book.

Allusive Myth and Legend

Against the better-known history and stories discussed above, Holdstock places mythological, legendary, and cultural references that I have called "allusive": "1: an implied or indirect reference especially in literature; *also*: the use of such references. 2: the act of alluding to or hinting at something" ("Allusion," *Merriam-Webster*). It is the second part of this definition that I wish to invoke. Holdstock uses a number of terms and names that the reader might well think refer to something, but most readers will, in all probability, not know what those referents are — although they might well feel that there is "something" to which Holdstock is alluding. Nor will their ignorance[4] of those referents impede either their reading or understanding of the story. In the same vein, the reader who does not know that the dwarf names in *The Hobbit* come from *The Poetic Edda* (or can be found in Snorri Sturluson's *The Prose Edda*) will not find that lack of knowledge a hindrance in reading Tolkien's novel. But for the knowledgeable reader, Holdstock, like Tolkien, weaves a rich, complex, and rewarding tapestry that reverberates with the resonances of actual, rather than invented, ancient tales. Holdstock's allusive elements come, primarily, from two sources: the Finnish materials found in the *Kalevala* and, in this first book in the series, materials from Welsh Celtic and Irish Celtic narratives.[5]

The words "Finland" or "Finnish" do not appear in Holdstock's text, although from the description of the bitter winter weather through which Merlin travels and from the strangeness of the place names and the people's names, any reader might assume that the setting is somewhere in Scandinavia — or a fictitious equivalent of Scandinavia. But allusive references to Finland and Finnish materials appear early. After the *Argo* takes Jason away "to a safe place of burial," there is the following section heading: "*The northern country of Pohjola, 700 years later*," and a bit farther on down the page, Merlin thinks about a year ago when he had first left the "plains and marshes of Karelia and crossed the ice-bridge to the mountains of the north" (Holdstock 4). Pohjola means "North Farm" in Finnish, but has occasionally been used to refer to an area of Finland and sometimes all of Finland itself, as Holdstock seems to use it here; and Karelia is "a large region on both sides of the Russo-Finnish border" and is the area in which most of the *Kalevala* materials were collected (Magoun 394). With these allusive references, as well as others, Holdstock places the action within a geographical context for the knowledgeable reader without confusing or destroying the context for the less knowledgeable reader who may think that these are invented names.

Other names Holdstock uses early in *Celtika* come more directly from Finnish mythology. One of Merlin's traveling companions mentions "Tuonela, the black lake" (Holdstock 18), which, too, appears in the *Kalevala*, sometimes as "Death's Domain," and it might also be the name of a god (Magoun 409). Lemkainon is the name of a Finnish mythological figure, usually spelled Lemminkainen in the *Kalevala*. Lemminkainen is, with Vainamoinen and Ilmarinen, one of the three major gods in the narrative. He is a warrior, an adventurer, and a lover; and he is sometimes characterized as irresponsible (395–96). Holdstock draws on the warrior part as Merlin tells the Finnish warriors he has just met that he "was the young warrior who had last come this way five generations ago and fought with their ancestor hero, Lemkainon, against the bear-skin shrouded Kullaavo, the dark spirit of the land" (Holdstock 11). But the reference to this figure from the *Kalevala* only appears once in *Celtika*.

Holdstock makes much more extensive use of the Finnish figure Mielikki in his novel. In the *Kalevala*, Mielikki is often referred to as "mistress of the forest" or "forest daughter-in-law" rather than by name (Magoun, poems 14, 32, and 46), and as such she is asked to help find or to protect various animals. She is also the wife of Tapio, himself a forest deity (404).[6] A more interesting aspect is her role in the creation of the bear (poem 46), for it places her in the company of other mythological women, usually hunter figures, like Artemis. In this first volume of the Merlin Codex, it seems to me that Holdstock, although he calls her "the Lady of the Forest" (Holdstock 92), draws on this fiercer aspect of Mielikki for his character. When the ship builder Lemanku is blinded while helping reconstruct the *Argo*, he says that Jason wanted the best wood, and so he, Lemanku, took a tree from Mielikki's grove and has been blinded by the goddess as punishment. "I thought I'd done everything right. I'll pay for that mistake with my life as well as the dark. You all will. You'll need gentle gods to help you if you sail in that ship now" (93). Mielikki's objection to her tree being used in the *Argo*, it seems, is that the boat is for foreigners, not for her own Finnish people, and throughout *Celtika* her presence in the *Argo* is both powerful — therefore, necessary — and dangerous.

After sailing from Tuonela, the Black Lake, and out into the Atlantic, Jason points the *Argo* towards Britain, "Alba" or "Ghostland" in *Celtika*, and although Mielikki and other Finnish elements continue to play major roles in the novel, by and large, Celtic allusions replace Finnish ones. Celtic characters, in the persons of Urtha, a Celtic chieftain, and his men, whom Jason has agreed to take home if they will help crew the ship, become more central in the narrative. In addition to the historical aspects already mentioned, Holdstock alludes to a great deal of Celtic literature and culture. When Urtha returns to his fort, he finds it burned to the ground; his father-in-law, one of the few survivors, asks him what he has brought back from his year-long quest, and the items he mentions ("Lugh's lance" and "the razor and tusks [from] the first of all bristle-backed hog-boars," for example) are allusions to the Irish stories of the Tuatha Dé Danann and to the successful quest of Culhwch found in the Welsh prose narrative, "Culhwch and Olwen," respectively (Holdstock 135–36). Urtha finds the body of one of his sons and says that he will bury the boy in "Herne's Grove" (129). Herne the Hunter is reputed to be the leader of the Wild Hunt, the hunt for unshriven souls. The deities watching over the field around Urtha's hill fort are named Scaithach and Morrigan (173), names which can be found in Irish mythology: the former belongs to the woman who taught Cuchulainn his warcraft, and the latter is the name of one of the prominent goddesses of war. As Urtha continues his journey with Jason and they leave Britain to follow the Celtic army that is heading for Greece, the narrator mentions that that army has been "gathering for more than two seasons under the watchful eye of Daanu" (173), a reference to Danu or Dana, the mother of the Irish divine race, the Tuatha Dé Danann, and therefore the head deity of the Irish pantheon. Needless to say, Holdstock makes none of these identifications; his use of these names and terms is, again, allusive.

Allusions to Celtic mythology and legend, as well as history and culture, come thick and fast in the last two-thirds of the novel. "Brigga's oak" and the oath "Brigga's blood!" (125, 172) refer to the Celtic goddess better known as Brigit. The "three cowled, cloaked matrons" who appear behind Urtha's children (151) are most likely an allusion to the Celtic triple goddess, a concept that appears throughout Celtic literature and art. Weapons are dedicated to Dana, Tuatates, and Nemetona, mentioned as "protecting gods" (196), although Holdstock does not explain Tuatates is associated with blood sacrifice or that Nemetoma is a deity of war. The "horse-head amulet, a bone carving of Epona" (153) invokes not only the goddess, but also her main totem, the horse, which could be a sacred animal among the Celts; in fact, toward the end of the novel, the Celtic leaders who break their forces off from the main army to seek wealth on their own swear to rejoin the main army, and to show how serious they are, each chief sacrifices his favorite horse. "The entrails were burned and the mane and its strip of hide cut from each, scraped of flesh and presented to the other as a belt" (322). Such allusions abound in this novel.

Conclusion

I chose "So many names in so many tongues..." (267), the words with which Holdstock refers to the Macedonian conqueror, Alexander the Great, as part of the title for this essay for two reasons.

First, there are, literally, many names in many tongues in *Celtika*. Holdstock draws from familiar stories about Jason and the Golden Fleece and about Merlin the Magician. They form the core of the narrative. In addition, as I have shown, the novel is full of names and terms from Greek, Finnish, and Celtic myth, legend, history, and culture. That Holdstock is able to weave these materials together in a coherent narrative is due in part to his artistry as a novelist and in part to the similarity such materials have from culture to culture and from age to age. As Joseph Campbell, among others, has shown, the Hero Tale, the magic tale, the Märchen, the legend, and the folktale are similarly structured and have similar themes throughout, at the very least, the western world. Thus, Holdstock can interweave a Greek tale with a Celtic/Arthurian tale secure in the knowledge that the two will fit together because they have similar structures and themes — and he has the ability to do it very well.

Second, and more important, perhaps, is what the inclusion of mythic and legendary materials brings to an original narrative. In his 1989 introduction to *The Mabinogion*, Gwyn Jones, discussing the specific elements in the stories in the Four Branches and in "Culhwch and Olwen," argues that these stories present us "not with myth but with the reminiscence of myth.... By virtue of these veiled and ancient sightings, imperfectly understood yet fully apprehended, The Mabinogion involves its readers in the wonders of time" (xxxv). Rather than "reminiscence," which sounds a bit wistful, I would say "reverberation" or, even better, "resonance" of myth. Similarly to the elements in the Four Branches that we do not fully comprehend or the fragments of tales referred to in "Culhwch and Olwen" the whole of which we will never hear, the allusions that Holdstock provides in *Celtika* resonate with the authority of ancient narrative because they have come to us, by the hand of Robert Holdstock, to be apprehended, not comprehended, from actual ancient narrative.

NOTES

1. Holdstock's Merlin Codex includes *Celtika, The Iron Grail,* and *The Broken Kings*. Although he referred to the Codex as complete, Holdstock had left the way open at the end of *The Broken Kings* for a fourth book — one he would never write.

2. For a complete discussion of the concept of "conscientious use," see my article, "Conscientious Use," available online at www.celtic-cultural-studies.com.

3. For Joseph Campbell's "Four Essential Functions of a Mythology," see Campbell's 1964 book, *Occidental Mythology,* 519–21.

4. I use "ignorant" here merely to categorize those readers who know little or nothing of Finnish or Celtic mythology and legend; I am not using it as a pejorative term.

5. I have chosen to give examples of the Finnish and Celtic allusions. There are, of course, allusions to Greek myths and legends as well, but as they are so much more widely known than the Finnish or the Celtic, it is difficult to see them having the same allusive quality as the other two.

6. Juha Y. Pentikainen identifies Mielikki as Tapio's daughter-in-law in *Kalevala Mythology,* 262.

WORKS CITED

"Allusion." *Merriam-Webster Online Dictionary.* 26 December 2009 <http://www.-merriam-webster.com/dictionary/allusive>.

Part Two: The Novels

Campbell, Joseph. *Occidental Mythology*. 1964. New York: Viking, 1970.
Herm, Gerhard. *The Celts*. New York: St. Martin's, 1975.
Holdstock, Robert. *Celtika*. New York: Simon and Schuster, 2001.
Jones, Gwyn, and Thomas Jones, eds. and trans. *The Mabinogion*. London: Dent, 1989.
Magoun, Francis P., Jr., trans. *The Kalevala*. Comp. Lars Lonnrot. Cambridge: Harvard University Press, 1963.
Pentikainen, Juha Y. *Kalevala Mythology*. Trans. Ritva Poom. Bloomington, IN: Indiana University Press, 1999.
Sullivan, C. W., III. "Conscientious Use: Welsh Celtic Myth and Legend in Fantastic Fiction." *Celtic Cultural Studies* 4 (2006). 26 December 2009 <http://www.celtic-cultural-studies.com/papers/04/sullivan-02.html>.

11

Thresholds, Polders, and Crosshatches in the Merlin Codex

Tom Shippey

Academic literary criticism has passed through several unsuccessful decades in the recent past, losing the intellectual prestige it once had in the United Kingdom, and losing a high proportion of its "market share" of students in the United States. By contrast, there seemed at the time when I entered the profession (1965) to be at least two potential growth areas, one being "narratology"—that is, the study of what makes a successful story, though the term itself was not invented till rather later—the other being the study of fantasy and science fiction, two of the most popular and also most distinctive literary forms of the twentieth century. Neither promise, however, was fulfilled. Narratology turned into something rather like the early modern art of rhetoric, with a bewildering variety of terms to describe rather obvious narrative devices, but no real insight into what made one rather than another powerful or appropriate.[1] The study of fantasy and science fiction (as of popular literature generally) meanwhile remained a marginal activity, unlikely to lead to prestige and promotion within the trade. It is true that some bold and hardy individuals continued to pursue their own interest, notable among them the founders and editors of *The Journal for the Fantastic in the Arts* (*JFA*), with its accompanying annual conference, held for many years in Fort Lauderdale, now in Orlando, Florida, and bringing together with unusual openness academics, writers, and publishers. It is also true that there have been some recent critical works both ambitious and well-informed, such as Brian Attebery's *Strategies of Fantasy* (1992) and now Farah Mendlesohn's *Rhetorics of Fantasy* (2008), but on the whole the current of post-structuralist writing has been in other directions, as critics have turned away from what has been a stunning and bewildering outpouring of creative talent within the various modes of "the fantastic" to the easier tasks of political exegesis, identifying with victim groups, and flirting with other disciplines, notably philosophy and linguistics.

How is one to define modern fantasy? For many years the approved academic definition was supplied by Tzvetan Todorov, who argued, in essence, that it dealt with events for which there were two possible solutions—either error or hallucination on the part of the observer/reporter, or some non-natural cause: "The fantastic occupies the duration of this uncertainty" (25). Like several other critical theses, this definition worked well enough for a very few literary cases, most of them short, safely canonical and well in the past, like Henry James's "The Turn of the Screw," Kipling's "The Man who would be King," de Maupassant's "Le Horla," and a few others one could add, such as the ending of James Blish's *A Case of Conscience* (1958) (though there it applied only to the ending and not the main body of the narrative). It did not fit at all well, however, with probably more than 99% of modern commercial fantasy. Still, it was expressed with careful academic rigor, had been invented by a respected critic, and had furthermore been written in the first place in French: it was accordingly repeated again and again by academic critics, to such an extent that the editors of *JFA* (it is said) imposed an effective embargo on any re-appearance. Does *The Lord of the Rings* maintain a thousand pages of uncertainty? Or Terry Pratchett's twenty-plus "Discworld" novels? One wonders why some similar question was not put to Todorov in the first place, before his book was ever finished.

Yet there is a sort of a point, a glimmer of understanding, which may be rescued even from Todorov's theorizing, and it is that modern fantasy does often deal with or find congenial what one might call boundary situations, so much so indeed that John Clute and John Grant's valuable *Encyclopedia of Fantasy* (1997) has done its best to categorize and clarify some of them. They introduce, for instance, the idea of "the polder," defined within fantasy as "enclaves ... demarcated by boundaries ... from the surrounding world" (772). It is part of the definition of the polder that these boundaries have to be maintained by some significant figure, the most familiar example being Tom Bombadil in Tolkien, with his little world within which his power is absolute, but whose boundaries he himself will not cross. As they define polders, however, Clute and Grant bring in other terms, such as "thresholds," "portals," and "crosshatches." Tracing these definitions introduces yet others including "wainscots"—the world of the magic-users in J. K. Rowling's Harry Potter sequence is probably the most prominent wainscot of modern times, though her books appeared too late to be included in Clute and Grant's discussion. Portal fantasies have been familiar since *Alice in Wonderland*, while a good example of a crosshatch might be the urban fantasies of Charles de Lint, where fantasy creatures co-exist with a modern Canadian setting. Yet, clearly, these terms overlap. What they have in common is the idea of crossing over from the mundane world to some sort of "otherworld" without—and this distinguishes them from the very common Tolkien mode of "heroic fantasy"—losing touch with the former. They do not inhabit a period of uncertainty, as Todorov said, but offer a continuing state of duality, or multiplicity, which they further suggest is knowable, or reachable, for some and under the right conditions.

One of the most original variations on this general theme is that of the mythago, as invented by Robert Holdstock. The term is discussed elsewhere in this volume, so I will indicate only the derivation from "myth" and "imago" (noted by Clute and Grant 674), to which I would add the obvious idea of "ago," of past time. Mythagos are "heroic legendary characters from our inherited unconscious" (Holdstock's own definition cited by Clute and Grant, loc. cit.), but in his work they inhabit a particularly varied polder called Ryhope Wood. One might note here the particular fascination which woods seem to have had for the English imagination, all the way from the enchanted wood of *A Midsummer Night's Dream* to T. H. White's Forest Sauvage or Tolkien's Mirkwood, Old Forest, and Fangorn, and taking in, among much else, the Wild Wood of *The Wind in the Willows* and the Hundred-Acre Wood of *Winnie the Pooh*. Why should this be so? Clute and Grant suggest that forests represent a barrier, while woods carry a "connotation of encounter and TRANSFORMATION" (362; note that small capitals in citations from Clute and Grant indicate that there is an entry under that heading elsewhere in their *Encyclopedia*). I would add that in both woods and forests one may easily lose one's bearings, physical and moral: they offer a kind of invisibility and with it irresponsibility, as in Shakespeare's Forest of Arden or Robin Hood's Sherwood Forest. The age of the trees, furthermore, their uncanny powers of reproduction, and the way they may be linked together all suggest powerful continuity, a feeling especially congenial to English authors in a crowded country where it is common experience to find childhood pastoral converted into suburb or estate.[2]

Woods have yet one further advantage as the site for a polder, which is that while they have very clear edges or boundaries, you can nevertheless go further and further into them, penetrating into "the heart of the wood" — which may also be, in a series of puns used prominently by Russell Hoban in *Riddley Walker* (1980), "the hart of the wood" (for harts are often magic animals which lead the huntsman into the world of the dead or the world of the fairies), and also "the heart of the would," the place where dreams (or nightmares) may take shape. The idea of deep penetration to darker levels which may, nevertheless, be rich in significance inevitably arouses Freudian or Jungian suggestions in modern minds, while for two hundred years the awareness has also been growing that fairy-tales, and the myths from which some think they developed, are not trivial or childish, but ways of expressing and dramatizing the most universal emotions and problems. They take us not only into the child-mind but the hindbrain beneath it, the area of instinct, the battleground of repression.

Holdstock's Merlin Codex trilogy, however, arguably takes us yet one stage further. It is not set in a polder, nor yet in a wainscot, and if it is a crosshatch, it is one of unusual complexity. The central character Merlin, the sorcerer-sage of the Arthurian tradition, is not, however, poldered in a cave, nor even very obviously associated with Arthur. Instead he is walking a Path, and the limits of the Path are especially obscure, both in time and space. The first book in the sequence, *Celtika*, opens with two scenes. The first is set in Greece, in "978 Old Era" (it is not clear whether this means "BC" or "BCE" or whatever else), and it describes the legendary death of Jason, hero of the *Argonautica*, finder of the Golden Fleece, killed by a falling spar from his ship the *Argo* twenty years after the murder of his and her sons by the witch-wife Medea. The scene then switches to "700 years later" and to "the northern country of Pohjola" (4). Pohjola is itself an Otherworld, the legendary country of those opposed to the heroes of the Finnish epic *Kalevala*: in the scene Merlin is heading for the Screaming Lake, where he will try to raise the rotting hulk of the *Argo*, last seen bearing its master Jason out to sea, and at the same time bring Jason back from the dead. The issue of "why?" may be set aside, for more immediate questions might well be "where and when?" Everyone knows (now) that Merlin is associated with King Arthur, who must have flourished somewhere round AD 500, and in Britain, of course — nowhere near Greece, nowhere near Finland, and though two dates have been given, it is hard to make either of them fit. Expectation is provoked, and simultaneously denied.

The title *Celtika* actually gives more of a fix on the imaginative location of the Merlin Codex, for the majority of it seems to take place within (our modern understanding of) the world of Celtic antiquity. Once the *Argo* has been raised and a crew found for her — it includes the birch-elemental Mielikki, who re-introduces the idea of the Heart of the Wood and the Heart of the Ship — Merlin sets off in pursuit of the sons of Jason, who, it seems, were not murdered by their mother after all, regardless of the traditional tale. But he does so in the track of a great raid on Greekland led by one Brennos, who has with him Orgetorix, one of Jason's sons now given a new name. All this has suggestions of history. Brennos, or Brennus, was the name of the Celt who (in the traditional history of Rome as given by Livy) sacked Rome some time in the fourth century BC. Orgetorix meanwhile has a name clearly of the same family as Vercingetorix, the Celtic enemy of Julius Caesar — the -ix suffix has become very familiar through the cartoon adventures of Asterix the Gaul, with his friend Obélix, the Druid Panoramix, the little dog Idéfix, and so forth. Among Merlin's companions on the trip, moreover, is the chieftain Urtha, who is pursuing his enemy Cunomaglos. Urtha is semi-familiar as a name, from Arthur's father Uther Pendragon, while Cunomaglos is recognizable as early British, the language which eventually became Welsh, some names in which have been recovered and made familiar once again by the activity of Celtic philologists; for instance, *Cunobelinos,[3] from which we get the Shake-spearean "Cymbeline." Urtha comes from Alba, and this name is carefully explicated:

> Urtha called his realm Alba, and this was a familiar enough dialect name for what various people of the south called Albos, Albon, Hyper-albora and so on, invariably meaning Whiteland, though the name was not necessarily derived from the chalk cliffs so easily visible from the territory of the Nervii on the mainland itself [107].

Alba is obviously Britain, or Albion, but not the Britain most of Hold-stock's readers live in. We are told that it "had been shrouded in mist for more than fifty generations," an "endless, timeless mist [that] concealed great storms that had pounded ceaselessly at the deeper forests and mountains," so that the island "had been a rain-land of terrifying darkness"

(107). This seems excessive as a description of even British weather, and we are told that another name for Alba has arisen, and this is "Ghostland."

> In Ghostland, the shades of the ancient dead ran, played, rode and hunted with the spirits of those yet to be born, bright elementals who always took adult forms and dreamed of the adventures and fates to come in their own far futures. For this reason, Ghostland was also known as the Land of the Shadows of Heroes [108].

Urtha has seen them, but he notes that "[t]hey have their sides of the rivers, their edges of the forests, their own valleys, which we leave well alone" (108). The shades and spirits can cross into the living world, but (at this point in the story) not the reverse. Is Alba "Ghostland," or does it *contain* Ghostland? There are clear boundaries, according to Urtha, but it's not clear which side (if either) is the polder. As with the names, so with the scenarios. Some things are familiar, some are not.

In further legendary relocations, Merlin and the new Argonauts move on to "the Hot Gates"—Thermopylae, that is—there not to meet Leonidas and the Spartans but instead to allow Urtha to fight a duel with Cuno-maglos. The intended Celtic flavor here comes through strongly, for most of the description consists of imaginative formal insults, combined with a very careful legalistic arrangement of conditions—weapons, ground, choice of weapons and ground, number of encounters. Merlin reflects: "Just when you think a combat is going to spring into action, the Celts stop for con-templation and insult" (273), while the start of the duel is further held up, after the exchange of insults, by the combatants embracing each other three times. Cathabach the druid explains that these are "[t]he Three Unavoidable Embraces: for a past shared; for a kind word shared; for a future when they will ride the same valleys in Ghostland" (274). With the duel over, the action of *Celtika* ends at another legendary location, the oak at Dodona, home of the oracle of Delphi and also the place where the wood for the *Argo* was cut. Here Jason's elder son, now using the Celtic name Orgetorix, confronts and appears to kill his father—though as with his own death centuries before, appearance is not reliable.

The point of these paragraphs is not at all to try to identify "sources" for Holdstock's vision, rather to indicate that even a moderately well-informed reader is bound to feel a constant ripple and surge of contradic-tion or anachronism. Thermopylae is not Spartan, it's Celtic. Brennos is not invading Rome, but Greece.[4] The Argo is not probing the shores of the Black Sea but the lakes of northern Finland. Merlin is not linked with Arthur but with Jason: and so on. In volume two of the sequence, *The Iron Grail*, the sense of constant blurring becomes, if anything, stronger. The opening place and time are much more precisely defined than was the case at the start of *Celtika*, "The Island of Alba, Territory of the Cornovidi, 272 BCE" (one notes that the date is now given in a recognizable form), but this certainty ebbs very quickly. In the opening scene Merlin is approaching the fortress of Taurovinda, "oldest of the Five Fortresses of Alba" (1). Where might that be? It guards the fords of "the mysterious river Nantosuelta" (1), which sounds as if it might be the Severn, but it is a boundary as described earlier by Urtha, where the land of the living touches not only the land of the dead but the land of the unborn as well. Merlin crosses the river in order to bring back Urtha's kidnapped children — a familiar motif from such legends as the Classical Orpheus and Eurydice, but also from its British medieval version, *Sir Orfeo*, where the lady has to be rescued not from the dead but from the fairies. But at some point (probably different places for different readers) one realizes that Ghostland is full of anachronisms as well. There are strikingly Celtic rituals of challenge and arming, reminiscent of the Urtha-Orgetorix duel in *Celtika*, a duel which is also retold with the characteristic Celtic rhetorical exaggeration, but then a squadron of horsemen appears wearing plain clothes rather than the tartans of the dead and are armed differently: they carry heavy lances, not javelins, and "[t]heir shields were narrow ovals, very plain, and carried at the horse's flank rather than slung over the warrior's back" (165). They must be Normans, and they come from the future: the whole history of Alba is available for recall (if recall can be the proper word for what is also foresight). Nor is this necessarily history. Other figures who appear and re-appear are two chariot-riding youths, who turn out to be the sons of the Celtic divinity Llew, who also materializes to punish them for stealing his chariot. Is that meant to be the Chariot of the Sun-god? Once again, different readers will jump to different conclusions. At a later stage Merlin necromantically raises a figure from the dead, and though he has been buried in the marsh where he was drowned as a sacrifice, enough is said about him for it to be clear that he is Brutus, in legend the eponymous founder of Britain — though no story known to me gives him a sacrificial end. But once again, not every reader will make the connection, or may make a different one. Other reminiscences include an "imram" sequence not unlike the Celtic stories of St. Brendan the Navigator, sailing to the west as Merlin does and there meeting strange creatures on various islands: in *The Iron Grail*, giant birds, tree-men, seal-women, while the recovery of Urtha's daughter Munda from a tangle of rosebriar resembles nothing so much as the (relatively modern) tale of Sleeping Beauty.

In Holdstock's writing, then, one encounters liminalities of every kind: borderlands of the living and the dead, the living and the unborn, switching between history and legend and myth, cross-overs between Greek legend and British legend and Finnish legend, with British legend furthermore stratified into (I think) perceptibly different time zones, though, as previously contended, no-one in these circumstances can entirely trust his or her own perceptions or assume that others will take them the same way. One explanation for this might just be that fantasy is by nature liminal (see above). Or one might argue that polders in particular are liminal. I would suggest, though, that there is a sense in which Hold-stock is here entering and exploiting a kind of readerly space, which one might call "intertextual liminality." It is, after all, a very common experi-ence nowadays, but also a distinctively modern one, created by a flood of books and commentaries and explanations, to switch in any evening's read-ing from one world to another: from King Arthur to the Trojan War, from Julius Caesar on druids to Robin Hood, and from any of them to *Star Trek* or *Star Wars*. They all now inhabit much the same kind of imaginative space, and it takes both quite a lot of knowledge and a certain talent for (or urge towards) organization to keep them in any way separate. A recent article on the way Northumbria is presented for the tourist trade noted a talk on King Arthur being interrupted by the fly-past of a Spitfire (Watson 239). King Arthur came from the fifth or sixth century, the warplane from the mid-twentieth, but for those watching they were all there at the same moment in 2000, and all part of the same (packaged) heritage. This is not "historical," and even less is it academic, but it is the way most people experience the past — the gap between academic and popular responses to the past indeed only gets wider, especially with reference to figures like King Arthur, and this is by no means always to the credit of the academic side of the divide.[5]

The last section of the third volume in the Merlin Codex, *The Broken Kings*, has as an epigraph a quotation from Tennyson's poem "Ulysses," "I am a part of all that I have met," and it could serve as a summary of the way Holdstock writes and the way modern readers read — eclectically, engaged in continuous mental bricolage as they fit together items which originally had no spatial or temporal or even literary connection, Greece and Britain and Finland, Jason and Merlin and the birch-spirit Mielikki. Is it just in the mind? Another development in *The Broken Kings* is the appearance of further borderlands, shadow-realms, or border areas: life and death are not sharply distinguished, says Merlin, for in between there comes "the 'ephemera' or the 'twilight time'" (170). Nor is Nantosuelta the only boundary, for there is something else besides Alba and the Ghostlands: "There are parts of the world ... where the land has echoes" (172). Merlin calls them "Echonians" and stresses the fact that

> they were not Otherworlds, or Ghostlands, or any sort of place where the Dead might journey to seek rest or rebirth.... They were ... the left-overs of play, the fragmented remains of exercises in charm, enchant-ment, magic and manipulation [173].

The echo realms were once guarded, Merlin says, and the entrances to them passed into the control of priests and priestesses who turned them into oracles, as at Delphi. But the idea of echoes of the past persisting is natural enough, especially in some areas of Britain, still marked on a field-by-field basis by tumuli, standing stones, old hillforts, and often enough by names which still seem to have significance but whose origin is forgot-ten. Names on the edge of memory indeed become a significant part of *The Broken Kings*, for when Merlin comes into contact, in the Ghostlands, with the Pendragon, who slowly becomes identified with Arthur rather than his father, his companions help to make that identification: Bedavor, Boros, Caiwain. Our familiar forms from Malory—Bedivere, Bors, Gawain—are close enough for the new ones to be recognized, but it should be noted, too, that most readers are by now acquainted with the idea that the familiar forms may not be right and may have been garbled over the centuries. In her Arthurian sequence, notably *Sword at Sunset* (1963), Rose-mary Sutcliff popularized the forms Bedwyr and (one clearly derived from the Celtic philologists) Gwalchmai, probably taking them over because they sounded convincingly Celtic, and so could be part of the "history behind the myth" which so many novelists and movie-makers (as well as academics) have reached out for. In the same way, when Holdstock's Pen-dragon describes a dream he has had of three women in a boat crossing a pool and vanishing into the mist, a man's arm just visible over the side of the boat, almost anyone will recognize the familiar scene from books and illustrations. "You think this was a dream of your death," suggests Merlin, and Arthur replies, "I'm certain of it" (271). But we all know — and so does Merlin — that it is a vision of the mysterious exit to Avalon. An Unborn is dreaming of himself Undead. Or, one might say, the whole sequence is taking place in "story space," like William Gibson's cyberspace, a "collective hallucination," but one for which there is a great deal more evidence than there is, even now, for cyberspace.

I earlier suggested that the Merlin Codex could be seen as, in Clute and Grant's terms, a crosshatch of unusual complexity, and parts of their account of crosshatches seem to be appropriate. Clute and Grant say that crosshatching may be restricted to a ribbon, a kind of buffer zone between two realities, but in some novels — they cite M. John Harrison's *A Storm of Wings* (1980) —

> the entire landscape is a crosshatch, quandaries of perception are rife, and anything at all may be a TROMPE L'OEIL ... when borderland conventions are absent, there is an inherent and threatening instability (>WRONGNESS) to regions of crosshatch; a sense of imminent METAMOR-PHOSIS [237].

Unlike quest-narratives, stories of this kind are unlikely to lead to firm conclusions, as indeed is the case with Holdstock's work. Strongly imagistic, strongly eclectic, the Merlin Codex sometimes seems to be penetrating deeper into the wood of the mythagos and the subconscious mind, while it sometimes also seems to be riffling through sets of memories, allusions, echoes, some of them this side and some on the other side of recognition. And, as previously maintained, even more than is the case with all literary works, no reader's experience can be the same. The effect may be summed up not in Tennyson's words but in those of another poet, Andrew Marvell, one of the great Green poets. In an English garden, he wrote, the mind withdraws into itself:

> The Mind, that Ocean where each kind
> Does straight its own resemblance find;
> Yet it creates, transcending these,
> Far other Worlds, and other Seas;
> Annihilating all that's made
> To a green Thought in a green Shade ["The Garden" lines 43–8].

Annihilation may not the right term for Holdstock, but he is undoubtedly a great creator of otherworlds, a great transcender of resemblances, a great voyager of the mind.

NOTES

1. I am thinking of works such as Gérard Genette's *Narrative Discourse: An Essay in Method* (1980). The most successful approaches to analyzing narrative that I know — they are very different approaches — are Derek Brewer, *Symbolic Stories: Traditional Narratives of the Family Drama in English Literature* (1988) and Leonard Jackson, *Literature, Psychoanalysis and the New Sciences of the Mind* (2000).

2. It is said that the oldest living creature in Europe is the Fortingall Yew in the churchyard at Fortingall, Perthshire, shown by its tree-rings to be some three thousand years old. The experience of urban sprawl destroying childhood playgrounds and pastoral memories has often been remarked: Tolkien and Orwell both wrote movingly about it, see further John Carey's *The Intellectuals and the Masses: Pride and Prejudice among the Literary Intelligentsia, 1880–1939*, 46–70.

3. The asterisk indicates a philologically reconstructed form, that is, one never recorded but deduced by modern scholars on the basis of analogous forms.

4. Readerly contradiction may be checked here, however, by awareness that a different Brennos is indeed said to have raided Delphi, as Holdstock well knew, see "Interview." All readings of these works are affected by what the reader recognizes, or fails to recognize, which will in every case be different.

5. For a subtle commentary on the way in which "King Arthur" is alternatively perceived by academics and even the well-educated general populace, see Ronald Hutton, *Witches, Druids and King Arthur*, 39–58.

WORKS CITED

Attebery, Brian. *Strategies of Fantasy*. Bloomington: Indiana University Press, 1992.

Brewer, Derek. *Symbolic Stories: Traditional Narratives of the Family Drama in English Literature*. London: Longman, 1988.

Carey, John. *The Intellectuals and the Masses: Pride and Prejudice among the Literary Intelligentsia, 1880–1939*. London: Faber, 1992.

Clute, John, and John Grant, eds. *The Encyclopedia of Fantasy*. London: Orbit, 1997.

Genette, Gérard. *Narrative Discourse: An Essay in Method*. Trans. Jane E. Lewin. Ithaca: Cornell University Press, 1980.

Holdstock, Robert. *The Broken Kings*. London: Gollancz, 2006.

_____. *Celtika*. 2001. London: Gollancz, 2006.

_____. *The Iron Grail*. London: Simon and Schuster, 2002.

Hutton, Ronald. *Witches, Druids and King Arthur*. London: Hambledon and London, 2003.

"Interview with Robert Holdstock." *Mythago Wood: The Robert Holdstock Website*. 25 March 2009 <www.robertholdstock.com/intervw1.html>.

Jackson, Leonard. *Literature, Psychoanalysis and the New Sciences of the Mind*. Harlow, Essex: Longman, 2000.

Marvell, Andrew. "The Garden." *The Poems of Andrew Marvell*. Ed. Hugh Macdonald. London: Routledge, 1952. 51–53.

Mendlesohn, Farah. *Rhetorics of Fantasy*. Middletown, CT: Wesleyan University Press, 2008.

Sutcliff, Rosemary. *Sword at Sunset*. New York: Coward-McCann, 1963.

Todorov, Tzvetan. *The Fantastic: A Structural Approach to a Literary Genre.* 1970. Trans. Richard Howard. Ithaca: Cornell University Press, 1975.

Watson, Steve. "Touring the Medieval: Tourism, Heritage and Medievalism in Northumbria." Tom Shippey and Martin Arnold, eds. *Appropriating the Middle Ages: Scholarship, Politics, Fraud.* Studies in Medievalism 11. Cambridge: Brewer, 2001. 239–61.

Robert Holdstock Bibliography

The Mythago Wood Cycle

Mythago Wood
UK: Victor Gollancz, 1984; hardcover.
USA: Arbor House, 1984; hardcover.
UK: Granada Panther, 1985; paper-
  back (special overseas edition).
UK: Grafton Books, 1986; paperback.
USA: Berkley, 1986; paperback.
UK: Grafton, 1990; paperback.
USA : Avon, 1991; paperback.
UK : Easton Press, 1996; hardcover
  (special leather-bound edition).
UK: HarperCollins Voyager, 1998;
  paperback.
UK: Earthlight, 2002; paperback.
USA: Orb Books, 2003; trade
  paperback.
UK: Gollancz, 2007; hardcover.
UK: Gollancz, 2009; paperback.

Lavondyss
UK: Gollancz, 1988; hardcover.
UK: Gollancz, 1988; hardcover (with
  slipcase).
UK: Gollancz, 1988; trade paper-
  back.
USA: William Morrow, 1989; hard-
  cover.
UK: Grafton Books, 1990; paperback.
USA: Avon, 1991; paperback.
UK: Earthlight, 2003; paperback.
USA: Orb Books, 2004; trade
  paperback.

The Bone Forest (short story col-
lection)
UK: Grafton Books, 1991; hardcover.
UK: Grafton Books, 1992; paperback.
USA: Avon Books, 1992; paperback.

The Hollowing
UK: HarperCollins, 1993; hardcover.
UK: HarperCollins, 1993; trade
  paperback.
UK: HarperCollins, 1994; paperback.
USA: ROC, 1994; hardcover.
USA: ROC 1995; paperback.
UK: Earthlight, 2003; paperback.
USA: Orb Books, 2005; trade
  paperback.

Merlin's Wood
UK: HarperCollins, 1994; hardcover.
UK: HarperCollins, 1995; paperback.
UK: Gollancz, 2009; trade paperback.

Gate of Ivory, Gate of Horn
USA: ROC, 1997; hardcover.
USA: ROC, 2001, paperback.
UK: Earthlight, 2002; paperback.
As Gate of Ivory (same novel)
UK: HarperCollins Voyager, 1998;
  hardcover.
UK: HarperCollins Voyager, 1998;
  paperback.

Avilion
UK: Gollancz, 2009; hardcover.

UK: Gollancz, 2009; trade paperback.
UK: Gollancz, 2010; paperback.

OMNIBUS EDITIONS OF THE MYTHAGO WOOD CYCLE

The Mythago Cycle: Volume 1
UK: Gollancz, 2007; trade paperback.

The Mythago Cycle: Volume 2
UK: Gollancz, 2007; trade paperback.

The Merlin Codex

Celtika
UK: Simon and Schuster Earthlight, 2001; hardcover.
UK: Simon and Schuster Earthlight, 2002; paperback.
USA: Tor Books, 2003; hardcover.
USA: Tor Books, 2003; paperback.
UK: Gollancz, 2007; paperback.

The Iron Grail
UK: Simon and Schuster Earthlight, 2002; hardcover.
UK: Simon and Schuster Earthlight, 2002; trade paperback
UK: Simon and Schuster Earthlight, 2003; paperback.
USA: Tor Books, 2004; hardcover.
USA: Tor Fantasy, 2005; paperback.
UK: Gollancz, 2007; trade paperback.

The Broken Kings
UK: Gollancz, 2006; hardcover.
USA: Tor, 2007; hardcover.
UK: Gollancz, 2008; trade paperback.

Science Fiction Novels

Eye Among the Blind
UK: Faber and Faber, 1976; hardcover.

UK: Pan; 1976; paperback.
NY: Doubleday, 1977; hardcover.
NY: Signet, 1979; paperback.
UK: Gollancz, 1987; paperback.

Earthwind
UK: Faber and Faber, 1977; hardcover.
UK: Pan Books, 1978; paperback.
USA: Timescape Pocket Fantasy Books, 1978; paperback.
USA: Pocket Books, 1982; paperback.
UK: Gollancz, 1987; paperback.

Where Time Winds Blow
UK: Faber and Faber, 1981; hardcover.
USA: Timescape/Pocket Books, 1982; paperback.
UK: Pan Books, 1982; paperback.
UK: Gollancz, 1988; paperback.

Other

Necromancer
UK: Futura, 1978; paperback.
NY: Avon Books, 1979; paperback.
NY: Time Warner Books, 1990; paperback.
UK: Futura, 1990; paperback.

In the Valley of the Statues (short story collection)
UK: Faber and Faber, 1982; hardcover.
UK: Gollancz, 1988; paperback.

The Emerald Forest (film novelization)
UK: Penguin Books, 1985; paperback.
NY: Zoetrope, 1985; trade paperback.
UK: HarperCollins, 1995; paperback.

The Fetch
UK: Orbit, 1991; hardcover.
UK: Warner Books, 1992; paperback.

As Unknown Regions
   USA: ROC, 1996; paperback.

Ancient Echoes
   UK: HarperCollins, 1996; hardcover.
   USA: ROC, 1996; trade paperback.
   UK: HarperCollins, 1996; paperback.
   USA: ROC, 1997; paperback.
   UK: Gollancz, 2009; paperback.

Bulman (based on scripts and the Granada television series by Murray Smith)
   UK: Futura, 1984; paperback.

Bulman 2: One of Our Pigeons is Missing (based on scripts and the Granada TV series by Murray Smith)
   UK: Futura, 1984; paperback

Short Stories

"Pauper's Plot" (1968)
"Microcosm" (1972)
"The Darkness" (1972)
"Ash, Ash" (1974) or "Ashes"
"The Graveyard Cross" (1976)
"Magic Man" (1976)
"On the Inside" (1976)
"The Time Beyond Age" (1976)
"Travellers" (1976)
"A Small Event" (1977)
"The Touch of a Vanished Hand" (1977)
"The Quiet Girl" (1978)
"In the Valley of the Statues" (1979)
"High Pressure" (1979)
"Earth And Stone" (1980)
"Mythago Wood" (1981)
"Ocean of Sound" (1982)
"Elite: The Dark Wheel" (1984)
"The Boy who Jumped the Rapids" (1984)
"The Other Place" (1985)

"Thorn" (1986)
"Scarrowfell" (1987)
"A Letter from Robert Holdstock" (1988)
"The Shapechanger" (1989)
"Time of the Tree" (1989)
"The Bone Forest" (1991)
"The Ragthorn" (1991) with Garry Kilworth
"The Silvering" (1992)
"Having His Leg Pulled" (1993)
"Merlin's Wood" (1994)
"The Charisma Trees" (1994)
"Infantasm" (1995)
"Going Home" (1998)

Editor

Stars of Albion (with Christopher Priest)
   UK: Pan Books, 1979; paperback.

Other Edens (with Christopher Evans)
   UK: Unwin Hyman, 1987; paperback.

Other Edens II (with Christopher Evans)
   UK: Unwin Hyman, 1988; paperback.

Other Edens III (with Christopher Evans)
   UK: Unwin Hyman, 1989; trade paperback.

Non-Fiction

Alien Landscapes (with Malcolm Edwards)
   UK: Pierrot Publishing Limited, 1979; Large format paperback.

USA: Mayflower Books, 1979; hardcover.
USA: Mayflower Books, 1979; Large format paperback.

Tour of the Universe: The Journey of a Lifetime (with Malcolm Edwards)

USA: Mayflower Books, 1980; hardcover.
UK: Pierrot Publishing Limited, London, 1980; hardcover.
NY: Mayflowers Books, 1980; trade paperback.

Realms of Fantasy (with Malcolm Edwards)

UK: Paper Tiger, 1983; hardcover.
UK: Paper Tiger, 1983; paperback.
USA: Doubleday, 1983; hardcover.

Lost Realms: An Illustrated Exploration of the Lands Behind the Legends (with Malcolm Edwards)

UK: Paper Tiger; 1984; hardcover.
UK: Paper Tiger, 1984; Large format paperback.
USA: Salem House Pub; 1985; Large format paperback.

Magician: The Lost Journals of Magnus Geoffrey Carlyle (with Malcolm Edwards)

UK: Paper Tiger/Dragons World, 1982; hardcover.
UK: Paper Tiger/Dragons World, 1982; paperback.

Encyclopedia of Science Fiction
UK: Octopus Books Ltd, 1978; hardcover.

Pseudonymous Work

Legend of the Werewolf (screenplay novelization — as Robert Black)
UK: Sphere Books, 1976; paperback.

The Satanists (screenplay novelization — as Robert Black)
UK: Futura, 1978; paperback.

THE PROFESSIONALS SERIES (AS KEN BLAKE)

Cry Wolf
UK: Sphere Books, 1981: paperback.

Operation Susie
UK: Sphere Books, 1982: paperback.

The Untouchables
UK: Sphere Books, 1982: paperback.

You'll Be All Right
UK: Sphere Books, 1982: paperback.

BERSERKER SERIES (AS CHRIS CARLSEN)

Shadow of the Wolf
UK: Sphere Books; 1977; paperback.

The Bull Chief
UK: Sphere Books; 1977; paperback.

The Horned Warrior
UK: Sphere Books; 1979; paperback.

NIGHT HUNTER SERIES (AS ROBERT FAULCON)

The Stalking
UK: Arrow; 1983, paperback.
USA: Charter; 1987, paperback.

The Talisman
UK: Arrow; 1983, paperback.
USA: Charter; 1987, paperback.

The Ghost Dance
UK: Arrow; 1983, paperback.
USA: Charter; 1987, paperback.

The Shrine
UK: Arrow; 1984, paperback.
USA: Charter; 1988, paperback.

The Hexing
UK: Arrow; 1984, paperback.
USA: Charter; 1988, paperback.

The Labyrinth
UK: Arrow; 1987, paperback.
USA: Charter; 1988, paperback.

OMNIBUS EDITIONS OF THE NIGHT HUNTER SERIES

The Stalking
UK: Century, 1987; hardcover.
UK: Arrow, 1987; paperback.

The Ghost Dance
UK: Century, 1987; hardcover.
UK: Arrow, 1987; paperback.

The Hexing and The Labryinth
UK: Legend, 1988; paperback.

RAVEN SERIES (AS RICHARD KIRK)*

Vol. 1: Swordsmistress of Chaos (with Angus Wells)
UK: Corgi, 1978; paperback.
USA: Ace, 1987; paperback.

Vol. 2: A Time of Ghosts
UK: Corgi, 1978; paperback.
USA: Ace, 1987; paperback.

Vol. 4: Lords of the Shadows
UK: Corgi, 1979; paperback.
USA: Ace, 1987; paperback.

Holdstock did not write volume 3 or 5 in this series

About the Contributors

Vera Benczik received her M.A. in English and her M.A. in Assyriology from Eötvös Loránd University, Budapest, where she is a Ph.D. candidate in American studies completing a dissertation on the voyage theme in Ursula K. Le Guin's science fiction. Her research area is postwar science fiction, with emphases on the quest narrative, the processes of narrating and reading, and the relationship between narrative construction and ellipses, which is reflected both in her essay in this volume and that on Le Guin's *The Left Hand of Darkness* in *Paradoxa* 21 (2008).

Stefan Ekman, a doctoral candidate at the University of Lund, Sweden, is finishing his dissertation on divisions of the modern fantasy landscape. He also teaches the fantasy and science fiction unit in the creative writing program at the University of Lund, works as fantasy specialist for one of Sweden's main fantasy publishers, and lectures on fantasy, manga, and role-playing games in schools and libraries.

Ildikó Limpár, assistant professor of English at Pázmány Péter Catholic University in Piliscsaba, Hungary, holds a Ph.D. in English language and literature and an M.A. in Egyptology. Her publications include *The American Dream Reconsidered: New World Motifs in Shakespeare's* The Tempest *and Their Transformations in American Literature* (2008) and several articles on Shakespeare, Marilynne Robinson, Linda Hogan, and Diana Abu-Jaber, Emily Dickinson's poetry, William Faulkner's concept of time, and J. D. Salinger's philosophy of art. Her play *Egy évben egyszer* [*Once a year*] won an award from the Hungarian Ministry of Culture in 2004.

Kálmán Matolcsy, teacher, translator, poet, and composer, focuses his research on the problems of epistemology and categorization in the cosmicist fiction of H. P. Lovecraft at the University of Debrecen, Hungary. He has published scholarly essays in Hungary, Romania, Great Britain, and the United States on the literatures of horror, science fiction, and fantasy, as well as on Japanese cinema. He has published poetry in English and Hungarian, produced music albums under various monikers distributed worldwide, and translated into Hungarian such works as Robert Holdstock's *Celtika* and *The Iron Grail* from the Merlin Codex.

About the Contributors

Donald E. Morse, university professor of American, Irish, and English literature, University of Debrecen, Hungary, and an emeritus professor of English and rhetoric, Oakland University, Michigan, has been twice Senior Fulbright Professor (1987–89 and 1990–92) and twice Soros Professor at the University of Debrecen. The author or editor of more than a dozen books and a hundred scholarly essays, he has lectured widely in Europe, the United States, and Asia. Among his books are *The Novels of Kurt Vonnegut: Imagining Being an American* (2003) and, with Csilla Bertha, *Worlds Visible and Invisible* (1994). He edits the *Hungarian Journal of English and American Studies* at the University of Debrecen and since 1984 has chaired the annual International Conference on the Fantastic in the Arts.

Marek Oziewicz, Ph.D., D.Litt., is an associate professor of literature and director of the Center for Young People's Literature and Culture at the University of Wrocław, Poland. He is also an adjunct assistant professor of education at Pennsylvania State University, teaching online courses in Penn State World Campus Children's Literature Program. A Fulbrighter (2005) and Kosciuszko Scholar (2006), he has published articles and edited collections on fantasy, mythopoeia, and young adult fiction. His *One Earth, One People: The Mythopoeic Fantasy Series of Ursula K. Le Guin, Lloyd Alexander, Madeleine L'Engle and Orson Scott Card* (McFarland, 2008) won the 2009 Mythopoeic Award in Myth and Fantasy Studies.

Andy Sawyer is the librarian of the Science Fiction Foundation Collection at the University of Liverpool Library, course director of the M.A. in science-fiction studies offered by the School of English, and reviews editor of *Foundation: The International Review of Science Fiction*. He has published widely on science fiction and fantasy — most recently with essays on Ursula K. Le Guin, Terry Pratchett, and the Liverpool horror writer Ramsey Campbell; contributions to the *Routledge Companion to Science Fiction* (2009); and (with David Ketterer) an edition of *Plan for Chaos*, a previously unpublished novel by John Wyndham. He is the 2008 recipient of the Science Fiction Research Association's Clareson Award for services to science fiction.

W. A. Senior holds a Ph.D. in medieval and Renaissance literature from the University of Notre Dame. A past president of the International Association of the Fantastic in the Arts and editor of *The Journal of the Fantastic in the Arts* 1998–2007, he has published articles on medieval literature, modern fantasy, and science fiction in journals such as *JFA, NYRSF, Mosaic, HJEAS, Extrapolation, Film Criticism,* and the *North Carolina Literary Review*; collections on J. R. R. Tolkien and William Gibson; and such reference works as the *DLB* and *The Encyclopedia of Twentieth Century Fiction*. He wrote *Stephen R. Donaldson's Chronicles of Thomas Covenant: Variations on the Fantasy Tradition* (1995).

Tom Shippey is a professor emeritus at St. Louis University, St. Louis, Missouri, and honorary research fellow at the University of Winchester, England. His many publications in the area of fantasy and science fiction include three books on Tolkien (beginning with *The Road to Middle-earth*, now in its fourth edition), two Oxford anthologies (*The Oxford Books of Science Fiction* and *Fantasy Short Stories*) and two edited or co-edited collections of critical essays (*Fictional Space* and *Fiction 2000*). He has also published extensively on medieval studies and the modern reception of the Middle Ages. His edited collection on Grimm's *Deutsche Mythologie*, *The Shadow-walkers*, won the Mythopoeic Society Award for Scholarship in 2008.

C. W. Sullivan III is university distinguished research professor of English at East Carolina University and a full member of the Welsh Academy. He is the author of *Welsh Celtic Myth in Modern Fantasy* (1989) and editor of *The Mabinogi: A Book of Essays* (1996), six other books of essays, and the online journal *Celtic Cultural Studies*. He is a past president of the International Association for the Fantastic in the Arts. His articles on mythology, folklore, fantasy, and science fiction have appeared in a variety of anthologies and journals, and he wrote the book *Fenian Diary: Denis B. Cashman on Board the* Hougoumont, *1867–1868* (2001).

Elizabeth A. Whittingham teaches English at the College at Brockport, State University of New York, and at Monroe Community College in Rochester, New York. Her expertise lies in medieval literature, classical mythology, fantasy literature, the Bible as literature, and literary analysis. She has given undergraduate and graduate courses on J. R. R. Tolkien and C. S. Lewis, and in 2009 lectured at the National Endowment for the Humanities Tolkien Institute. Her book, *The Evolution of Tolkien's Mythology: A Study of the History of Middle-earth* (McFarland, 2008), examines nearly six decades of J. R. R. Tolkien's writings. She has written, directed and performed adaptations of scenes from *The Lord of the Rings* and has presented and participated at numerous conferences.

Index

Index

Index

Index